Seeking the Woman
in Late Medieval and
Renaissance Writings

Seeking the Woman in Late Medieval and Renaissance Writings

Essays in Feminist Contextual Criticism

Edited by Sheila Fisher and Janet E. Halley

The University of Tennessee Press / KNOXVILLE

For Dana and Libby

Library of Congress Cataloging in Publication Data

Seeking the woman in late Medieval and Renaissance writings :
    essays in feminist contextual criticism /
    edited by Sheila Fisher and Janet E. Halley. — 1st ed.
    p. cm.
    Includes bibliographies and index.
    ISBN 0-87049-591-7 (cloth: alk. paper)
    1. Women in literature.   2. Women and literature.
3. Feminist literary criticism.   4. Criticism, Textual.
5. European literature—Medieval, 500–1500—History and
criticism.   6. European literature—Renaissance, 1450–1600—
History and criticism.   I. Fisher, Sheila.   II. Halley, Janet E.,
1952–   .
PN98.W64S44 1989
809'.93352042—dc 19   88-22802   CIP

Contents

Illustrations

Acknowledgments

A collective and collaborative project such as this receives crucial help at each stage of its progress from an idea shared in an afternoon of conversation to the finished book. Early on, Evelyn Torton Beck gave sound and smart advice on the process of getting a collection of essays off the ground. Susan Squier encouraged us to contact Carol Wallace Orr, Director of the University of Tennessee Press, who has become a friend as well as an editor.

Throughout the various stages of making this book, Carol Orr has generously provided us with good advice, practical suggestions, and an enormous amount of encouragement. Our work has been made immeasurably easier because of her insight. We would also like to thank Bettie McDavid Mason, our copyeditor, and Kim Scarbrough, acquisitions assistant at the University of Tennessee Press, for their attention to the final stages of preparing this manuscript. Patricia Ryan of Trinity College worked with us on the index, and we are very grateful for her help.

A number of people and institutions are to thank for the illustrations that appear in Margaret Maurer's essay, "Reading Ben Jonson's Queens." Teresa Taylor and Stephen Orgel gave us invaluable assistance in locating photographic archives. Bryn Mawr College and the Trustees of the Chatsworth Settlement generously permitted us to reproduce the images in their custody; the Courtauld Institute swiftly provided a key photograph. Funding from Colgate University has subsidized the reproduction of this material, and Trinity College generously defrayed other necessary expenses.

Through all the stages of this project, Libby Potter and Dana Brand have listened, talked, edited, criticized, encouraged, and celebrated with us. We want to thank them both for sharing their intelligence, their fine judgment, and their equally fine sense of humor with us. Without them, doing this book would not have been nearly as much fun.

Introduction

The Lady Vanishes:
The Problem of Women's Absence
in Late Medieval and Renaissance Texts

Sheila Fisher and Janet E. Halley

> The difficulties in writing on the history of women have been
> rehearsed many times, and nothing in the future will ever
> remove them. . . . Writers' hopes of documenting women's
> lives will always outrun the possibilities of achievement.
>
> —Joan Thirsk[1]

A problem shared by medieval and early modern scholars is the difficulty
of understanding an area of history whose accessibility is limited by the
loss of material to time and to the vagaries of script and early print
culture. But when we try to study the history of women's lives and of
their subjective experience during these periods, the problem of lost
material and of insufficient sources and resources is intensified in specific
ways. Despite social, institutional, and technological changes, the basis
—or rather, the bias—of the written record continually problematizes
attempts to determine women's subjective experiences. Not only must
scholars contend with the widespread illiteracy of women themselves,
but they must also confront the vexed relationship between the lives and
subjectivities of "real" women and the ideological re-presentation of
them in whatever remains of the textual tradition. By using contextual
criticism and postmodern literary theory to examine earlier writings,
the new feminist essays in this volume address the special problem of
medieval and early modern women's relationships to the textual record
of these periods. In the end, the common denominator characterizing

these relationships is absence, in both its literal and its literary-theoretical meanings.

Notwithstanding the postmodern critique of the concepts of the self and the subject, the self has been a crucial historical category for men and for women. The periods we are studying shared a deep-seated belief in an essential self, locating it in and calling it variously the soul or the heart or the mind. From Augustine and Aquinas to Descartes, the result was a massive production of theological and philosophical writings that defined and formulated theories of the self, its workings, and its relationship to its world: theories of the self that influenced not only literate audiences but also, primarily through the pulpit, illiterate ones as well. In different ways at different times and in different settings, people of these periods doubtless experienced themselves as having "selves" of historically specific kinds.

This tradition must be approached skeptically by those seeking the historical self of women, however. For, although the Christian program of spiritual redemption posited the equality of women's and men's souls, theological and philosophical writings, in their formulations of the female self, did not often show a convincing belief in that equality. The idea of spiritual equality was further diminished, and indeed erased, by the legal and political structures erected on the basis of, and justified by, Christian orthodoxy and its theorizings about women. This historical context requires us to proceed very carefully, therefore, when we wish to know what constituted the self or selfhoods of women, and how women, depending upon their class, their education, and their occupations, experienced those selfhoods.[2]

The nature and repercussions of medieval and early modern women's absence from the textual record are further clarified if we compare the process of doing Women's Studies scholarship in earlier and later periods. Feminist literary criticism of nineteenth- and twentieth-century writings has been able to establish itself as one of the cornerstones of Women's Studies for many reasons, not the least of which is that the sheer availability of resources offers ample material for feminist investigation. Not only is there much more written, and written about women, in these periods, but there is much more written by women themselves. In the nineteenth and twentieth centuries, women began, for the first time, to produce a sustained written record of their own experiences, both in noncanonical writings such as letters and journals, and in the more privileged genres of the literary canon. From these writings by women, we can attempt to determine what women thought of themselves, their roles, their education, and their lives. Their writings provide us with the voices and experiences of individual women as well as the chronicles of collectivities of women, which can counter and inform the interpretations of women made by men.

When we turn to the medieval and early modern periods, however, we find drastically fewer records left by women of their own experiences. Female illiteracy is not the only cause of this virtual silence. Women who were literate did not, by and large, conceive of themselves as writers, or, if the textual record is any indication, they rarely conceived of their writing as sufficiently important to consume the wealth necessary to the production of books. Certainly, there were medieval and early modern women who wrote—and who wrote about their experiences as women in their societies.[3] But attempts to map the range and variety of women's subjective experiences cannot be based on the textual evidence left by the extraordinary few whose proximity to power and influence allowed them to write—and publish—in the first place. Even if we could overcome problems of the disproportionate representation of aristocratic and propertied women among the literate, and of the pressure of male interests in preserving and destroying literary remains, still we would not find that writing women of these periods took up the pen as an unproblematic medium. As Patricia Francis Cholakian's essay in this volume shows, the successive editions of Marie de Gournay's *Proumenoir de Monsieur de Montaigne* attest to the female author's search for an authorizing audience, beginning with her adoptive father Michel de Montaigne and moving painfully and only partially towards an audience of women. The peculiar challenge facing all those who attempt to study women's subjectivities in these periods, then, is determining the ways in which women themselves, even those who did write, were silent and silenced by their exclusion from the patriarchal institution of literacy.

Nor, by and large, can the literary writings of these periods allow us access to women's subjective experience, even though many versions of "woman" populate medieval and early modern texts.[4] The expectations surrounding literary genres, styles, and conventions as well as the modes of production of literature itself meant that authors, the overwhelming majority of whom were men, had little stake in representing the reality of contemporary women's personalities and experiences. Indeed, as many of the essays in this volume demonstrate, re-presentations of women in literature hardly represent women in life. In this light, reading women in male-authored texts of these periods requires a special attention to the problematic of referentiality as it has been defined by postmodern literary theory. Regardless of our own affection for or interest in such characters as the Wife of Bath or Milton's Eve, there is no Wife of Bath or Eve, no "she" or "her." [5] These characters do not refer to real women, and it is misleading to adopt the strategy of traditional (and some nontraditional) literary criticism and to discuss them as if they did.

They must be doing something else instead. As Elaine Tuttle Hansen suggests in her essay on *The Legend of Good Women*, for a male author to write women in these periods was to refer not to women, but to men—to desire not relationship with women, but relationship to the traditions of male textual activity, and, by extension, of male social and political privilege. And as Janet E. Halley argues in her discussion of John Donne's actual social practices of sharing textual images of women with his male friends, homosocial literary activity had profound social as well as literary implications. In the medieval and early modern periods, perhaps more than at any other time, the production of literature was a fundamentally male "homotextual" activity: one in which male writings referred to, responded to, manipulated, and projected desire upon other men and other men's writings as much, if not more, than they claimed to represent the extraliterary world and the women in it. Thus these texts, as Roberta Krueger's essay on thirteenth-century French wager romances demonstrates, cannot be read as simple reflections of women's historical or subjective experience, even and especially when they seem to exalt women and whatever power the texts ascribe to them.

If figurations of women within male-authored works do not allow us access to historical women's selfhoods, feminist criticism of these early writings can offer us a sense of the ideological function of literature in these periods by charting the positions and positionings of female characters within the textual tradition. As many of the essays in this collection argue, literary texts were often complicit in replicating and upholding a social, economic, and political *status quo*. In her essay on

Sir Gawain and the Green Knight, Sheila Fisher shows how the poem's textual inscriptions of women constitute a strategy for displacing and thereby containing women within feudal ideological structures that were distinctly homosocial.[6] But, as the marginalization of Morgan la Faye in this poem suggests, early texts often displace the figure of the female in order to assert the ascendancy of the male specifically because women are perceived to have and are associated with a "feminizing" power threatening to male sociopolitical and literary interests. As Adrienne Munich has recently written, feminist literary criticism of male-authored texts need not rest with alerting us to the mythologizing of women in patriarchy. Feminist readings of these texts can also explore the implications about women's power, perceived or actual, that these writings attempt to submerge. Or, in Munich's words, "Suppression, distancing, alteration or any other defences against woman's role in a text's creation are compelling examples of women's history, and are therefore a vital subject for feminist criticism."[7]

To make such observations is to go beyond much mainstream work on women, with its focus on the questions of a given author's feminism or antifeminism and on the criteria for defining what a medieval or early modern "feminist" might be. Such studies can simplify the relationship of reader to text, author to meaning, and sexuality to textuality. They presuppose the stability not only of female identity and thus of women's interests, but also of textual reference to that identity and those interests. Finally, they elide the more pressing problem: the textual history of women's absence.

Postmodern literary theory is useful to scholars who would go beyond mainstream studies of medieval and renaissance "feminism" because it provides a means of assessing and describing that absence at the same time that it can register the textuality in social interaction, and the valence of gender in both. As Anne J. Cruz demonstrates in her essay on the Spanish female picaresque, the female speaker invented by a male author is the mark of female absence, because the male author is speaking not through, but across the female in order to address other men. And Elaine Hansen's discussion of Chaucer traces the way in which efforts to fix authorial politics (in either direction, and especially for a "major" writer) can become, in effect, a projection of the reader's own desire upon the text. These two essays exhibit a postmodern sensitivity to textuality as it engenders the historical self.

It is here, however, that we encounter another boundary: that between postmodern conceptions of the self and those implicit in this volume. The female absence analyzed in these essays is not the result of deconstructive pressure applied to a self experienced or represented as historically sovereign: that is possible only in the analysis of male identity. In her essay, Marguerite Waller discusses this female absence by showing the ways in which Sir Thomas Wyatt's sonnet "Whoso list to hunt" *and* its recent new-historicist reading by Stephen Greenblatt conceal their appropriation of the female voice. Through the assumption of a male, heterosexual reading of history and ideology, the new historical project reveals its stake in what Waller calls "the epistemology of authority." In the process, it underwrites female absence, and the absence of historical women, once again.

STUDY OF MALE-AUTHORED TEXTS of these periods suggests, then, that the representation of women does not merely distort or interpret but can altogether ignore the historical existence of real women and their experience of selfhood. In order to understand these literary constructions of women, it is necessary to assess them against the materiality of women's lives—the conditions in which they grew up, worked, worshiped, married, gave birth, and learned. It is here, obviously, that contextual criticism becomes crucial to the project of this book.[8] Yet understanding this historical background requires literary-critical decoding of the various means by which women's material and subjective experiences can be occluded. In other words, when we study historical background, we must also forefront what is, essentially, the textuality of social context. In so doing, we can begin a radical critique of the extraliterary textual constructions that presented their own readings of medieval and early modern women: the contemporary economic, legal, political, and religious systems and codes articulating the parameters of women's access to power and self-determination.

By contending that such codes were, like literary writings, male textual activities without reference to or unrepresentative of women's selfhoods or their subjective experiences, we are not suggesting that these codes did not exert a powerful influence over the lives of real women. Awareness of the textuality of these systems does, however, reveal their primary grounding in masculinist interests, even when they claim to work for "women's good." Elizabeth Robertson's analysis of the *Ancrene Wisse*, a thirteenth-century spiritual guide for anchoresses, points usefully to the ways in which the *Wisse*-author's received conceptions of women influenced the form, structure, and imagery of a work intended to address the very issue of women's subjectivities. Indeed, her essay can serve as a model for analyzing the pressure exerted upon historical women by the textuality of social context. The various codes and systems of the world around them necessarily limited most women's access to power, but we must ask—although this is a question we can probably never answer: in what ways did these textual constructions of women influence women's conceptions of themselves?[9]

Of course, historical, if not fictional, women worked in, around, and beyond these systems, responding to the demands of their lives, their personalities, their minds, and their desires.[10] Yet only recently have we been able to obtain a clearer picture of women's lived experience in these periods and of their movement within formal articulations of their place and power. With the establishment of Women's Studies as a field of inquiry and the project of developing a feminist historiography, medieval and early modern women are, to quote the title of an important contribution to this enterprise, "becoming visible." [11] As influential as that title has been, it is also dangerous: it represents and exerts a temptation to reify textual constructions of historical women. It is here that postmodern literary theory, with its radical critique of the self, of semiological systems, and of textuality, can inform feminist historical analyses of women and their lives. Two prominent contributions to the study of medieval and early modern women—Eileen Power's *Medieval Women* and Joan Kelly-Gadol's "Did Women Have a Renaissance?"— suggest the kinds of questions that feminist literary theory can raise and must ask of the conclusions and assumptions drawn from the historical context.

Power's posthumously published study emerges from the Cambridge school of social and economic history, rather than from the late twentieth-century project of feminist historiography. Essentially descriptive in its approach, this study offers important insights into the material conditions of medieval women of the three estates. Power's descriptions, however, can produce misleading conclusions about women's "status" and welfare, as, for example, when she represents the position of bourgeois and peasant women in relation to that of their aristocratic counterparts:

> As we descend the social scale, we do not find the role of women declining. On the contrary her activity, if she is alone, her importance in the life of the family, if she is married, is all the greater for the modesty, indeed exigency, of her income and possessions.[12]

Power's recognition of women's contributions to feudal and emerging capitalist economies is important indeed if we are to see the history of working women as anything but a sequence of victimizations; if, in other words, we are to locate the ways in which women actively participated in their societies.[13] Yet Power's statement raises a number of questions about the degree to which the "importance" of these historical women was valued. Are we to understand from Power's interpretative description that bourgeois and peasant women were, in some way, "better off" than women of the aristocracy? As significant contributors to domestic and national economies, were they allowed access to the economic benefits of their work? Did relative equality in productive labor significantly influence the lives of women who, because of their class, constantly confronted "exigency," poor diets, dangerous pregnancies, and the burdens of the unremitting labor that gave them whatever claim they might have had to "equality"? And, because the textual record is especially silent about the experiences of women in these classes, how can we know whether they had any conception of what we would call "equality," or whether, given the conditions of their lives, they would have valued it?[14] Power's observation is founded upon the assumption, as Penny Schine Gold has described it, "[t]hat there is a unitary status of women in every society that can be measured over time and compared cross culturally." [15] And while we may never be able to answer many of these questions, by the same token, we must resist the conclusion to which Power's assumptions about status and about a coherent and unitary female self might lead us: a conclusion romanticizing the power or prestige of women who worked alongside men in shops or fields.

Joan Kelly-Gadol's "Did Women Have a Renaissance?" dates from the beginning of the feminist historiographical project. In this influential essay, Kelly-Gadol argued that women in the early modern period experienced a curtailment of the autonomy, power, and self-determination enjoyed by their medieval foremothers.[16] Indeed, there is evidence that, with the development of capitalism, government by bureaucracies, and increased professionalization of fields like law and medicine, early modern women did in fact wield less influence outside the home, in the structures of urban government, than had their aristocratic and upper-middle-class counterparts on the manor or in the guild.[17] In the construction of her argument, however, Kelly-Gadol adduces a good deal of her evidence about the relative power and prestige of medieval and renaissance women from literary texts.[18] The result can be statements overvaluing the influence and self-determination of women within the feudal aristocracy:

> Renaissance ideas on love and manners, more classical than medieval, and almost exclusively a male product, expressed this new subordination of [renaissance] women to the interests of husbands and male-dominated kin groups and served to justify the removal of women from an "unladylike" position of power and erotic independence.[19]

By assuming the facticity and referentiality of medieval courtly love literature, Kelly-Gadol could posit the "power and erotic independence" of medieval women. Yet, as Roberta Krueger and Sheila Fisher demonstrate in their essays in this volume, literary ascriptions of this kind of privilege did not coincide with the relative lack of power accorded aristocratic medieval women by the laws and customs of feudal society. In formulating her conclusions about renaissance women, Kelly-Gadol elides the implications of courtly ideology for both medieval and early modern women, and thus misses the significant fact that, by and large, the codes and conventions of courtly love were articulations not of women's "erotic independence," but of masculine desire.[20] Kelly-Gadol's argument, then, asks us to believe in a direct referentiality between literary text and historical reality: "Insofar as images of women relate to what really goes on, we can infer from them something about that social reality."[21] But, as feminist literary critics know, the relationship between the textual record and historical experience is too problematic to allow us to read literary images as representations of women's lives and of their subjectivities.

These two important studies suggest the dangers of "finding" the historical women whose lives are often absent from the textual records contemporary both to their world and to ours. They also demonstrate that, if historical study is necessary for understanding women's place in earlier literature, then feminist literary theory is necessary for examining historical interpretations. As Power's work shows, historiography that claims "objectivity" can often end by encoding assumptions about women and class within its arrangements of data and descriptions. And, while Kelly-Gadol's essay locates itself squarely within feminist ideology, its own reluctance to examine carefully the ideology of texts results in an interpretative representation of women that obscures the material conditions of women's lives and the legal and political systems—the nonliterary textual constructions—that positioned women in their societies. Finally, writings like those of Power and Kelly-Gadol occlude the absence of women's subjective experience from the textual records of these periods. By failing to engage the textuality of social, legal, and literary constructions of women and by assuming a coherent self, they fail to illuminate the subjectivities of real women or the difficult processes of reading which these largely vanished subjectivities demand of us.

THE PROBLEMS CONFRONTING THE EFFORT to locate historical women in the periods we are studying place special pressures on what Elaine Showalter has called "gynocritics"—on the criticism of the literary activity of women themselves.[22] The critical desire to seek in early texts by women the harbingers of "the woman's voice" presupposes an essential female self, and reintroduces into feminist discourse that repressive identity which has been so evident in the masculinist literary canon and criticism.[23] But even more obviously here than in work on the male literary tradition, the problem of real women's subjective experiences of selfhood is the decentered pole around which our thinking should rotate elliptically. Without denying the importance of Showalter's central question—"What is *the difference* of women's writing?"—we must acknowledge that earlier writings by women demand that we pose a prior question: what are the relationships of historical women to the forms of power mediated by writing?

This question suggests a continuum between women silenced by illiteracy and women struggling within the institutions of literature. In her essay, Anne J. Cruz places the Spanish female picaresque—a male literary tradition—in the historical context of contemporary prostitution not to establish a referential link between them, but rather to show how literature reaffirms ideology *about* women. Unlike the subversive *pícaro,* the *pícara* is a "deviant insider" defined by a collusion between dominant morality and economics. Cruz's analysis shows the literary text colluding with a symbolic system that contributed directly to the actual oppression of real women. Janet E. Halley's essay focuses on Anne More Donne, the wife of the famous poet John Donne, to expose the social and poetic significance of Anne Donne's illiteracy. Halley argues that the exclusion of this historical woman from her husband's social practice of literary exchange is persistently part of the meaning both of that exchange and of the texts it circulated. Margaret Maurer takes the next step, by selecting a text which allows her to examine the insertion of real women into the production of literary meaning. She discovers a tension between the court ladies who participated in Ben Jonson's *Masque of Queens* and the roles Jonson gave them to play. As these masquers resist the forms of meaning assigned to them, Jonson's deeply misogynous poetic strategies contain that resistance. Finally, Maurer argues, Jonson engenders meaning itself as male, rendering the Queen and her ladies silent in their own self-representation. Margaret Maurer's, Janet Halley's, and Anne Cruz's essays suggest the ways in which real women can be absent even when they are the reference of or, indeed, *participants in* literary production.

These three essays further suggest that a particularly fruitful place to focus work on women as readers and authors in these periods is where the problematics of their participation are sharpest. When we consider that, despite widespread illiteracy, there were literate women who could not only provide the audience for but also be the authors of texts, how can we go about gauging the existence of something that we can call "women's literature" in these periods? Efforts to formulate a "gynocritics" for earlier writings must pay special attention to what Showalter, following Susan Lanser and Evelyn Torton Beck, calls the "double-voiced discourse" of women writers:[24] the muted voice of women's culture and the dominant voice of masculine authority are so intertwined that closely contextual study is required if we are to hear them. In her essay, Elizabeth Robertson, for instance, examines the extent to which an important body of Middle English prose, addressed to historical anchoresses, but written by a man, constitutes a "women's literature" and a peculiarly female contribution to the continuity of vernacular prose. And Patricia Francis Cholakian, as she follows Marie de Gournay through repeated revisions of her text, demonstrates that the paternal "authority" of her adoptive father Michel de Montaigne pervades the woman writer's self-definition, even when she keeps him in his place as audience and even when she speaks past him to an audience of women.

THE ESSAYS COLLECTED HERE STAND, then, at the intersection of Anglo-American empirical historicism and French theories of textuality. In different ways, they work at the limits imposed on criticism by a feminist awareness that historical women were real in ways that must necessarily be absent from the textual record: they inhabited subjective realities and real subjectivities. The dangers of *forgetting* the woman-who-is-not-referred-to in the pursuit of postmodern reading are suggested by Gayatri Spivak, who assesses what "we-women" might think on reading Derrida's claim in *Éperons* that he is a "woman." By stepping into the position that Nietzsche assigned to woman, that of the impersonator, and by claiming that shifting, decentered, unstable identity as his own, Derrida both destabilizes phallocentrism and, as Spivak argues, displaces historical women yet once more:

> "we-women" . . . cannot dismiss our double displacement by saying to ourselves: "In the discourse of affirmative deconstruction, 'we' are a 'female element,' which does not signify 'female person.' " [25]

The double displacement of woman that Spivak discerns in affirmative deconstruction is echoed, as Roberta Krueger's essay argues, in male-authored literary texts in which a female voice is created to speak for the author to other men: it can be echoed again in critical efforts to appropriate the feminine in early texts to pure textuality. Without asserting a biological determinism, we can insist that the historical presence of people living in female bodies and experiencing the historical pressures applied to them places constraints on the analysis of textuality as feminine and requires careful analysis of the social uses of literary texts.

In answer to Foucault's famous question, "What matter who's speaking?"—with which he predicted the quiet apocalypse that will free us of the repressive Western subject[26]—we agree with Nancy K. Miller that

> This sovereign indifference . . . is one of the "masks . . . behind which phallocentrism hides its fictions": the authorizing function of its own discourse authorizes the "end of woman" without consulting her. I would answer it matters, for example, to women who have lost and still routinely lose their proper name in marriage, and whose signature—not merely their voice—has not been worth the paper it was written on; women for whom the signature—by virtue of its power in the world of circulation—is *not* immaterial. Only those who have it can play with not having it.[27]

Refusing to abandon the historical existence of women, Miller calls for "a female materialism" involving a "decentered vision (*theoria*) but a centered action that will not result in renewed invisibility" of academic or literary women[28]—or, we would add, of those historical women whose illiteracy has made their silence irrevocable. For feminist literary critics working on texts in the "earlier" literatures of Europe, Miller's argument calls for the development of approaches that hold a certain ambivalence firmly in mind. We know that medieval and early modern women lived: we know that they marshalled their wits and resources, that they endured, triumphed, suffered, and died in the silence we now hear when we listen for them. We need a literary method—or methods—that will respect the many forms of their presence in history, while developing ways of gauging or describing their absence from the literary record. We should not displace them again; but neither should we simplify their presence, create them in our own image, or romanticize their occlusion by "restoring" them.

The essays collected here are rooted in a feminist awareness that the historical self of women is a compelling and yet elusive subject of study. But since we, as readers, are also historical women, we should recognize that an adequate approach to this study may require placing both the text and the reader back into historical motion, in an activity destabilizing the text and the self. Marguerite Waller's essay, in its insistence on the inconclusiveness of context and in its rejection of imperial selfhood, exemplifies this activity. Waller's critique of new historicism destabilizes her own reading project and resists creating presence where none exists. Margaret Maurer forefronts this problem by entitling her essay "*Reading* Ben Jonson's *Queens*" (emphasis added). She finds herself confronted with a poet for whom the poetic idea was a property of the masculine mind, and with the historical fact that his masque was enacted by women conveniently (apparently) indifferent to the meanings he made of them. In the double bind of *Queens*, Maurer observes, feminist critics find themselves figured in the antimasque hags—Impudence, Ignorance, Bitterness—who, under the leadership of Mischief, expose the distortions of women on which traditional poetical meaning depends. Thus revisionist reading works its own distortions on the critics themselves. Reading women in canonized texts, she suggests, may reliably offer us only "occasions to calculate the price we pay to participate in significant discourse."

This volume, then, offers not a solution, but a problem. It is a problem that we have begun to define by casting our sights widely to include not only literary, but also historical writings, not only major male-authored works of the established canon, but also female-authored work, noncanonical texts, and writings which the academy has considered "minor," tangential or ancillary to the defined currents of the western literary tradition. Moreover, this volume presents not a monolithic methodology, but a collective argument for a multifaceted contextualism. Methodological diversity constitutes, we believe, the strength of feminist theory—a theory that, because it participates in many methods, ends by resisting the hegemonics of any unitary theory.[29] And methodological diversity is, as the critics in this volume demonstrate, the only adequate method for mapping the complexity of the problem that they are presenting here.

NOTES

1. Joan Thirsk, "Foreward," *Women in English Society, 1500–1800*, ed. Mary Prior (London and New York: Methuen, 1985), 2.

2. A concise but thorough analysis of the effects of patriarchal social, political, economic and intellectual systems on the groups these systems marginalize can be found in the "Introduction" by Margaret Ferguson (with Maureen Quilligan and Nancy J. Vickers) to *Rewriting the Renaissance: The Discourses of*

Sexual Difference in Early Modern Europe (Chicago: Univ. of Chicago Press, 1986), xv–xxxi.

3. A trove of works by medieval and early modern women has been made readily available in recent years. Among the new texts: Joan Goulianos, ed., *By a Woman Writt* (Baltimore: Penguin Books, 1973); Mary R. Mahl and Helene Koon, eds., *The Female Spectator: English Women Writers Before 1800* (Bloomington: Indiana Univ. Press, 1977); Betty Travitsky, ed., *The Paradise of Women: Writings by Englishwomen of the Renaissance* (Westport, Conn.: Greenwood, 1981); Margaret L. King and Albert Rabil, eds., *Her Immaculate Hands: Selected Works by and about the Women Humanists of Quattrocento Italy* (Binghamton, N.Y.: Center for Medieval and Early Renaissance Studies, 1983); Katharine M. Wilson, ed., *Medieval Women Writers* (Athens: Univ. of Georgia Press, 1984); and Moira Ferguson, *First Feminists: British Women Writers, 1578–1799* (Bloomington: Indiana Univ. Press; Old Westbury, N.Y.: Feminist Press, 1985).

4. On the obfuscations and dangers attendant upon the category of "woman," see Sheila Ryan Johansson, " 'Herstory' as History: A New Field or Another Fad?" in *Liberating Women's History*, ed. Berenice A. Carroll (Urbana: Univ. of Illinois Press, 1976), 402–3. And for a sustained examination of this problem, see Catherine Belsey, *The Subject of Tragedy: Identity and Difference in Renaissance Drama* (New York: Methuen, 1985), particularly her chapter on "Silence and Speech," 149–91.

5. See H. Marshall Leicester, Jr., "Of a Fire in the Dark: Public and Private Feminism in the *Wife of Bath's Tale*," *Women's Studies* 11 (1984): 175. Elaine Hansen considerably expands the implications of the Wife of Bath's non-referentiality in her essay, "The Wife of Bath and the Mark of Adam," *Women's Studies* 15 (1988): 77–94.

6. Eve Kosofsky Sedgwick, *Between Men: English Literature and Male Homosocial Desire* (New York: Columbia Univ. Press, 1985).

7. Adrienne Munich, "Notorious Signs, Feminist Criticism and Literary Tradition," in *Making A Difference: Feminist Literary Criticism*, ed. Gayle Greene and Coppélia Kahn (New York: Methuen, 1985), 244. See Gerda Lerner's discussion of the need to assess both the victimization and the contributions of women to their own and to their societies' histories in her essay, "Placing Women in History: A 1975 Perspective," in *Liberating Women's History*, 358–59.

8. For an exercise of such contextualism, see Linda Woodbridge's excellent study of the *hic mulier* controversy in Renaissance English life and literature, *Women and the English Renaissance: Literature and the Nature of Womankind, 1540–1650* (Urbana: Univ. of Illinois Press, 1984). Taken as a whole, a useful new anthology of essays edited by Mary Beth Rose—*Women in the Middle Ages and the Renaissance: Literary and Historical Perspectives* (Syracuse, N.Y.: Syracuse Univ. Press, 1986)—examines the interplay of historical and literary analysis.

9. Further work along the lines suggested by Robertson's essay could find no better place to begin than the richly descriptive bibliography compiled by Suzanne W. Hull, *Chaste, Silent, and Obedient: English Books for Women, 1475–1640* (San Marino, Calif.: Huntington Library Press, 1982).

10. See Thirsk; also see Shulamith Shahar, *The Fourth Estate: A History of Women in the Middle Ages*, trans. Chaya Galai (New York: Methuen, 1983).

11. *Becoming Visible: Women in European History*, ed. Renate Bridenthal and Claudia Koonz (Boston: Houghton Mifflin, 1977).

12. Eileen Power, *Medieval Women*, ed. M. M. Postan (Cambridge: Cambridge Univ. Press, 1975), 53.

13. Lerner, 358–59.

14. Penny Schine Gold, *The Lady and the Virgin: Image, Attitude, and Experience in Twelfth-Century France* (Chicago: Univ. of Chicago Press, 1985), xviii. See also p. xx.

15. For the value placed on the life of the peasant woman, see Emily Coleman's study of female infanticide, "Infanticide in the Early Middle Ages," in *Women in Medieval Society*, ed. Susan Mosher Stuard (Philadelphia: Univ. of Pennsylvania Press, 1980), 47–70.

16. Joan Kelly-Gadol, "Did Women Have a Renaissance?", *Becoming Visible*, 137–64.

17. See Hilda Smith, "Feminism and the Methodology of Women's History," *Liberating Women's History*, 381–82.

18. For another estimate of the problem posed by Kelly-Gadol, and another suggestion that literary texts provide direct evidence of women's "mentalities," see Stuard, "Introduction," *Women in Medieval Society*, 10.

19. Kelly-Gadol, 161.

20. For astute critiques of courtly love and its implications for medieval women, see E. Jane Burns and Roberta L. Krueger, "Introduction," *Courtly Ideology and Woman's Place in Medieval French Literature*, ed. Burns and Krueger, spec. issue of *Romance Notes* 25, no. 3 (Spring 1985): 205–19; and Toril Moi, "Desire in Language: Andreas Cappelanus and the Controversy of Courtly Love," in *Medieval Literature: Criticism, Ideology, and History*, ed. David Aers (New York: St. Martin's, 1985), 11–33.

21. Kelly-Gadol, 144.

22. Elaine Showalter, "Feminist Criticism in the Wilderness," *Writing and Sexual Difference*, ed. Elizabeth Abel, spec. issue of *Critical Inquiry* 8, no. 2 (Winter 1981): 185. This essay was republished in *Writing and Sexual Difference*, ed. Elizabeth Abel (Chicago: Univ. of Chicago Press, 1982), 1–35.

23. See Maria C. Lugones and Elizabeth V. Spelman, "Have We Got a Theory for You!: Feminist Theory, Cultural Imperialism, and the Demand for 'The Woman's Voice,' " *Hypatia, A Journal of Feminist Philosophy*, spec. issue of *Women's Studies International Forum* 6, no. 6 (1983): 573–81.

24. Susan Lanser and Evelyn Torton Beck, "[Why] Are There No Great

Women Critics? And What Difference Does It Make?" in *The Prism of Sex: Essays in the Sociology of Knowledge*, ed. Evelyn Torton Beck and Julia A. Sherman (Madison: Univ. of Wisconsin Press, 1979), 86; Showalter, 201.

25. Gayatri Chakravorty Spivak, "Displacement and the Discourse of Woman," in *Displacement, Derrida and After*, ed. Mark Krupnick (Bloomington: Indiana Univ. Press, 1983), 174.

26. Michel Foucault, "What is an Author?", in *Language, Counter-Memory, Practice*, ed. Donald F. Bouchard (Ithaca, N.Y.: Cornell Univ. Press, 1980), 138.

27. Nancy K. Miller, "The Text's Heroine: A Feminist Critic and her Fictions," *Cherchez la femme*, spec. issue of *Diacritics* 12 (Summer 1982): 53.

28. Miller, 53.

29. For a discussion of this diversity, see Elaine Showalter's introductory essay, "The Feminist Critical Revolution," in *Feminist Criticism: Essays on Women, Literature, and Theory*, ed. Showalter (New York: Pantheon, 1985), 3–17.

Part One

Exchanging Women:
Male Texts and Homosocial Contexts

Double Jeopardy: The Appropriation of Woman in Four Old French Romances of the "Cycle de la Gageure"

Roberta L. Krueger

I. Woman, Metaphor, and History

The relationship of the heroine of twelfth- and thirteenth-century Old French romances to the "real" aristocratic women who may have read or heard these stories has been much disputed. The early view held that the privileging of the lady in romance reflected the tastes and status of historical courtly ladies, whose "clairvoyante sagesse" (in the words of a female scholar)[1] or whose "charme," "beauté féminine," and "instruction" (in the words of a male critic)[2] had opened the way for "une autre race féminine."[3] Despite its persistent appeal, this simple "reflection" theory appears inadequate in several respects to the complexities of history and the romances themselves.[4]

First, the new historical thesis that woman's social influence declined significantly under the new primogeniture and marriage systems imposed by the male aristocracy and the Church in this period argues strongly against the myth of medieval woman's power.[5] It suggests rather that the idealization of woman in romance masks her social degradation in history. Secondly, the notion of strong feminine influence underemphasizes the fact that the vast majority of courtly texts were written by male clerics for "seigneurs" and other "clercs" as well as for ladies. As Joan Ferrante has reminded us, the woman in most courtly texts is a masculine construct that tells us more about male fantasy than about the reality of female experience.[6] Finally, such a view oversimplifies the poetics of courtly romance. Far from being straightforward "romans à thèse" idealizing chivalry or femininity, many romances are self-conscious literary creations that reflect upon and question the very amorous or social ideology they purport to espouse. To read the inscription of woman in Old French romance as any less problematic than her appearance in, for example, the work of Stendhal or Sand is to discredit the literary sophistication of the earliest French *romans*.

At the other extreme of the critical spectrum from the reflection theory is the recent view, held by some French critics, that the woman in medieval romance provides no information at all about her historical counterpart. No flesh and blood character, the romance woman is a *sign* who calls forth an extended meditation on (male) writing and desire. According to Jean-Charles Huchet, the desire for woman is the very condition of romance: "Support du désir, la femme permit au roman de parler du désir d'écrire et de l'amour de la langue là où il parlait du désir et de l'amour."[7] Woman in romance is "woman," a metaphor for the poetical discourse of men who write romance. "Grâce à la femme," says Huchet, "le roman découvre la théorie et, au défaut des traités de rhétorique, énonce au féminin une 'poétique' du roman."[8]

Such a conception of woman, whose debt to poststructuralist and psychoanalytic theory is evident, offers an important corrective to the literal historicizing of early critics. It helps to mark the limits for a feminist reading of woman in medieval literature. If woman in romance is a metaphor, then we can never reconstruct the "real" medieval woman from her literary representations. The question with which Georges Duby concludes *Le Chevalier, la femme, et le prêtre*—"Que sait-on d'elles?"— remains unanswerable for literary texts in the light of woman's absence.[9]

But, from the perspective of feminist criticism, the reading of woman as metaphor is also a dangerous practice. If undertaken uncritically, such a reading erases the gap that woman's absence inscribes. It ignores the implications of metaphorization for the historical women who were an indisputable part of the audience. Reading woman as a sign of male discourse within patriarchal ideology, a feminist analysis can explore the very process of woman's metaphorization as an aspect of her cultural "subjection."

To take woman as a metaphor, and to make of her a pretext for literary discourse, is to appropriate and displace the subjectivity of the absent "real" woman. As Gayatri Spivak has said of woman's position in deconstructive discourse, woman's transformation into the "subject" of male critics and philosophers is a move that "doubly displaces" the figure of woman.[10] She is displaced first as a female who is not-a-man, but the object of male desire, and second as the marginal subject through which the male thinker can stand in opposition to phallocentric culture. This displacement, says Spivak, has its historical roots in the project of phallocentric culture to appropriate female reproductive power and affirm patriarchal law:

> The institution of phallocentric law is congruent with the need to prove paternity and authority, to secure property by transforming the child into an alienated object named and possessed by the father, and to secure property by transforming the woman into a mediating instrument of the production and passage of property.[11]

To ignore the question of "real" woman's absence in twelfth- and thirteenth-century texts is to overlook the historical implications of romance narrative's appropriation of woman. Insofar as "woman" exists as a construct of masculine thought that generates *male* discourse, the power of historical women to produce and to reproduce their own meaning has been appropriated. Duby has shown that romance arises at the same period that primogeniture affirms the father's line as determinant of family order. Can we not consider the displacement of woman and the appropriation of her power as a central problem—or project—in romance?

II. The Wager

> Le but des histoires de ce cycle était la glorification de la vertu de la femme et on peut les opposer aux contes qui tâchaient de s'en moquer et de l'avilir.[12]

Four thirteenth-century romances from the "cycle de la gageure" (the wager cycle) provide an excellent locus for an analysis of this problem.[13] These stories—*Le Roman du Comte de Poitiers*; Gerbert de Montreuil's *Le Roman de la Violette*; *Le Roman du Roi Flore et de la Belle Jehane*; and Jean Renart's *Le Roman de la Rose ou de Guillaume de Dole*[14]—

participate in a broad tradition of narratives in which an innocent woman is falsely accused and later vindicated.[15] They have been hailed by some critics as a celebration of feminine virtue and ingenuity in a century noted for its literary misogyny.[16] But their common "glorification de la vertu de la femme" masks a displacement and appropriation of female sexual power by means of narrative strategies that invite our investigation.

The romances recast, in various ways, the common wager plot: an evil knight challenges a husband (or fiancé) to bet on the sexual fidelity or chastity of his wife (or fiancée); both knights place their land and their honor at stake. When the challenging knight claims to have seduced the woman and offers false signs of her sexual favors, the innocent lady immediately loses her honor and her position at court. In many cases, she is threatened with death by her knight or another relative. After a series of episodes in which she proves her devotion and exemplary virtue, the lady is vindicated, the rival punished, and the couple reunited or married.

Rather than read the trials of virtuous heroines as a reflection of the high moral status accorded to historical women, let us consider the evident displacement of woman's sexual and reproductive autonomy that the romances inscribe. Each story revolves in some way around the threat female sexuality poses to chivalric honor, a threat whose ultimate realization would produce illegitimate male heirs. The heroine's role is that of an object of exchange between two knights who use her as a testing ground for their own honor.[17] Insofar as they are genealogical narratives, we can group these texts within the "matrimonial cycle" of French romances that problematize patrilineal succession.[18] Unlike other romances in this group, where the threat to the patriarchal order arises from consensual love, the danger in the wager romances is located solely in the woman's body. The villain's articulation of female sexuality in a sign—a ring, a rose, a violet—disgraces the husband/fiancé whose honor depends on her fidelity or chastity. The wager romance is a "test" of the chivalric system's ability to contain and control the threat of female sexuality.

In its own way, each narrative dramatizes what historians have described as aristocratic woman's role as an exchange object in the marriage system.[19] The anxiety about female chastity underlying the wager reveals the crucial role of the chaste woman as guarantor of legitimacy in primogeniture. Furthermore, the legal bind in which the heroines find themselves—they are unable to assert the truth of their denial against the false signs of the self-proclaimed seducer—reflects woman's incapacity within the medieval legal system. A married woman could not bear testimony or make an appeal without her husband's sanction;[20] a maiden could not appeal without a champion because, as Beaumanoir says, "feme ne se peut combatre" [woman cannot fight].[21] Although the vindictive cruelty of the husband or relatives who attempt to kill the calumniated woman oversteps the bounds of corporal punishment permitted by customary law in cases where a wife is "en voie de fere folie de son cors, ou quant ele desment son mari ou maudit" [committing a folly with her body or when she lies to or curses her husband] (here her punishment should be "sans mort et sans mehaing" [without death and without wound][22]), it is not out of keeping with the punishment accepted for adultery *in flagrante delicto,* where both wife and rival may be killed.[23] (The wife or friend is of course never caught in the act, but is entirely innocent.) The crude exchange of the woman in the wager and the violence or threatened violence against her that ensue are fictional configurations of historical woman's physical vulnerability in the face of the sanctioned sexual dominance of the feudal aristocracy.[24]

It will not be difficult to show how the following wager plots recast the appropriation of female sexual autonomy. But to read these texts only as an evident figuration of historical woman's oppression will not take us far beyond the "reflection" function of romance; we will merely be reading the reflection on the dark side of the mirror. A more compelling question for feminist criticism is to ask how it is that this primary appropriation is *itself* displaced (embellished/ obscured/ mystified) in particular ways by narrative strategies that appear to privilege and glorify the "heroine."

For in each of our texts the heroine vindicates her honor, either by submissive devotion—in *Le Roman du comte de Poitiers* and *Le Roman de la Violette*—or by ingenious manipulation of the system—in *Le Roman du roi Flore et de la Belle Jehane* and *Le Roman de la Rose ou de Guillaume de Dole.* The differences between the passive heroines in *Poitiers* and *Violette* and their active counterparts in *Flore et Jehane* and *Guillaume de Dole* are striking, as are the differences in their narrators' stances toward the chivalric system and their literary art. The narrator whose heroine is "passive" reaffirms the justice of the chivalric ethic without seriously questioning the system. The "active" heroine, as we shall see, accompanies a more critical analysis of courtly relationships and of woman's place. Most remarkable is the forceful *mise en question* of the courtly system effected by Lienor in Jean Renart's *Guillaume de Dole*, a work that surpasses the others in its self-reflective scrutiny of language and literary form. Yet, despite their literary and ideological divergences, each of these stories appropriates the heroine in its examination of a system to which she is always reassimilated. Like the knight within the story who stakes his honor on a woman's body, the narrator and his implied audience use the figure of woman to test the honor of their courtly discourse.

The narrative appropriation of woman is reflected in the very structure of these stories: each text embeds the crisis of female virtue within an overarching narrative of male honor. In each case, the narrator's exploration of his female character's dilemma allows him to test and to scrutinize the courtly values which he espouses. The stories' celebratory exemplification of female virtue, be it active or passive, obscures the fact of woman's primary appropriation in the feudal marriage system; the crude terms of the wager are apparently reversed in the happy ending. Even in that romance where the narrator's social critique and his heroine's autonomy are the most remarkable, the *Guillaume de Dole*, the heroine remains above all an object of the narrator's appropriation and mystification.

III. Passive Virtue: *Le Roman du Comte de Poitiers*

The dynamics of appropriating glorification are straightforward in *Le Roman du Comte de Poitiers*, which recasts the most "primitive," if not necessarily the oldest, version of the "gageure." [25] In this text, the division between the plot of female virtue and that of male honor is clear. After describing the perils of the heroine and her vindication (ll. 1–1229), the romance recounts her son Gui's succession to the throne of Constantinople (1230–1719). The heroine's passive devotion, unswerving chastity, and wifely subservience shore up the "honor" of the male line in the overarching genealogy.

The narrative's appropriation begins with a vulgar boast, when the

Count brags in court that his sexual exploits with his demanding wife are more heroic than Pepin's feats, and that his exclusive possession of her makes him richer than the King:

> "Plus avés fait k'ainc ne fist nus,
> Mais jo gis quant je vuel tous nus
> Avec la plus bele del mont.
> Adés me prie ele et semont
> Et tart et tempre et main et soir
> Que de li face mon voloir."
>
> (41–46)

[You have done more than anyone, but I lie naked when I wish to with the world's most beautiful woman. She always begs and invites me, early and late, day and night, to do what I want with her.]

> ". . . Rois Pepins, miex valt sa biautés
> Que ne face vo roiautés.
> Par tant sui plus rices de vous,
> Et si n'en sui mie jalous."
>
> (65–68)

[King Pepin, her beauty is worth more than your royalty. I am so much richer than you, and I am not jealous.]

Such a performance effectively puts the wife into discursive circulation. Its arrogant claim prompts the wager of the Duke of Normandy who bets, staking the lands of Normandy against those of Poitou, that he will have carnal knowledge of the faithful wife within a month's time (70–79). By accepting the seducer's terms, the husband negotiates his wife's body as a sign of his honor: her chastity stands metonymically for his fortune. When the Duke crassly attempts to seduce the Countess, by handling her food at table and fondling her (she here threatens to strike him!), the Countess says that she would rather be killed, burned, or drowned than disgrace the Count. As her husband had done by accepting the wager, she stakes her body for his honor:

> Laissiés ester vo legerie.
> Anchois soie jo mise en biere,
> Ou jetee en une caudiere
> Toute plaine de plonc boullant,
> Les piés deseur, la teste avant,
> U es ondes de mer noïe,

Arse, ventee et garallie,
Que hounesisse mon signor
Qui m'a porté si grant honor.

(186–94)

[Stop this nonsense. I would rather be put in a bier, or thrown in a cauldron full of boiling lead, feet up head down, or drowned in the waves of the sea, burned, and grilled and thrown to the winds, than shame my lord who has brought me such great honor.]

It matters little that the Duke has failed to possess the wife's physical body. As a master of the discursive system, he is able to appropriate parts of her—ten hairs, a ring, and a piece of her dress—with the help of a duenna, parts that become "signs" ("ensagnes") of possession when he displays them at court. His duplicitous discourse prevails over the Countess's brief protestation of innocence, and Pepin rejects her plea for a trial by ordeal: "Vous ensagnes vous ont provée" [your signs have proved you] (432). The sexual double standard is evident. The seducer, who has ostensibly forced a violation of the marital bond and is as much an "adulterer" as the wife, is honored with the holdings of Poitou; the woman is led away to be killed by the husband she has dishonored. "Car jou me vengerai de li," he threatens (460).

Le Roman du Comte de Poitiers boldly states the power of female sexuality to destroy the patrimony. The Count laments that he has lost "ma cointe cite de Poitiers" [my delightful city of Poitiers] for his love of a woman (504–6), and he accuses the Countess of being pregnant by the Duke as he prepares to kill her (501–33). But this appropriating narrative works to contain the threat of female sexuality within an ideology of male chivalry and feminine passivity. The Countess's identification with Mary, chaste Mother of God, whom she claims to serve as her "ancele lige" [faithful servant] (425) and whose name she repeatedly invokes as witness and protector of her chastity (424–25; 545; 647–52; 1059–62), reinforces her subservient humility.[26] In words that echo her service to Mary, she pleads innocence, devotion, and servitude to her assailant husband—"Je sui vo feme et vo ancele" [I am your wife and your servant] (543). Even when threatened with death, she shows mercy: she warns her husband of a lion who is about to attack him just as he has raised his sword to slay her.

The plot of feminine virtue compounds examples of wifely devotion in the section that describes the Countess's perils in the hands of Harpin, who attempts to force her to marry him. Twice more she wishes for death or torture rather than dishonor her husband (654–58; 984–88). When she is brought against her will to the altar, the narrator's *descriptio* (933–68) portrays someone whose resplendent beauty and purity surpass those of all other women (966). The Count, having learned that she is blameless, comes to his wife's rescue at the moment that Harpin has struck the reluctant bride and bloodied her face on the marriage altar (991–94). The romance figures woman's virtue as a martyrdom that preserves the integrity of man's land and honor.

Despite the manifest misogyny and violence of the romance's male characters, the narrator ultimately deploys the Countess's passive subservience to validate knighthood and feudal justice. Paradoxically, the Countess depends upon her husband to save her from the very victimization his complicity in the wager created. She is ultimately vindicated by a form of male-to-male violence sanctioned by the social and divine orders, a *judicium Dei,* or trial by combat between the Count and the Duke.

Such an outcome fulfills the narrator's previous promises to his public that God always punishes "mortex traïson" [mortal treason] and that God will lead the Countess to a safe harbor (868). The deceitful Duke and duenna are assigned gruesome punishments appropriate to feudal treason. Pepin bestows Normandy on the Countess, who becomes the "dame des Normans." [27] That night, the reunited couple conceives their son Gui, whose rise to emperor is narrated in the final five hundred lines of verse. This narrative of paternal lineage appropriates the "chaste" female body as an irrefutable sign of legitimacy and celebrates subservient feminine devotion.

IV. A Woman's Consolation:
Le Roman de la Violette

Like her counterpart in the *Roman du Comte de Poitiers,* the heroine of the *Roman de la Violette* exemplifies passive virtues that reaffirm the justice of feudal institutions. Gerbert de Montreuil recasts the basic plot of *Poitiers* in an enlarged and embellished courtly frame addressed, significantly, to a female reader. Dedicated to a woman whose lands were confiscated by Philippe-Auguste, the *Roman de la Violette* presents an exemplary heroine whose "fois et loyauté" [faith and loyalty] were rewarded with the return of her former high status and happiness.[28] When Gerbert states in his Epilogue that the Countess de Ponthieu regained her lands through her "fois et loyauté," he makes explicit the connection between his heroine's *exemplum* and his dedicatee's travails. Since both women ultimately win back what they had lost by waiting and feudal justice ultimately restores their losses, their common victimization appears to be an error or a temporary lapse in justice rather than a failure of the system itself.

The *Violette* embellishes the material of *Poitiers* with numerous inserted lyric fragments[29] and amplifies the plot with an extensive love quest undertaken by the hero, which occupies the central section of the romance. Perhaps in deference to its female audience, it softens some of the cruder elements of the wager plot. Gerart, for example, pronounces his initial boast in the form of a lyric praising his lady, and the King tries to dissuade the villain from placing the bet, declaring righteously, "Nous veons souvent avient/ Que cil ki velt hounir autri,/ Que li maus revertist sour lui" [We see that misfortune often backfires on someone who tries to shame another] (286–88). Lisiart's seduction attempt is considerably more refined than the awkward gropings in *Poitiers*. He too utters a lyric poem, a "complainte," which is promptly rejected by Euriaut as "fause et fainte" [false and feigned]. Rather than adduce a tangible object as proof of his seduction, he offers a verbal account of a violet he has seen on her breast.[30]

These rhetorical refinements do nothing to alter the basic structure of the wager. Gerart refuses to believe his friend when she protests her innocence, and threatens to punish her "as she deserves":

> "Par foi, ne vous valt escondire,
> Que les ensaignes bien connois;
> Escondis n'i vaut pas deus nois,
> Que terre tolue m'avés;
> Mes tel loier com vous devés
> Arés vous voir prochainnement.
> Or tost montés isnielement."
>
> (980–86)

[In faith, it is not worth it for you to protest, since I recognize the signs; your denial is not worth two cents, since you have taken my land away; but in truth you will get the payment you deserve very soon; now quickly mount.]

As does his counterpart in *Poitiers*, Gerart leads Euriaut into the forest to kill her and spares her life only when she warns him of a serpent that is about to attack. Woman's fate is equally perilous in the "courtly" version of the wager.

Indeed, the *Violette's* principle amplification of the *Poitiers* material —a 4,500-line account of Euriaut's perils in the hands of the Duke de Metz, and Gerart's quest for her after he realizes her innocence— intensifies the heroine's victimization at the same time that it heightens Gerart's valor. In her desperate plight, Euriaut comes to need the very man whose wager initially jeopardized her. Such a "glorification de la vertu féminine" becomes a vindication of the knight who rescues the helpless woman he has endangered.

When Gerart abandons his *amie* in the forest after she has saved his life, Euriaut immediately falls prey to the Duke de Metz, who wants to take her as his woman (1170). By pretending to be a loose woman of low birth, she manages to frighten the Duke's people, who exercise a restraining influence on the lovestruck knight. Then worse misfortunes befall her. She is framed as the murderer of the Duke's sister by the evil knight Meliatir who had intended to slay *her* because she resisted his attempted rape and kicked in three of his teeth (3979–81). If in *Poitiers* the wife repeatedly wishes for martyrdom through corporal mutilation, in *Violette* the heroine comes close to undergoing it. Charged with the murder of her host's sister, she faces the death at the stake.

The grim events of the female subplot are intercalated with Gerart's more profitable adventures. Gerart not only rescues maidens from distress and defends the honor and landholdings of noble families; he also attracts a number of female admirers, one of whom manages to waylay him for a year by means of a love potion. These episodes lessen the brutality of Gerart's complicity in the wager; by portraying the knight as the admired champion of women, rather than their misogynist foe, Gerart's adventures rescue the compromised plot of chivalric romance and make it serve women well once again.[31]

Gerart's active quest joins Euriaut's arduous test at the very moment she has been brought "trestoute nue en sa chemise" [completely naked in her shift] to be burnt at the stake; her only recourse is a sustained prayer which invokes Eve, Mary, and Mary Magdalen (5182–5331). Gerart's defeat of Meliatir in judicial combat proves the efficacy of feudal justice to answer a woman's prayers. The romance restores female honor as the *raison d'être* of chivalry. "M'amie Euriaut" (6009, 6029) becomes Gerart's battle cry during a tournament upon his return to court. Later, he defeats the treacherous Lisiart in judicial combat. Gerart's and Euriaut's marriage, embellished by the lyric accompaniment that has provided an intermittent courtly background in this romance, completes and redeems the model of the chivalric quest that the wager had perverted.

The romance concludes with a celebration of the powers of feminine faith and fidelity. Gerart tells Euriaut that her "fois et loiautés" (6625–26) have saved their love, just as the narrator says that Marie de Ponthieu's "fois" and "loiautés" have restored her lands to her (6657–58). The conclusion that women who wait patiently and loyally will be rewarded with the protection they deserve vindicates the chivalric system as the solution to, rather than the cause of, women's perils. It contains the threat of female sexual autonomy within an ideology of feminine virtue whose passivity necessitates the intercession of controlling male action. By holding up the heroine of the *Violette* as a model for a historical reader, Gerbert implies that other women might also console themselves with the sufficient justice of this system. To the extent that the female reader did identify with the heroine of the *Violette*, she may have found her own autonomy appropriated by the conservative ideology of this romance.

V. Female Privilege: *Flore et Jehane*

At first glance, the late thirteenth-century prose romance, *Li Contes du Roi Flore et de la belle Jehane*, appears to be a more feminocentric text. Certainly, the heroine's ingenuity and active manipulation provide a welcome contrast to the earlier impoverished female portraits. Rather than submit to the system that has defeated her by passively waiting, Jehane takes steps to effect her own vindication. Like some other thirteenth- and fourteenth-century heroines who seek escape from the destiny of gender, Jehane disguises herself as a man.[32] When her husband abandons her (there is no attempted slaying), the clever transvestite collects her money, catches up with her husband on horseback, and offers her services as his squire: "je vous siervirai à mon pooir" [I will serve you as best I can] (p. 114). Squire Jean proves to be considerably more resourceful than her master. She purchases food for them both with her cash reserves; she finances a bakery in Marseille through the sale of their horses; and she quickly sells more than the best bakers in town. With two years' savings—100 *livres*—she opens an inn, earning over 300 *livres* within four years. By the seventh year, the couple has saved enough to return to Flanders, where Jehane plans to punish Raoul, the knight who unjustly accused her.

Because of her resourcefulness within an essentially commercial, bourgeois framework, Jehane has been hailed as a reflection of the relative freedom and privilege of the bourgeois woman in thirteenth-century society.[33] For Sheila Delany, Jehane foreshadows and surpasses Chaucer's Wife of Bath. Unlike the Wife, Jehane "is always dignified, capable of rising to the heights of courtly manners and achieving a social status to which Alice could never seriously aspire."[34] According to this reading, when Jehane later marries King Flore and bears him children denied him by his [two previous] sterile wives, her fertility symbolizes the prosperity of the "newly-rich haute bourgeoisie of merchants, commodity dealers and financiers whose rivalry with the ancient landed nobility brought it into a new and fruitful relation with royalty."[35]

By comparison with the passive victims in *Poitiers* and the *Violette*, Jehane does demonstrate an autonomy that makes her a compelling character for modern female readers, and probably for medieval ones as well. The narrator's insistence on her resourceful activities may well reflect an appreciation of the value of "hard work and thrift, investment and social mobility" displayed by the new bourgeoisie. But to exalt Jehane as an accurate reflection of the superior status of the thirteenth-century *bourgeoise* is to ignore the narrator's appropriation of the heroine to the overarching masculine courtly ideology and aristocratic genealogy of the romance.

The notion of Jehane as a symbol of female privilege overlooks the obvious paradox that she achieves "freedom" not as a woman but as a man. During her period of activity, Jehane's social identity is as Jehan, a *bourgeois* rather than a *bourgeoise*. Moreover, the enterprising squire acts as a palimpsest for the subservient role through which Jehane proves her marital devotion. At night, she sleeps at her master's feet (p. 115). When Robert claims that the money Jehan has earned belongs to him, the servant insists that her savings belong to the master: "il sont vostre; car vous iestes mes drois sires, ne james, se Dieu plaist, ne vos cangerai" [they are yours; for you are my rightful lord, and never, please God, would I change] (p. 129). The romance limits the transvestite's sphere of activities to supportive, not combative, roles. Robert refuses to let Jehan take up arms against Raoul, as the squire has boldly requested.

After the wife is vindicated and returns to her husband, but before she explains her previous disguise, Robert laments that he has lost a squire who has done more than any man had done for another. Jehane's reply perfectly expresses the wife's marital *obligation* underlying the squire's apparent generosity; such service was Robert's due: "Sire, se il a fait pour vous, il a fait que sages: il le devoit bien faire" [Lord, if he did this for you, he acted wisely; he was supposed to do this] (p. 145). Jehane's resourcefulness is contained within a subordinate role which generously enhances, and never threatens, male authority, even when that authority is embodied in someone as weak as *mesire Robiers*.

Ultimately, the critic's desire to celebrate Jehane's privilege overlooks the heroine's inscription within the genealogical narrative that frames the wager tale. The agent within this overarching structure is not Jehane but King Flore, who repudiates his first wife when he realizes that she will bear him no heirs and who is attracted by Jehane's exemplary marital devotion. In the frame story, female sexuality is controlled by the feudal male aristocracy, whose members arrange marriages (e.g. Jehane's first marriage) and repudiate wives on the grounds of their infidelity (Jehane) or their sterility (Flore's first wife).

After Jehane's first husband dies (their marriage remained happy but childless for ten more years), King Flore, still seeking an heir after the death of his second wife, hears of Jehane's goodness and sends a messenger to invite her to court. Jehane's gracious refusal to present herself as a marriage candidate at the King's command, like a mercenary bride for sale, is both forceful and "correct." She insists that the King come to her, explaining that lords must woo ladies, and not vice versa:

"Ciertes, je ne sui mie soudoiière pour aler à son coumant; mais dites à vostre Roi, s'il li plaist, k'il viegne à moi, se il me prise tant et ainme, et se li soit biel se je le vuel prendre à mari et à espous; car li segnor doivent rekesre les dames, ne mie les dames les segnours" (p. 153).

[I am certainly not a mercenary to go at his command; but tell your king, if it pleases him, to come to me, if he esteems me and loves me so much and if it would please him for me to want to take him as husband and spouse; for lords must seek out ladies, and not ladies lords.]

In a romance that began with a crude wager between two knights on a bride's sexual fidelity, and in which a daughter was exchanged and a wife repudiated, Jehane's proud stance represents a vindication of feminine virtue and an improvement of woman's lot. It may further reflect the respect due a woman of social importance, be she aristocrat or bourgeoise, as Delany suggests.[36] But the very courtliness of Jehane's formulation bespeaks a pattern of female passivity and male activity familiar to readers of romances: it is knights who seek out ladies, and not ladies knights. Back in her female garb, Jehane assumes the stance of the courtly heroine who waits in her chambers to be beseeched by a worthy man. Despite its compelling exemplification of "active" female virtue, the text assimilates its heroine to a male aristocratic lineage enhanced by her dignity and legitimated by her fidelity.

VI. Subversive Femininity and the Clerk's Manipulation

> For a woman could never become just a sign and nothing more, since even in a man's world she is still a person, and since insofar as she is defined as a sign she must be recognized as a generator of signs.
>
> —Claude Lévi-Strauss[37]

The dynamics of the heroine's appropriation through glorification find their most complex inscription in Jean Renart's *Le Roman de la Rose ou de Guillaume de Dole*. This sophisticated, self-reflexive narrative goes far beyond the three romances we have examined thus far in using its heroine to critique the ideology of courtly love and to point up the injustice of the courtly system to women. It is the only one of these romances wherein the lady's honor is decided ultimately *not* by judicial combat between two knights but by the heroine's ingenious verbal manipulation. As critics have noted, Jean Renart uses Lienor not only to accuse her alleged seducer of treachery, but also to point up the deceptive nature of courtly language.[38] More than *Poitiers*, *Violette* or *Flore et Jehane*, this romance calls into question the discursive and social system in which women are exchanged as objects. Yet, for all the text's demystification of courtly ideology and of woman's place within it, Jean Renart's narrator subtly appropriates his heroine in a way that diffuses the historical question of woman and displaces the historical female subject from the story's center.

The romance's most striking displacement is its suppression of the wager itself. Rather than begin with an account of the crude bet between two knights, Jean Renart commences with a lengthy description of the Emperor Conrad and his amorous life. The moment when the seneschal's jealousy incites him to disgrace Conrad's *amie* (which corresponds to the villain's reaction to the arrogant boast of the wager plot) is delayed for over three thousand lines that recount how Conrad falls in love with a woman he has never seen and how he courts not Lienor but her brother.

The effect of the wager's omission is complex.[39] The narrator replaces the bet with a sophisticated textual performance intermingling lyric and narrative modes, and historical and fictional personages. Such a presentation invites the readers to reflect on the nature of literature itself. For Michel Zink this "glissement" of modes and registers is itself the subject of this romance, "qui consiste en un jeu formel sur les formes littéraires et qui confirme ainsi que ce roman est un roman sur les mots." [40]

While it is true that Jean Renart directs the reader's attention to a profound analysis of literary language, the wager's tensions are by no means absent from the first two-thirds of the romance. On the contrary, Jean's courtly embellishment is a self-conscious mystification of sexual relations that focuses our attention on the deceptive games and discourse which entrap both men and women. The romance explores the way language manipulates woman as a sign and appropriates her to the male fantasies of lyric poetry. But, at the same time that the narrative *reveals* this process to the discerning reader, it also participates in it, implicating the reader in the narrator's game. For the very sophistication and ambivalence of Jean Renart's poetry obscure the question of the "real" woman whose oppression is figured in the crude wager.

Jean Renart's ambivalent presentation of the Emperor Conrad describes a ruler of temperance and justice who is, ironically, "ruled" by his youthful passions to the extent that he would rather flirt than follow his barons' advice to marry: "Mes genvrece qui en lui regne/ ne l'i lessoit pas acorder" [But the youthfulness that ruled him would not let him agree with them] (136–37). In addition to being "sage" and "courtois" (53), Conrad is "sage" and "voiseus" [crafty] (173). Although the narrator insists that Conrad's "biaus gieus" are "sanz vilonie," the object of his pursuit is clear: he wants each of his companions to "fera amie" and to procure a lady for himself. This good, noble knight, we are told, knew all the tricks of love: "il savoit toz les tors d'amors" (161).

Conrad's principle "tour" consists of equipping the elderly and jealous men with gear and leading them into the woods to hunt game. Meanwhile, he sneaks away by back roads to join his young companions to pursue ladies. As the old hunters track down "cers" [stags], the gallant knights relish "biax cors" [beautiful bodies] (197). The ladies "chevex ondoianz et sors," their "biax cors sanz mantiaus," their "genz cors et lor mameletes" are all actively admired by the narrator. His first-person interventions underscore the ladies' hyperbolic beauty and invite his audience to share his vicarious enjoyment: "Ja mes, voir, en lieu ou *ge soie,* / ne *verrai* gent a tel solaz, / ne tante dame" [never, indeed, anyplace will I see such happy people, nor such ladies] (194–96, emphasis mine); "lor genz cors et lor mameletes / les font proisier de *ne sai quanz*" [their beautiful bodies and their breasts made I do not know how many people esteem them] (207–8, emphasis mine). As the centerpiece of Conrad's courtly and youthful entertainment, the ladies are objects of desire not only for the courtiers within the romance but for the public of listeners beyond it.

Readers cannot fail to remark that the courtliness of the feast and the guests contrasts with the crudity of the hunt and the hunters. More significantly, the feast/hunt juxtaposition highlights a similarity between the flirting knights and the hunters who chase their game. Jean Renart's analysis shows us how man's impulses to chase his amorous quarry and to exchange women as booty have been refined into a sophisticated game more genteel than the hunter's brute sport. It also raises uneasy questions about those "refined impulses."

Jean Renart's courtly omission of the wager in fact reveals its underlying sexual tensions. In two direct interventions, the narrator insinuates that the knights who stay home pursue their quarry as successfully as the hunters. First, when he describes the ladies coming to the knights, who hold out their arms and pull them "sous les covertors," the narrator exclaims: "Qui onques fu en tels estors / bien puet savoir quel siecle il orent" [Whoever waged such battles well knows what kind of time they had!] (214–15). The military conceit "estors" [battles] with its rhyme "covertors" [covers] underscores the sexual tensions, rather than sexual reciprocity, within the silken tents. When the narrator alludes to his audience's understanding of such exploits, he implicates them in the subtle objectification of women effected by "courtly" culture.

In the second passage, Jean Renart explicitly links the knights' enjoyment of the ladies' "biaus cors" to the seneschal's later appropriation of Lienor. Again, he implicates his audience in a similar practice. As he describes the pleasures of the knights with the ladies after feasting, he tells how the knights placed their hands on the ladies' thighs when the ladies offered their chemises instead of towels, and concludes with the ironic comment that he does *not* say that he who asks for more is courtly:

> Or ne sai ge que riens lor faille:
> as dames, en lieu de touaille,
> empruntent lor blanches chemises;
> par ceste ochoison si ont mises
> lor mains a mainte blanche cuisse
> (je ne di mie que cil puisse
> estre cortois qui plus demande).
>
> (277–83)

[Now I do not know of anything they lacked; in the place of towels, they borrowed the ladies' white chemises, and in that manner put their hands on many a white thigh (I do not say that he could be called courtly who asks for more).]

Michel Zink, among others, insists on the propriety of this scene: "ce n'est pas pareil de mettre la main à la cuisse et de mettre la main à autre chose; l'un est courtois, . . . l'autre ne le serait pas." [41] But the equivocal rhetoric of Jean's *double entendre* encourages the audience to imagine further sexual activity, as Zink suggests. The narrator says, after all, that the knights lack nothing. The knights' literal handling of white thighs places these women in a position analagous to Lienor's, whose "rose" the seneschal claims to have seen upon her *blance cuisse* (a body part echoed in 3361, 3365, 3588, 3724).

By omitting the wager and focusing instead on Conrad's amorous games, Jean Renart shifts his analysis of woman's appropriation to another register. He recasts the physical manipulation of woman into a refined *linguistic* manipulation that mystifies its objectification of women. Such is the mechanism of the "courtly love" exemplified by Conrad when he falls in love with Lienor "par oïr dire" [by hearing about her]. Conrad hears his minstrel Jouglet tell a story about a valiant knight and a "dame de Perthois." [42] When Conrad asks if such a lady might be found (and we note that his desire is for a fiction), Jouglet describes Guillaume's sister so seductively that Conrad succumbs to the power of the woman's name, "Lienor": "Amors l'a cuit d'une estencele/ de cel biau non mout pres del cuer" [Love set him ablaze with a spark of this beautiful name very near the heart] (793–94). He is seduced by the language of Jouglet's *descriptio* and, already obsessed, begs that Jouglet describe her again: "Si te consaut Dieus, or me rembeliz la pucele" (803–4).

What Conrad loves, as Rey-Flaud has remarked, is not a woman but the name of a woman, a sign that inscribes the desired woman as an absence. [43] Deciding that he can never marry the woman herself because of his kingdom and his honor (although he later changes his mind and engages himself), he enjoys a vicarious love by meditating ("panser") on her while he courts her brother. His love becomes a purely linguistic affair, lived through the language of the *grant chant courtois* whose tropes perfectly express his desire for an absent, unattainable woman and his desire for her absence.

Le Roman de la Rose ou de Guillaume de Dole makes clear that the place of woman in the knight's world is as an absent figure of his fantasy whom he contemplates in the presence of other knights, as Conrad does with Guillaume. The romance's structure reflects the dominance of the homosocial bonds between Conrad and Guillaume. The central section recounts the friendship between emperor and knight which results from Guillaume's generosity and chivalry at Saint-Trond. [44] Conrad receives from Guillaume the promise of the "pucele" whom her brother has joyously guarded as his "joiaus" (he lets no man see her in his absence). The exchange of a woman bonds Conrad to Guillaume, and it is the men's exclusive and constant proximity, not Conrad's love for Lienor, which incites the seneschal's jealousy:

> Mout resgarda la vie et l'estre
> dou prodome et de son segnor
> *qui li porte si grant honor*
> *qu'il ne poënt s'ensamble non:*
> *en champ n'en bois në en meson,*
> *toz jors sont ensamble lor voel.*
>
> (3153–58, emphasis mine)

> [He [the seneschal] often watched the life and behavior of the gentleman and his lord who showed him such honor that they could do nothing unless they were together: in the fields or the woods or house, they always wanted to be together.]

The seneschal contrives to break the bonds of homosocial desire by devaluing the "pucele" who unites them: as in the standard wager plot, he appropriates the sign of the woman's sexuality, the knowledge of the "rose vermelle" upon her "cuisse blanche et tendre" (3364–65). The seneschal's divulgence of the "mout veraie ensaigne," his utterance of the secret of female sexuality, destroys Conrad's poetic system, which was based on woman as an *absence*.

Lienor's "pucelage" would have guaranteed the legitimacy of Conrad's empire; her empty body, her sexual lack, was the necessary pre-text for male social exchange. That the seneschal's lie about Lienor's active sexuality suffices to undermine the Emperor's illusion of an unattainable absence indicates the extent to which Lienor's value is coined by the male speaker who invents her truth. Conrad's discourse and his politics regulate a manipulative game in which he strives to be the principal ruler and assigner of meaning. His first words about Lienor's disgrace are a lament that no king has ever before lost his queen, his "fierce" or chess queen, before he has been able to lay out the pieces of the game: "Onques mes rois ne perdi fierce / ainçois que ses gieus fust assis" [Never before has a king lost his queen, before his play was moved] (3592–93).

Deprived of their female pawn as soon as they hear the "word," Conrad and Guillaume wallow passively in shame and sorrow. Conrad intones two final, sorrowful *chansons courtoises:* "Por quel forfet ne por quel ochoison / m'avez, Amors, si de vos esloignié" [For what misdeed or for what reason, Love, have you distanced me from you] (3751–52) and "Ja de chanter en ma vie / ne quier mes avoir corage" [I will never seek the will to sing again in my life] (3883–88).

In the context of these multiple appropriations of woman as object/ sign, and in contrast to the men's passivity, Lienor's ascension as an active subject in the last third of the romance is remarkable. In the other wager narratives we have seen, the woman's sexuality is ultimately contained and vindicated by legal combat. In Jean Renart's romance, Lienor's threatening sexuality is transformed into textual manipulations that propel the narrative to its end. When accused by a cousin who sets off to kill her of "ribaudie" [debauchery], she rouses her family from despair "par son grant sens" [by her great intelligence] (4060) and vows to regain "le grant segnorage" [the important seigniory] promised her and to avenge her brother. She resorts to the same verbal strategies that have ensnared her and turns the invention of female signs to her own advantage. To adapt Lévi-Strauss' formulation, if Lienor is merely a sign in the first two-thirds of the romance, in the final episodes she becomes a generator of signs.

Like Jouglet and Conrad, Lienor creates a female fiction, a story of female desire about the Châtelaine de Dijon who loves the seneschal. Surpassing the seneschal in his own ruse, she supports her fiction with false "ensaignes" whose meaning she manipulates. She gives her messenger a brooch, a belt, and a ring in a purse—sexually charged love-tokens—instructing her emissary to tell the seneschal to wear them for love of the lady. When Lienor arrives at court incognito to accuse the seneschal of robbing her of her "pucelage" and her "jewels," she usurps the male appropriative function by assigning *herself* the value of her sexuality and the seneschal's. To do so, she resorts to a prevalent male fiction, borrowed from the *chanson de toile;* she casts herself in the role of the compromised object, the passive lady, who was engaged in her sewing when the seneschal raped her: "vient en un lieu par aventure / ou ge fesoie ma cousture" [He came by chance to a place where I was sewing] (4781–82).

By means of a perverted feminine fiction, Lienor empowers herself to mount her own suit, in seeming defiance of medieval woman's legal incapacity. The narrator comments that she could not have better pleaded her case had she spent five years studying law (4768–4773). Her verbal manipulations not only unmask the seneschal's deception, but also point out the injustice of a legal system that favors bonds between male peers. As Lienor comments later, the barons' sympathies for one of their own prevailed over the fact of the belt upon the seneschal's body when the barons demanded, and were accorded, the trial by ordeal which ironically damned him (5071–82). (In Lienor's case, we recall, a "word" alone was enough to disgrace her and warrant her death.) Lienor's clever deployment of fictional conventions demystifies the structure of a courtly ideology which, in Althusser's terms, is the subject's imaginary relationship to the real conditions of his existence.[45] When, in response to Conrad's question, she utters "N'en doutez mie, ce sui ge bele Lienors" [Don't doubt that I am beautiful Lienor] (5096–97), the reader might well believe, with Conrad, that the "real" woman has finally revealed herself.

Such, indeed, has been the critical reception of Lienor's unmasking of the seneschal. For Rey-Flaud, Lienor becomes the "maître du jeu qu'elle dirige," in the final scene, "comme le montreur ses marionettes, au premier rang desquelles il convient de compter Conrad."[46] For Zink, the poignant moment when Lienor's wimple falls back, spreading her blonde hair on to her shoulders, as she pleads her case before Conrad, is an involuntary undressing allowing "sa vraie nature" to shine forth, much as a knight reveals his identity by taking off his helmet; "heaume" and "ventaille" are the words which here describe Lienor's headdress.[47] For Marc-René Jung, Lienor "en chaire et en os et non pas son mirage, vient à la cour, où la fiction s'effondre—pour se réaliser."[48] It is a tribute to the narrative art that Jean Renart vaunts in his Prologue that the illusion of a "real woman" is created in the final verses of the *Roman de la Rose*.

Because Lienor, of course, remains a fictional being, a figure of the narrator's seductive *descriptio:* "bele Lienor." As she prepares herself lavishly for court, we are aware of the dressing and undressing of the narrator's rhetoric. Here, as at the *fête champêtre,* the eye focuses on the "biaux cors" revealed beneath the silk and ermine: "El ot un poi basses les hansches, / et grailles flans, et biau le pis" [She had hips that were a little low, and thin sides, and a beautiful chest] (4359–60). "Tout avoit, desus la ceinture, descovert le piz et le cors" [Above her belt, she had completely uncovered her chest and her body] (4530–31);

"Et savez qui mout l'abeli? qu'el ot descovert son visage," [And do you know what made her more beautiful? that she had uncovered her face] (4533–34). Figurative language and literary allusions embellish her "simple" countenance. She is compared to Berthe aux grands pieds and to Aude (4509–10); she has an angel's voice, a "vois d'angre" (4538); she resembles the *puceles* who used to come to Arthur's court (4617–19); she appears as a "mervelle tote droite," between "fee ou fame" (4689), and is hailed by the townspeople as the Queen of May, the embodiment of springtime sensuality, herself: "Vez mai, vez mai, / que cil dui chevalier amainent!" [See May, see May, whom the two knights lead forth!] (4605–06). Far from being accidental, Lienor's revelation of her "natural" beauty before Conrad is a highly self-conscious moment of narrative mystification.

That moment allows the narrator to create the fiction of a "true love" between the Emperor and his future bride even as he uses Lienor's voice and actions to deconstruct the *mensonge* of another kind of love. But, for all the text's subversion of literary conventions and self-conscious deconstruction of courtly discourse, the romance's conclusion re-inscribes Lienor in the place to which Conrad and Guillaume's exchange had initially assigned her: as the Emperor's wife. When she marries Conrad amidst a profusion of May songs and *caroles,* the feminine voice becomes re-assimilated to the redeemed chivalric ethic. Like the figure of Helen whose abduction by Paris is woven in golden images on her imperial robe (5332–51), Lienor's resemblance to a historical female subject and her meaning for a modern female reader are displaced from their point of origin, irrecoverable as a "reality," inextricable from the tensions of gender which recuperate her to the world of rival heroes. Jean Renart has of course not created a "real" woman in Lienor, and we cannot infer from her any direct image of the power or influence of her historic counterpart, the aristocratic woman who may have identified with the fictional character. The narrator has instead appropriated "paroles de femme" to tease at the fibers of courtly discourse while preserving his own authority as speaker; Lienor's feminine subversion of the "tors d'amors" is the narrator's "tour de force," the game of a wily clerk who conceals his name, and hides his "renardie," in an anagram in his final verses:

> Et cil se veut reposer ore
> qui li jor perdi son sornon
> qu'il ENTRA en REligion.
>   (5653–55, emphasis mine)

[And now he who lost his surname the day he entered into religion wishes to rest.]

VII. Medieval Gynesis and the Female Audience

> Grâce à la femme, le roman découvre la théorie et, au défaut des traîtés de rhétorique, énonce au féminin une "poétique" du roman.
> —Jean-Charles Huchet[49]

> To accept a metaphorization, a semiosis of woman . . . means risking once again the absence of women as subjects in the struggles of modernity.
> —Alice Jardine[50]

Ultimately, the Lienor who was a generator of signs becomes reinscribed as a *sign* of femininity manipulated by the narrator for the courtly pleasure and instruction of the audience. Like many postmodern male critics who use the feminine as a trope to subvert phallocentric culture and language—a process Alice Jardine has aptly named *gynesis*—Jean Renart uses Lienor as a narrative device to demystify courtly conventions. Unlike the deconstructive critics, Jean Renart reaffirms cultural norms in the end with Conrad and Lienor's marriage of "true love." But what is significant about both the medieval cleric's and the modern theorists' inscription of "woman" is that they deploy her to explore a crisis in male culture. Precisely because historical woman is marginal to the structures of masculine power, the figure of "woman" comes to represent opposition and subversion. Precisely because the real woman is absent from the scene of writing, the attempt to represent her generates literature. Male critics and clerics embody their highest poetic aims in the metaphor of woman.

Our reading of *Guillaume de Dole*'s conclusion has brought us back to the woman as a figure of male desire. Even as Lienor demystifies the deceptive discourse of Conrad's court, the narrator remystifies her as a superlative beauty worthy of Conrad's adoration. The spunky heroine is ultimately appropriated by the male aristocracy to the project of royal lineage; she becomes, in the end, a sign legitimating Conrad and Guillaume. What becomes, then, of history? Does the "real" female context recede irretrievably when we take Lienor as an instance of male mystification?

Our examination of thirteenth-century wager narratives suggests that if we cannot hypostatize historical woman's *presence* in romance, we must evaluate the implications of her *absence*. We have seen how the harsh reality of woman's status as an object of exchange—clearly exemplified by the wager—is mystified by diverse narrative strategies which glorify feminine virtue. Whether that virtue is conceived as passive devotion or as clever ingenuity, the female figure serves to embellish aristocratic and clerical culture. We have seen how the sign of woman is appropriated to buttress male fantasies of honor and desire. Contemporary medieval critics who read "woman" as the springboard for the male poetic imagination without understanding her appropriation adopt the trope of medieval mystification themselves. They do not question the effect of gynesis on the historical female subject, the displaced reader of these texts.

Yet, as feminist historical criticism can remind us, the historical woman is always implied by these texts as one component of the romance's implied audience. Her reception of these appropriated heroines may well have been different from that of male nobles and clerics. She may have assented to her cultural mystification or, like the modern feminist, she may have offered critical resistance. This essay offers an analysis of narrative strategies that displace the female reader as one form of critical resistance. It invites discussion of the female reception of these texts—a question no less haunted by the spectre of the absent woman—as the next step in the feminist interpretation of romance.

NOTES

I would like to express my thanks to E. Jane Burns, Janet Halley, Nancy Jones, Nancy Rabinowitz, and Thomas Bass for their helpful suggestions at various stages of this paper's redaction. Portions of this work were presented at the

Kentucky Foreign Language Conference and at the Fordham Conference on Women and Power in the Middle Ages in 1985, and at Hobart and William Smith Colleges in 1986.

1. Myrrha Lot-Borodine, *De l'Amour profane à l'amour sacré: études de psychologie sentimentale au Moyen Age* (Paris: Nizet, 1961), 19.

2. Reto Bezzola, "La transformation des moeurs et le rôle de la femme dans la classe féodale du XIe au XIIe siècle," *Les Origines et la formation de la littérature courtoise en Occident, 500–1200*, pt. 2, vol. 2 (Paris: Champion, 1960), 461.

3. "Une autre race féminine vient d'apparaître sur la scène; et ses représentantes, au seuil de la jeunesse, voient s'ouvrir devant elles, dans la poésie, sinon dans la vie, une véritable voie triomphale" [A new feminine race has just arrived on stage, and its members, on the threshold of youth, see a truly triumphant route open before them, in poetry if not in life]. Lot-Borodine's valorization of aristocratic women and their influence is characteristic of early assessments of women's place in courtly ideology. *De l'Amour profane à l'amour sacre*, 16.

4. More recent positive assessments of women's role in courtly literature and of historical woman's power and influence include Joan Kelly-Gadol, "Did Women Have a Renaissance?" in *Becoming Visible: Women in European History*, ed. Renate Bridenthal and Claudia Koonz (Boston: Houghton Mifflin, 1977), 137–64; Rita Lejeune, "La femme dans les littératures françaises et occitanes du XIe au XIIIe siècle," *Cahiers de civilisation médiévale* 20, nos. 2–3 (April–Sept. 1977): 201–17; June Hall McCash, "Marie de Champagne's 'Cuer d'ome et cors de fame': Aspects of Feminism and Misogyny in the Twelfth Century," in *The Spirit of the Court: Selected Proceedings of the Fourth Congress of the International Courtly Literature Society, Toronto 1983*, ed. Glyn S. Burgess and Robert A. Taylor (Cambridge: D. S. Brewer), 234–45. For a critique of approaches that draw parallels between woman's "positive" image in literature and her status in history, see Penny Shine Gold, *The Lady and the Virgin: Image, Attitude, and Experience in Twelfth-Century France* (Chicago: Univ. of Chicago Press, 1985), xv–xxi.

5. This thesis has been advanced by Georges Duby, *Le Chevalier, la femme, et le prêtre* (Paris: Hachette, 1981); supporting evidence for the decline or circumscription of women's power in this period is offered by Suzanne Wemple and Jo Ann McNamara, "The Power of Women through the Family in Medieval Europe: 500–1100," *Feminist Studies* 1 (1973): 126–41. For a cautious assessment of the status of noblewomen in the twelfth and thirteenth centuries that evidences the range of difference in women's condition, see Robert Hajdu, "The Position of Noblewomen in the 'pays des coutumes,' 1100–1300," *Journal of Family History* 5, no. 2 (Summer 1980): 122–44.

6. See Joan M. Ferrante, *Woman as Image in Medieval Literature: From the Twelfth Century to Dante* (New York: Columbia Univ. Press, 1975).

7. Jean-Charles Huchet, *Le Roman médiéval* (Paris: Presses Universitaires de France, 1985), 218.

8. Huchet, *Le Roman médiéval*, 222.

9. Duby, *Le Chevalier, la femme, et le prêtre*, 304.

10. Gayatri Chakravorty Spivak, "Displacement and the Discourse of Woman," in *Displacement, Derrida and After*, ed. Mark Krupnick (Bloomington: Indiana Univ. Press, 1983), 169–95; see esp. 171–75.

11. Ibid., 184.

12. Douglas Labaree Buffum in the "Introduction" to his edition of Gerbert de Montreuil, *Le Roman de la Violette* (Paris: Champion, 1928), liv.

13. For an analysis of the cycle, see Gaston Paris, "Le cycle de la gageure," *Romania* 32 (1903): 481–551. The group Paris analyzes includes a tale from Boccacio's *Decameron* (II, 9), Shakespeare's *Cymbeline*, three other French versions, and numerous European analogues.

14. All references in this paper are to the following editions: *Le Roman du Comte de Poitiers: poème français du XIIIe siècle*, ed. Bertil Malmberg (Lund: C. W. K. Gleerup, 1940); Gerbert de Montreuil, *Le Roman de la Violette ou de Gerart de Nevers*, ed. Douglas Labaree Buffum (Paris: Champion, 1928); *Li Contes du Roi Flore et de la belle Jehane*, in L. Moland and C. D'Héricault, *Nouvelles françoises en prose du XIIIe siècle* (Paris: Jannet, 1856); Jean Renart, *Le Roman de la Rose ou de Guillaume de Dole*, ed. Félix Lecoy (Paris: Champion, 1977).

15. For a description of other medieval romance cycles in which the innocent woman is accused, see Alexandre Micha, "La Femme injustement accusée dans les Miracles de Notre-Dame par Personnages," in his *De la chanson de geste au roman: études de la littérature médiévale* (Geneva: Droz, 1976), 479–486.

16. See Paris, "Le cycle de la gageure," 550, and Buffum, *Violette*, liv. On negatively portrayed thirteenth-century female figures, see Jean-Charles Payen, "La destruction des mythes courtois dans le roman arthurien: la femme dans le roman en vers après Chrétien de Troyes," *Revue des langues romanes* 78 (1960): 213–28.

17. On the woman as an object of exchange in another romance, see my own "Love, Honor, and the Exchange of Women in *Yvain*: Some Remarks on the Female Reader," *Romance Notes* 25, no. 3 (Spring 1985): 302–17. The social and theoretical implications of the primacy of the male "homosocial" bond in such triangulated relationships have been fully discussed (albeit for post-medieval English literature) by Eve Sedgwick, *Between Men: English Literature and Male Homosocial Desire* (New York: Columbia Univ. Press, 1985).

18. For an enumeration of other matrimonial romances, see R. Howard Bloch, *Etymologies and Genealogies: A Literary Anthropology of the French Middle Ages* (Chicago: Univ. of Chicago Press, 1983), 193–94. Bloch's analysis emphasizes the disruptive effects of adulterous desire or of consensual love upon the ideology of paternal lineage in such romances as *Aucassin et Nicolette* and

Béroul's *Tristan* (see 174–97). His "anthropological" method subsumes gender within the categories of kinship, class, economic and linguistic structures. The wager romances allow us to see to what extent *woman* is the focal point of the discursive disruption Bloch describes in romance, and to what extent courtly romance problematizes the sex-gender system.

19. For a general discussion of the noblewoman's role as an object of exchange in marriage and as a reproducer of male heirs during the feudal aristocracy's aggrandizement in the eleventh and twelfth centuries, see Duby, *Le Chevalier, la femme et le prêtre*, and Bloch, *Etymologies*, 64–91. A concern for legitimacy and female chastity underlies aristocratic ideology well into the Renaissance; see, for example, Kelly-Gadol, "Did Women Have a Renaissance?" 156–59.

20. According to medieval customary law, daughters fell under the legal jurisdiction of their fathers; married women came under the guardianship of their husband and had no autonomous legal capacity. See Robert Hajdu, "The Position of Noblewomen in the *pays des coutumes*," 123–25. For example, see Philippe de Beaumanoir, *Coutumes de Beauvaisis*, ed. A. Salmon, 2 vols. (Paris: Picard, 1899–1900), par. 1175, 1287, 1330, 1378, 1796. See also Pierre Petot and Andre Vandenbossche, "Le statut de la femme dans les pays coutumiers français du XIIIᵉ au XVIIᵉ siècle," in *La Femme: Recueils de la Société Jean Bodin pour l'histoire comparative des institutions* (Brussels: Libraire Encyclopédique, 1959–62), vol. 12, pp. 243–54.

21. Beaumanoir, *Coutumes*, par. 1795.

22. Ibid., par. 1631. See also Petot and Vandenbossche, "Le statut de la femme," 245. On the husband's physical authority as an accepted principle in canon law, see René Metz, "Le statut de la femme en droit canonique médiéval," in *La Femme: Recueils de la société Jean Bodin*, vol. 12, p. 89.

23. Killing wife and rival in adultery was acceptable if the husband found them *in flagrante delicto* ("en fet present") or if they were found alone in a private place and there was other evidence of their crime, see Beaumanoir, *Coutumes*, par. 933–34; a maiden ("pucele"), however, ought not to be killed for fornication, par. 934. Beaumanoir cites the example, during Philip Augustus' reign, of a husband killing a rival who announced "Vous estes cous et de moie meisme" [You have been cuckolded, and by me]; the husband was not punished, par. 932. (Beaumanoir does not mention killing the wife in this case.) The threatened slaying of the wife in the *Comte de Poitiers* seems exceptionally harsh, even under the severe terms of medieval customary law; the threatened slaying of the *amie* in the *Violette* and in the *Guillaume de Dole* is expressly outlawed by Beaumanoir. (There is no threatened punishment in *Flore et Jehane*.)

24. For discussion of the literary inscription of male sexual violence against women in another genre, see Kathryn Gravdal, "Camouflaging Rape: The Rhetoric of Sexual Violence in the Medieval Pastourelle," *Romanic Review* 76, no. 4 (Nov. 1985): 361–73.

25. The dates and the relative chronology of these romances have been much

disputed. See Gaston Paris, "Le cycle de la gageure," *Romania* 32 (1903): 532–41; Rita Lejeune-Dehousse, *L'Oeuvre de Jean Renart* (Paris: Droz, 1935), 73–130; Buffum, *Le Roman de la Violette*, xl–xlii; Michel Zink, *Roman rose et rose rouge: Le "Roman de la Rose ou de Guillaume de Dole" de Jean Renart* (Paris: Nizet, 1979), 9–14, 69–77. There is some recent consensus for the following order: *Comte de Poitiers* (last quarter of the twelfth century?), *Guillaume de Dole*, *Roman de la Violette*, *Flore et Jehane* (last half of the thirteenth century). My analysis, however, does not follow the probable historical chronology of the romances but instead groups these stories in terms of the critical problems they present.

26. Mary incarnates two contradictory ideals for twelfth-century man: chastity and motherhood. On the portrayal of Mary as submissive and humble in Gothic art, in contrast to earlier presentations, see Penny Shine Gold, *The Lady and the Virgin*, 61–68.

27. Under customary law, this land would fall under her husband's jurisdiction; see Hajdu, "The Position of Noblewomen," 125–29.

28. Comtesse Marie de Ponthieu's husband was exiled in 1214 for having fought against Philip Augustus at Bouvine; the King then confiscated Ponthieu, which Marie had inherited from her father. Louis VIII returned most of her inheritance to her in 1225 and pardoned her husband in 1230. See Buffum, *Violette*, lv–lvii. On the loss of property rights of a wife whose husband has been banished, see Beaumanoir, *Coutumes*, 931.

29. Like the *Roman de la Rose ou de Guillaume de Dole* which it imitates, the *Violette* includes refrains and fragments from the courtly lyric tradition which are voiced by characters to intensify or comment upon themes and sentiments. There are forty such lyric insertions in the *Roman de la Violette*; for a full enumeration, see Buffum, lxxxii–xci.

30. The verbal "ensagne" or sign of female sexuality occurs in three of the four romances. Here it is a violet on the breast, in the *Guillaume de Dole* a rose on the thigh ("cuisse"), in *Flore et Jehane* a black mole "pres de sa nature."

31. Norris Lacy has commented upon the double purpose of the *Violette* quest: Gerart avenges himself against Lisiart, but he also symbolically expiates the wrong he has done his wife. See Norris J. Lacy, "Spatial Form in Medieval Romance," *Yale French Studies* 51 (1974), 162.

32. On transvestism in thirteenth-century romance, see Michele Perret, "Travesties et transsexuelles: Yde, Silence, Grisandole, Blanchandine," *Romance Notes* 25, no. 3 (Spring 1985): 328–40.

33. See Sheila Delany, "*Flore et Jehane*: A Case Study of the Bourgeois Woman in Medieval Life and Letters," *Science and Society* 45, no. 3 (Fall 1981): 274–87.

34. Delany, "*Flore et Jehane*," 276.

35. Delany's Marxist analysis rejects the usefulness of a "strictly feminist" approach (275). One could object that a feminist historical method would raise precisely the questions Delany does about class identification. I would also

qualify her identification of Jehane as a "bourgeoise." She is the daughter of a knight, and her husband, the squire, becomes ennobled through marriage with her ("Robin" becomes "Robiers"). During her period of entrepreneurship, she is disguised as a man; she and her husband earn just enough to return to vindicate her. After her rehabilitation as a lady, the couple accrues wealth by aristocratic means: Robert wins at tournaments, and they inherit her parents' landholdings (147–48). Jehane's position when Flore marries her is that of a wealthy aristocratic *Dame*. However, whether she is a successful *bourgeoise* turned noblewoman, or a noblewoman who adopted a bourgeois role, Jehane's autonomy as a *woman* is equally troublesome.

36. Delany, *"Flore et Jehane,"* 280.

37. Claude Lévi-Strauss, *The Elementary Structures of Kinship* (Boston: Beacon Press, 1969), 496.

38. See, for example, Marc-René Jung, "L'Empereur Conrad chanteur de poésie lyrique: fiction et vérité dans le *Roman de la Rose* de Jean Renart," *Romania* 101, no. 1 (1980): 35–50.

39. Although the wager's omission appears in other versions of the tale, it is possible that they are adaptations of the *Guillaume de Dole*. Jean Renart's story may be the first in which the bet is suppressed; see Lejeune, *Jean Renart*, 54–55.

40. Michel Zink, *Roman rose et rose rouge* (Paris: Nizet, 1979), 67. Cf. Norris J. Lacy, "'Amer par oïr dire': *Guillaume de Dole* and the Drama of Language," *The French Review* 54, no. 6 (April 1981): 779–87.

41. Zink, *Roman rose*, 78.

42. The resemblance of this couple to the couple in Jean Renart's *Le Lai de l'ombre* underscores the seductive power of courtly language.

43. "A la place du corps, *Le Roman de la rose* met d'abord le *nom* de la femme comme cause du désir." Henri Rey-Flaud, *La Névrose courtoise* (Paris: Navarin, 1983), 89.

44. The terms of Sedgwick's analysis in *Between Men* again prove useful in describing the privileged bond between men who use a woman—here, quite literally the "sign" of a woman—as a means of solidifying their homosocial relationship.

45. "Ideology represents the imaginary relationship of individuals to the real conditions of existence." Louis Althusser, "Ideology and Ideological State Apparatuses (Notes towards an Investigation)," in his *Lenin and Philosophy and Other Essays* (New Left Books, 1971), 153.

46. Rey-Flaud, *La névrose courtoise*, 104.

47. Zink, *Roman rose*, 107–8.

48. Jung, "L'Empereur Conrad," 49.

49. Huchet, *Le Roman médiéval*, 222.

50. Alice Jardine, *Gynesis: Configurations of Woman and Modernity* (Ithaca, N.Y.: Cornell Univ. Press, 1985).

The Feminization of Men
in Chaucer's *Legend of Good Women*

Elaine Tuttle Hansen

> "No, I don't want to destroy you, any more than I want to
> save you. There has been far too much talk about you, and I
> want to leave you alone altogether. My interest is in my own
> sex; yours evidently can look after itself. That's what I want to
> save."
>
> Verena saw that he was more serious now than he had been
> before, that he was not piling it up satirically, but saying really
> and a trifle wearily, as if suddenly he were tired of much talk,
> what he meant. "To save it from what?" she asked.
> "From the most damnable feminization!"
>
> —Henry James, *The Bostonians* [1]

Basil Ransom's confession of interest in his own sex corresponds felici-
tously to what I will argue are the motives and concerns of a literary
character imagined more than five hundred years earlier, the narrator of
Chaucer's *Legend of Good Women*. While the latter never stops "piling it
up satirically," he speaks, like Basil Ransom, "a trifle wearily" about the
whole subject of women, and both male characters are in fact obsessed
with redeeming themselves and their sex from the "damnable feminization" that this tired talk can serve at once to foster and to obscure. As
readers acquainted with both texts may recognize, the correspondence
between the modern novel and the medieval poem might be pursued a
bit further; I invoke it here, however, only to anchor my use of the term
"feminization" in a familiar literary scene and language, and to acknowledge from the outset what probably goes without saying to any reader of

this volume. In reading Chaucer, I seek in part to appropriate a historical masterwork into a twentieth-century context, making the old text a field on which currently interesting battles can be waged (and where a number of live mines, to extend a borrowed metaphor, can be expected to blow up[2]). While this approach breaks the rules of one familiar variety of historicism, it is sanctioned by the recent pronouncements of eminent theorists of another kind of literary history. Hans Robert Jauss, for example, affirms that "the tradition of art presupposes a dialogue between the present and the past, according to which a past work cannot answer and speak to us until a present observer has posed the question which returns it from its retirement."[3] The *Legend of Good Women* is the text among Chaucer's poetic works that has been comparatively in retirement for centuries. The question that brings it most dramatically out of its relative seclusion is the one that feminist observers of canonical authors, at once steeped in a historical tradition of male writing beginning long before Chaucer and continuing long after James and yet vitally engaged in the contemporary investigation into the concepts of "woman" and "gender," are obliged to pose.

In an earlier consideration of this poem's tone and its author's gender politics, I have already taken up this question once, the question of how a contemporary feminist scholar might approach one of the least interpreted and—on the question of "woman"—most interesting of Chaucer's masterworks.[4] In this second assay, I want first to develop what I noted in passing in my original focus on Chaucer's treatment of his traditional heroines: the narrator's equally problematic treatment of his traditional heroes, his consistent debunking of men, and his increasingly harsh attacks on "fals lovers," which I read as both mask and symptom of the narrator's overriding interest in his own sex. Specifically I want to argue now that this concern is directed toward precisely the kind of feminization that Basil Ransom deplores, the feminization of men who indulge in heterosexual adventures, and who talk with and about women. In the second part of this essay, I want to take issue with the notion, implied by my earlier reading, that we can redeem that putative historical subject we call "Chaucer" as either a feminist or a humanist; and to underscore briefly why in looking both at the Chaucerian canon and at "woman" in history and in literature, we should bring the *Leg-*

end of Good Women out of retirement to play a more central part in the current conversation between the present and the past.

In arguing for the relevance of a modern usage of a term like "feminization" to our study of a fourteenth-century poem, I do of course lay my argument open to the charge that it ignores historical differences. To avoid this, I might have begun not with Henry James, but with some discussion of the ways in which medieval authorities viewed the problem. A well-known passage in Orderic Vitalis' *Historia Ecclesiastica* might have made a better epigraph; here, Orderic deplores the unmanly and impious behavior of the younger generation in the late eleventh-century court of King Rufus, noting in particular the tight shirts and long, womanly hair of these *effeminati* and *catamitae:*

> Tunc effeminati passim in orbe dominabantur indisciplinate debachabantur sodomiticisque spurciciis foedi catamitae flammis urendi turpiter abutebantur. Ritus heroum abiciebant, hortamenta sacerdotum deridebant, barbaricumque morem in habitu et uita tenebant. Nam capillos a uertice in frontem discriminabant, longos crines ueluti mulieres nutriebant, et summopere comebant, prolixisque nimiumque strictis camisiis indui tunicisque gaudebant.

> [At that time effeminates set the fashion in many parts of the world: foul catamites, doomed to eternal fire, unrestrainedly pursued their revels and shamelessly gave themselves up to the filth of sodomy. They rejected the traditions of honest men, ridiculed the counsel of priests, and persisted in their barbarous way of life and style of dress. They parted their hair from the crown of the head to the forehead, grew long and luxurious locks like women, and loved to deck themselves in long, over-tight shirts and tunics.][5]

Germane to my discussion of feminization in Chaucer's world, too, is Orderic's conflation of charges of homosexuality *and* excessive heterosexual interest; a few sentences later in this same passage, for example, he adds:

> Femineam mollitiem petulans iuuentus amplectitur, feminisque uiri curiales in omni lasciuia summopere adulantur.

> [Our wanton youth is sunk in effeminacy, and courtiers, fawning, seek the favours of women with every kind of lewdness.][6]

Or I might have begun by surveying the recent work of certain literary critics and historians, broadly interested in sociopolitical approaches to literature, who have begun to supply a medieval context in which to speak of the issues involved in the study of what we now call feminization. Toril Moi, for instance, building on Marc Bloch's earlier observations concerning the influence of noblewomen on aristocratic males of the *courtoisie*, explains the feminization of the knightly classes from the twelfth-century on as strategic to the naturalization of class differences:

> Signalling their cultural superiority, the "effeminisation" of the aristocracy paradoxically enough comes to signify their "natural" right to power. It is precisely in its insistence on the "natural" differences between rulers and ruled that courtly ideology achieved its legitimising function, a function which operates long after the feudal aristocracy has lost its central position in society.[7]

Without explicitly speaking of feminization, Eugene Vance similarly reads the twelfth-century romance as serving the interests of a new class and ideology. Most interesting for the purposes of my argument, Vance considers the identification of one poet with his fictional female characters, the silk workers in the Pesme Avanture episode of Chretien's *Yvain*, and suggests that it reveals the male author's anxiety that the worker of texts, like the weaver of textiles, will be exploited by the new ideology.[8] R. Howard Bloch has also made a persuasive case for the association in authoritative medieval discourse of the mutability of gender and improper sexual differentiation with the indeterminacy of meaning and improper writing attributed to poetic discourse.[9] And R. H. Green, without raising the question of gender himself, describes the situation of the fourteenth-century court poet in ways that might enable us to understand a part at least of his feminization: like woman, he is a marginalized figure at court, who must be careful not to offend those of higher rank and authority; he seeks, like a wife or daughter, to please and entertain those who have power over him.[10]

Both the historical evidence and the richness of such recent scholarly investigations are more complicated, however, than the preceding paragraphs can even begin to suggest, or than I can pursue in this brief essay. Its working assumption, then, is that what I call "feminization" —the occupation of a position associated with what is conventionally identified as feminine in a given social world—is a long-lived problem with specific historical contours extending throughout the centuries of western culture. In studying this problem, we need to analyze both continuities and disjunctions between its manifestations at particular historical moments and in particular texts. In this essay, I undertake only a small part of this analysis, which is in turn only one aspect of a broad investigation into the cultural interaction of class and gender. My limited aim is to show in some detail, first, how one text embodies and turns on the problem of feminization and then to sketch out much more briefly how this problem resonates throughout the later Chaucerian canon and speaks to certain pressing concerns of late twentieth-century feminist literary criticism.

DESPITE ITS TITLE, WHAT DRIVES THE *Legend of Good Women* from its opening dream vision to its arguably strategic incompletion is not the subject of women, good or otherwise, but the subject of two kinds of men: legendary heroes who become involved with women, and male authors who traffic in stories about women. As I have argued elsewhere, the narrator of this poem is writing both for and against a male audience, at once defending himself and his poetry against the criticism of a male tyrant, the God of Love, while identifying with masculine interests and privilege.[11] To borrow some useful nomenclature from a recent study of similar issues in (again) later texts, we can say, in other words, that the subject of the *Legend of Good Women* is "male homosocial desire." In *Between Men: English Literature and Male Homosocial Desire*, Eve Sedgwick recasts the work of twentieth-century theorists like Lévi-Strauss and Girard from a feminist perspective to shed light on the literary representation of a wide continuum of male bonds, ranging from the homophobic to the homoerotic, and pays particular attention to "triangular transactions" between men in which women figure not as subjects but as objects of exchange.[12] With a consistent awareness of the socioeconomic and political contexts in which homosocial desire takes literary shape, Sedgwick reminds us that the texts she examines come from a specific place and culture and were written over a relatively short span of time; she also suggests, however, that her insights have wider application. She does not "delineate a separate male homosocial literary canon," Sedgwick argues, because "the European canon as it exists is already such a canon, and most so when it is most heterosexual."[13] Chaucer's entire *oeuvre*, I would suggest, provides early support for this large claim, and a closer examination of the classical tales of hetero-sexual adventure retold in the *Legend of Good Women* is crucial to our understanding of how this is so. In this poem, heterosexual union is clearly presented not as a good or even attainable end, but as a seri-ous and even insuperable problem, a necessary yet perilous part of the quest for stable masculine identity and homosocial bonds between men. And what is most dangerous about heterosexual desire, according to the Legends, is the more or less feminine position—vulnerable, submissive, subservient and self-sacrificing, on the one hand; crafty and duplicitous, on the other—that men in love or lust for a woman seem forced to assume.

The actual centrality of men in a poem ostensively devoted to women's stories is made possible in part by the agenda set out in the Prologue, where the first-person speaker of the poem, self-dramatized as a poet of love but not (much of) a lover, recounts a dream-vision in which he meets Cupid, here a grown-up God of Love, accompanied by Queen Alceste and a large band of literary ladies all "trewe of love" (G. 193).[14] The God of Love castigates the dumbstruck poet at length as a heretic who has encouraged people to transgress the laws of Love, in particular by telling stories of wicked women like Criseyde instead of celebrating the countless hordes of faithful heroines. After rebuking the God for his overly hasty and tyrannical judgment, the good Alceste prescribes a specific literary penance for these alleged sins against women: the poet is ordered to tell stories both "Of goode wymmen, maydenes and wyves, / That weren trewe in lovyng al hire lyves" and "of false men that hem bytraien, / That al hir lyf do nat but assayen / How many women they may doon a shame" (F. 484–88). The God of Love commands the poet to begin with the story of Cleopatra, and again reminds him that his charge is to contrast the heroic sufferings of women with the failings of men in love: "For lat see now what man that lover be, / Wol doon so strong a peyne for love as she" (F. 568–69).

But in fact, neither of the first two legends, of Cleopatra and then of Thisbe, quite fits the bill, for each features a leading man, Antony or Piramus, who proves his "truth" in love by committing suicide even before the heroine has a chance to do so. This fact may retrospectively undermine the God of Love's judgment in calling for the story of Cleo-patra to begin with, and thus unwittingly permitting the narrator to show

us a "true" man, by Love's standards. The narrator's commentary at the
end of *Thisbe* calls even more explicit attention to the subversive and
"male-identified" stance he will continue to take throughout the rest of
the poem:

> And thus are Tisbe and Piramus ygo.
> Of trewe men I fynde but fewe mo
> In alle my bokes, save this Piramus,
> And therfore have I spoken of hym thus.
> For it is deynte to us men to fynde
> A man that can in love been trewe and kynde.
> Here may ye se, what lovere so he be,
> A woman dar and can as wel as he.

> (916–23)

The narrator's primary concern, as suggested by his telling of the first
two legends and confirmed by this passage, is to be pleased as a man,
to please other men, and hence to make clear his own gender identity,
his right to the first-person plural pronoun of line 920. In the last two
lines here the ostensive motive of the poem, the celebration of women,
is added—as I believe it indeed is related to the poem as a whole—as
an afterthought, and virtually a nonsequitur.

But if the narrator wants to identify and bond with "us men," why
does he go on to debunk the truly "false" heroes of the next seven
legends? Why does he make most of them even more despicable than
traditional story demands, and why does he claim to respond with increasingly strong, personal disgust—actually weeping, for instance, as
he heaps invective on Tereus, brother-in-law and rapist of Philomela—to
their well-known betrayal of his increasingly passive, shallow heroines?
Perhaps, after some initial show of resistance, he is simply trying to ac-
quit himself as quickly as possible in the God of Love's (and Alceste's)
eyes. But a more interesting possibility emerges if we consider Antony
and Piramus as early object lessons in the fate of men who give themselves wholeheartedly to a heterosexual passion, or to the idea of one.
In different ways, both are utterly unmanned by their submission to the
service of Love. For the love of Cleopatra, Antony loses his reason, his
freedom, and his public position: "love hadde brought this man in swich
a rage, / And hym so narwe bounden in his las . . . That al the world he
sette at no value" (599–602). The defeat at Actium inevitably follows,

and the narrator clearly implies that Antony's motive in killing himself is not so much the loss of Cleopatra as it is the loss of manly honor, prowess, and rationality that he has suffered on account of love: " 'My worshipe in this day thus have I lorn,' " he says; and in the very next line the narrator adds, "And for dispeyr out of his wit he sterte, / And rof hymself anon thourghout the herte" (660–61).

Piramus is presented as a less tragic figure, in that he has less manly worship to lose in the first place. He is an adolescent about whom we are told very little; he seems to fall in love because Thisbe lives next door, and because his father and hers forbid the affair. From his unexplained tardiness in arriving at Nynus' tomb, we can only infer that he is not so bold or appetitive or eager as Thisbe, not so able and willing to leave the domestic sphere—"al to longe, allas! at hom was he" (824). Revealing his own fear of women and heterosexuality, he misreads Thisbe's bloody veil as a sign of her death; it more accurately represents, in this version of the story, her confrontation with the feminine aggression and appetite figured in the lioness, forces that the nubile maiden also hides from but is not undone by. In his only speech in the legend, Piramus is less concerned with the loss of Thisbe than with his own failure as a man to protect her (833–41), and his immediate response, when faced with this blow to manly pride, is, like Antony's, suicide.

For both Antony and Piramus, unbearable flaws in their masculine identity—as warrior/ruler in Antony's case, as sexually mature and independent adult male and defender of helpless women in Piramus'—appear to have been caused or at least exposed by their honest efforts to establish and maintain a heterosexual relationship. They consequently choose suicide not because they cannot live without the women they love, but because they cannot live with themselves in the emasculated state to which they have been reduced. But ironically, of course, their suicides simply confirm that they have been feminized by love. Suicide is after all defined by the poem and the larger traditions it draws on[15] as the ultimate act a woman can have recourse to when she is raped or abandoned or otherwise troubled by the vagaries of heterosexual relations, or when like Alceste she can sacrifice herself for her husband. The fate of the only two "good" men the narrator can think of thus signals from the outset the pervasive problem that the *Legend of Good Women* examines: the incompatibility of the roles of adult male and true lover in a world where the latter is by definition feminized in one way or other. Antony and Piramus further introduce the real agenda of the Legends by representing the danger to men in love at either end of the masculine life cycle: Antony is the mature hero lamentably feminized by ungoverned (and of course adulterous) heterosexual desire, Piramus the boy who does not make it to manhood because he rushes (admittedly not quite fast enough) into the dangerous path of love before he is equipped to negotiate the perils along the way, and notably without his father's guidance, let alone approval.

If the first two Legends suggest that manhood is thus difficult both to attain and to maintain, the remaining stories extend the problem of feminization for the fourteenth-century aristocratic male from those men who try to serve Love to a number of men who are not so naively loyal to women or to the God of Love's ostensively woman-centered code. Most of the remaining heroes, older than Piramus and wiser than Antony, seem to know that heterosexual union is sometimes a pleasant or necessary diversion—it confirms one element of their manhood, and often saves their lives—but a dangerous state to settle down in, a place in which the manhood they are supposedly proving is in fact deeply threatened. Unlike Antony or Piramus, the rest survive the mortal dangers of Love by betraying women, but the problem of feminization is not so easily solved. For the very strategies these men use to escape any permanent heterosexual bond are in turn ironically feminizing ones, almost as characteristically so as suicide. In fact femininity, pervasively associated in medieval culture with passivity, weakness, irrationality, self-indulgence, and deceitfulness, seems to be an almost inescapable condition for all the men in the world of the poem, something either inherent in the "human" condition or in the social organization into which all are born.

All of the remaining heroes are in the first place presented as characters caught up—like women—in the plots of other men, constrained by forces beyond their control and unable to rule their own destinies. Theseus is literally imprisoned (in a story about sons who, like daughters in most stories, are objects of exchange between noble fathers); Eneas (another son of an incapacitated father) is defeated, exiled, and lost to boot; Demophon is shipwrecked; Jason and Lyno are conspired against (like Theseus) in the dynastic struggles of elder male relatives. Those few males who are circumstantially freer, apparently more in control of their lives, are actually even more inescapably in bondage to the ir-rational effect of what is characterized as innate, gratuitous male lust. Tereus rapes Philomela because of an unexplained, unmotivated, per-haps involuntary and brutalizing desire; Tarquinius rapes Lucrece on account of a somewhat more explicable passion, as male competition routed through women (who has the most faithful wife?) fuels the fires of his lust and violence. The male characters' status as victims and pawns —like women, again—of external and/or internal forces beyond their rational control is also emphasized and aggravated by the frequent rever-sal of roles anticipated in the story of Piramus and Thisbe, where Thisbe is, as we have seen, more aggressive, eager, even "manly" than her lover —or at least as capable of taking care of herself in the woods. Although the narrator sometimes downplays the unfeminine characteristics of his heroines in order to make them fit the model of "good woman" he is constructing here, we still see that most of them (Dido, Ariadne and Phaedra, Medea, Phyllis, Hypermnestra) are or could be in positions of power over their lovers. The sexual anxiety this circumstance generates in men is brought into the open in the plot of the last story, the legend of Hypermnestra, when Hypermnestra's father gives her a knife on her wedding night and commands her to kill her husband (who is also his nephew) in their nuptial bed. But like Hypermnestra, who is said to be congenitally unable to wield a blade, all the women of the narrator's tra-dition and devising are uninterested in using their power except to rescue men from life-threatening situations, usually in the hopes of marrying them afterwards.

Although the heroes who come after Antony and Piramus are com-pletely uninterested in stable domestic relationships, the Legends go on to demonstrate that men are always entrapped by heterosexual relations —if not in the lady's arms, then in a vicious circle of feminization. When he has been feminized by circumstances, fate, or innate weakness in the first place, the strategies a hero can subsequently use to escape this status in fact only confirm it. To secure a more powerful woman's assistance, for instance, a hero is often forced, like any victim, to play up his weakness: Eneas weeps and threatens suicide, Theseus begs and bribes and makes false promises; Jason is as "coy as is a mayde" (1548), while his friend Hercules, in Chaucer's version of the story, serves as his pimp. Tarquinius and Lucrece's husband Colatyne leave their post in the Roman camp to steal into the "estres" (1715), the inner spaces, of Lucrece's chamber; in that feminine enclosure Tarquinius' proper masculine reason and honor are defenseless against "his blynde lust" (1756). Tereus, enflamed by the vulnerable beauty of Philomela, uses his "wiles" (2294) to take her from her father's protection; and again the feminizing quality of his lust is imaged by the underscored interiority of the space where the rape occurs, in a "derke cave" within a forest (2310–12). After prostituting himself to win (with little effort) the lady's undying affection, or removing himself to a feminine place where he can indulge in his lust, the hero must then attempt to recover his masculine position—his independence, nobility, and devotion to more important issues—by eschewing the heterosexual union in which he is dependent on a woman. And yet the process of abandoning a woman, like the earlier process of seducing one, is emasculating in one way or another, as men's infidelities and betrayal of women in this poem always involve them once again in lies and storytelling, wiliness and other feminine duplicities, ignoble escapes out the window, and the complete failure of chivalric obligations to protect the lady herself.

By the end of the poem we might well conclude that feminization in this world is hard to avoid because the rules of patriarchy are incompatible with the rules of courtly love, and that men are caught in the consequent contradiction as they try to establish stable gender identity. Whereas patriarchy devalues the culturally feminine and insists on the difference between men and women as well as the power of the former over the latter, the heterosexual union idealized by the laws of Cupid values traits associated with femininity such as irrationality, self-sacrifice, submission, and service, and thus diminishes in theory both the difference and the power differential between male and female. The problematic lack of difference that such a conception of love entails is made clear in various ways: for example, the women in the poem who give themselves utterly to men are in fact all attracted not by otherness and virility, but by the male's temporary or apparent sameness, his passivity, coyness, vulnerability, and dependence (and even, in the case of Jason, his looks)—those very characteristics that also signal the heroes' feminization. In the cases where women are raped, there is no suggestion of their sexual interest or complicity—or even, in the case of Lucrece, of their consciousness. What might be construed as the women's unconscious desire, like the men's, to bond with their own sex cannot be gratified for long by the hero, who for his part must necessarily be unfaithful if he is to demonstrate his manhood, his independence and freedom and difference. And the actual loss of gender differentiation that a successful heterosexual union might bring about, if two actually became one, is perhaps hinted at in the essential similarity of the most innocent and "true" lovers in the poem: Piramus and Thisbe, who speak in one voice, both "wex pale" and are separated only by the cold wall their fathers have built (apparently in vain) to keep them apart.

But if the poem suggests, as so many readers with otherwise different interpretations agree, that there is something wrong with the laws of Love,[16] it also reveals a serious problem in the rule of the fathers. Fathers are in theory at least men who have negotiated that treacherous path of heterosexual desire, and the institution of patriarchal rule should facilitate the next generation's passage to adulthood: hence a father must at once protect his daughters and pass proper standards of manliness on to his sons. But the contradiction in this charge is brought out in the Legends by the fact that all the men of the fathers' generation fail in one way or another to see their offspring to sexual maturity, either through absence, incapacity, or malevolence. Cleopatra's story, as told by this narrator, tellingly begins "After the deth of Tholome the Kyng" (580), and so too we are reminded early in the linked stories of Medea and Ysiphile that Eson, the father of their common seducer, Jason, is dead. Living fathers are in some instances too weak (like Anchises and Pandeon) to protect their sons and daughters; or as is more often the case, they cause active harm, intentionally or not, to the next generation. Thisbe's and Piramus' fathers inexplicably prohibit love, and so indirectly cause their childrens' deaths. Oetes, by contrast, unwittingly seals his daughter Medea's doom when he bids her to sit at the table with Jason. Theseus passes on his good looks and his false ways with women to his son Demophon, while Jason and Lyno are both schemed against by jealous uncles. In the latter story, we also see a strong suggestion of incest in Egiste's bizarre speech to his daughter Hypermnestra: in the same breath the father vows his love and threatens to kill the girl if she doesn't murder her bridegroom-cousin Lyno, and it is difficult to avoid the conclusion that this is the story of a Lear-like father who cannot let his daughter grow up and sleep with another man. The public, institutional consequences of such unresolved Oedipal situations—of the patriarchal failure to help sons become men—reaches epic proportions in the legend of Lucrece, where the narrator frames his story with reminders that Tarquinius' irrational lust brings an end to the whole line of Roman kings (1680–84, 1862–64).

I have thus far been arguing from the evidence of the Legends alone that this is a poem for and about men and their anxieties about sex and gender: each alleged heroine's story is embedded in a plot and told in a way that underscores the greater interest and value of masculine affairs; in this world heterosexual love is always emasculating (if not lethal), and the generation of the fathers fails to provide whatever young males might need to escape the pervasive threat of feminization. I want to return briefly now to the figure of the dreamer/poet himself as it is characterized in the Prologue, for there in retrospect we find arguably sufficient explanation for the narrator's only partially concealed antipathy toward women and his complex anxieties about the infectious feminization of the Court of Cupid and its literary servants.

The narrator of the *Legend of Good Women* presents himself in the well-known opening lines (F. 1–209, G. 1–103), before the dream-vision, as a bookworm who is drawn from his fanatic devotion to reading by only one "game": the cult of the marguerite. This emphasizes both the literary man's prior disinterest in actual heterosexual love and his professional obligation to take part in an elaborate courtly word-game, in which the explicit substitution of the daisy for the loved one at once covers over and underscores the unimportance or irrelevance of women.[17] The dream that follows suggests the multiple anxieties of the court poet in such a situation, including his fear of a tyrannical male ruler who (perhaps to demonstrate his own superior sensitivity and potency) blames his servant for writing antifeminist poetry and also calls attention to that servant's emasculated status: "Thow . . . art therto nothyng able," the God of Love says (F. 320, G. 246). Like so many of the heroes of the Legends, the poet is further feminized by the intervention of a powerful, aristocratic woman who speaks the kind of rational words he for some unexplained (but psychologically and historically plausible[18]) reason cannot. The poet's disinterest in real women can perhaps turn to active antipathy when he is, in effect, treated like a woman himself, not recognized as a man by the male ruler and blocked from proving his manhood either by loving an actual female or by ignoring the subject of women altogether. Again, as in the case of the heroes of the Legends, the only strategy the poet can use to subvert the censure and embarrassment revealed in the dream actually requires behavior widely viewed as feminine—wiliness and duplicity—as he apparently submits and then subtly betrays Cupid's purposes and writes to his own end. Perhaps as part of this subversion, moreover, the poet already suggests through his recounting of the dream that feminization in the Court of Cupid is a corruption spreading right to the top. The God of Love himself, dressed in embroidered robes with a garland of rose leaves on his head (F. 226–28, G. 158–61), also stands corrected for his irrational anger (motivated by what he sees of himself in the daisy worshipper?) by the words of an articulate, rational woman, who admonishes him to act in a more manly, less willful and self-indulgent way.

THE QUESTION THAT "RETRIEVES" THE *Legend of Good Women* from its "retirement" and brings to light a coherent and interesting reading of the Prologue and the Legends together is, then, the broad question of what "woman" or women—both absent and present, as characters, images, metaphors, as readers and as critics—have to do with this text, written like most other masterworks by and for men. In the belief that this question also raises others that I cannot address in detail in the present essay, I want to turn now to a more general discussion of two ramifications of my argument that suggest how the *Legend of Good Women* can be fruitfully brought more directly to the center of attention of certain current critical investigations as well as of contemporary approaches to Chaucer's more well-known poems.

Pursuing as I have done the import of the narrator's obsession with the feminization of men who try to love or to write first provides a necessary caution to the modern critic's own obsession, brought into the open in the last decade or two, with determining the sexual politics of Chaucer or any other canonical male author. In my own earlier reading of the Legends, I stressed the inherent and extensive antifeminism of both the narrator and the God of Love he is forced to serve, an antifeminism noted by earlier critics, more or less repressed for obvious reasons, and then made manifest again by the question that feminist scholarship asks of any text. So marked is this antifeminism, I argued, that it cannot be attributed to the implied author, Chaucer, first because his "subtle intelligence," displayed in his work as a whole, could not conceivably produce a text that reduced so easily to conventional satire, and second because any discussion of the antifeminism of the poem also reveals its simultaneous critique of men and the masculinist bias of the God of Love, the court, and the poet who serves both. Without retracting the conclusion that this poem is not trying to perform conventional antifeminist satire or that it does criticize less subtle forms of misogyny, I do want to challenge the naive assumption on my part that a critique of the "socio-gender system" and its constraining effects on male identity and freedom amounts to a "pro-woman" position, and hence to take back the implicit support my earlier views offer to current attempts to reconstruct a Chaucer who is either a feminist or—more perniciously, perhaps—a humanist who transcends through art the constraints of a gendered voice and point of view.[19]

It is easy to understand why critics of varying persuasions might want to construct either kind of Chaucer; the apparently unavoidable drive to divine the author's (or the text's) sexual politics, or to go one step further and reclaim the author's (or the text's) greatness on the grounds that he (or it) has no sexual politics, reveals less about the ostensive end of such projects—"meaning" and "intention" disclosed—than about the constitutive force of our own needs and desires. Fifteen years ago, in an essay entitled "Crocodilian Humor: A Discussion of Chaucer's Wife of Bath," David Reid broached what has since been an untenable critical position: he suggested that Chaucer's brand of humanism involved "baiting women and the middle classes," and that since times have changed— "we are middle class . . . and women are not to be baited really, for their place has changed"—now we cover our "embarrassment" at Chaucer's unacceptable views and practices with an "elaborate misunderstanding" of the Wife and her significance.[20] My rereading of the *Legend of Good Women* might suggest that this poem and its critical reception can offer as much or more support for Reid's view of Chaucer's antifeminist humor and our willful misunderstanding of it as does the Wife's *Prologue* and *Tale*. The *Legend*'s rich representation of the feminization of men, although surely a critique of the arbitrariness of gender stereotypes and of crude antifeminism, nevertheless offers nothing "for" women: it does not revalue the feminine, which is even more clearly a pathological condition, nor celebrate woman as a sign or subject; its author does not refuse to traffic in stories about women, but simply insists on doing so on his own terms.

But Chaucer's attitude remains finally inaccessible and irrelevant, and Reid's claim becomes more interesting and even urgent if for a moment at least we pursue not the differences but the similarities between Chaucer's times and our own. I would argue that there may be more real and crucial continuity between the humanism of the *Canterbury Tales* and of our day than Reid wants to believe, more actual commonality between "curmudgeonly and old-fashioned" jokes about women like the Wife of Bath or Cleopatra and the fundamental position of modern criticism. Recent feminist and other broadly speaking "deconstructive" critiques clearly suggest that criticism as we have learned it is as threatened by their challenges to claims of universality, objectivity, certainty, and humanity (or humaneness) as Chaucer's representative fourteenth-century man of letters, the Clerk, say, is threatened by the Wife of Bath "and al hir secte"—or as the men of the *Legend of Good Women*, narrator and characters alike, are threatened by the kind of feminization they experience. Such feminization involves, as this text teaches us, both the real presence and the heightened consciousness of external and internal limits; the paralyzing, even fatal recognition that the position represented by ideals of adult male power, courtly or patriarchal, is unattainable by the most heroic of men; as well as the further, more frightening and barely visible perception that such power is itself, like clear gender distinctions, unstable, even illusory, at the same time that both the constraints and uncertainties of sex roles are inescapable. The primal fear of feminization, it might be said, is the fear that men might be women. Akin to this, I submit, is the fear that all criticism might in fact be or become feminist. Criticism might have to become aware, that is, that the gender of reader, author, and critic always matters, affects interpretation, and establishes what gets read by whom in ways we will never fully understand but must no longer ignore; that textuality and sexuality are, as Janet Halley and Sheila Fisher suggest so clearly in their introduction to this volume, related with an unsettling complexity that insists on the continued relevance of questions about the silencing, displacement, and impersonation of women's voices, past and present, in male-authored texts; that the myth of the great poet's (or the great text's) androgyny or transcendence *is* a myth.

Implicit in the broad claims of the preceding argument is the more specific point that the *Legend of Good Women* is central to our understanding of Chaucer's other works. Here I can only sketch out what amounts to a prolegomenon to a certain kind of reading of the *Canterbury Tales* that privileges the question of gender and the problem of feminization. Other critics have read the Legends as a kind of apprenticeship in storytelling, a prototype of the framed narrative that comes to fruition in the later, more well-known work, or a failed or flawed experiment that turns out better next time.[21] Situating my reading of the Legends in a similar position, I would stress less its failure or its experimental nature, more its key role in identifying and accounting for the Tales' collective exploration of the complex relation of gender and voice, or again of sexuality and textuality.

Viewed through the perspective foregrounded by the Legends, the pilgrims and the characters they create in their narratives repeatedly reveal the same feminine pathology diagnosed and dissected in the stories of "good" women. All are self-conscious and constrained by the felt and real limits of sex roles, and they notably present us with unmistakable images of divided, illusory, and absent selves. From the beginning of the poem, although all speakers are later seen to be anxious to attain "maistrie" over women (and/or the "woman" in themselves) by one route or another, all also desire to submit to a dominant, more powerful, and markedly masculine judgment: namely, the rule of the Host, Harry Bailley, who "of manhod . . . lakkede right naught" (I. 756). Promising them the power of a voice, the freedom and pleasure of speaking ("confort ne myrthe is noon/ To ride by the weye doumb as a stoon," I. 773–74), he ironically enforces their silence, when he wants it, from the beginning: "Hoold up youre hondes, withouten moore speche" (I. 783), he commands, and within three lines they consent. The Host continues to define his position openly as that of the tyrant, just like Cupid: he censures the pilgrims' tales and their critical responses to them beforehand by announcing that he will be the sole judge of their merit; they not only assent but beg him to do as he has decreed (I. 810–14).

The Host's subsequent and sustained concern with the masculinity of his subjects (and hence by implication of himself) and the antifeminism of his literary taste is well documented in the linking matter, and a brief catalogue may suggest those tales in which the problematic feminization of men in love or lust is most markedly at issue. The *Knight's Tale*: Palamon and Arcite, imprisoned cousins, barely conceal their frustrated desire to compete with each other by falling in love with the same vision of woman seen from their prison window; in different ways each proceeds to suffer equal loss of identity; their competition is finally given a much-celebrated public forum, and the winner in battle must die while the final winner in love must give up claims of prowess. The *Miller's Tale*: three men—silly and presumably impotent old John, effeminate Absalon, and wily Nicholas—are further unmanned in their pursuit of Alison (and a similar trio, busy trading corn, women, and even a cradle, appears in the matching *Reeve's Tale*). The *Man of Law's Tale*: evil maternal figures easily trick their ineffectual sons, and Constance (like Alison) is passed from one man who can't hold onto and protect her to another. And so forth: The *Wife of Bath's Tale* stars the knight-rapist who is saved first by the Queen and then by the preachy old Hag; the *Clerk's Tale* actually rewrites the *Legend of Good Women* in complex and misunderstood ways;[22] the *Merchant's Tale* returns to the scene of the old man who fails at all levels to play an adult male role in his belated marriage. The ending of the *Franklin's Tale* transforms the story into a competition, again, among three men, routed through the innocent Dorigen; the *Physician's Tale* centers on the father who cannot protect his daughter from the Tarquinius-like judge, Apius, whose irrational lust destroys him as well as its object; and all this is followed by the complex self-presentation of the "feminoid" Pardoner and the nun-pecked Nun's Priest and his Chauntecleer. Desired, satirized, impersonated, displaced, and damned, the feminine, in the *Canterbury Tales*, turns out to be more or less the human norm, and hence the central source of instability for the narrative as well as for the culture it represents.

NOTES

1. Henry James, *The Bostonians* (New York: Modern Library, 1956), 342–43.

2. The allusion is to Annette Kolodny's "Dancing Through the Minefield: Some Observations on the Theory, Practice, and Politics of a Feminist Literary

Criticism," *Feminist Studies* 6 (1980): 1–25; apropos of my point here, see the first of Kolodny's "three crucial propositions" to which a feminist approach gives rise: "Literary history (and, with that, the historicity of literature) is a fiction" (8).

3. "Literary History as a Challenge to Literary Theory," in *New Directions in Literary History*, ed. Ralph Cohen (Baltimore: Johns Hopkins Univ. Press, 1974), 27.

4. "Irony and the Antifeminist Narrator in Chaucer's *Legend of Good Women*," *Journal of English and Germanic Philology* 82 (1983): 11–31.

5. Both Latin text and translation are taken from Marjorie Chibnall, ed. and trans., *The Ecclesiastical History of Orderic Vitalis*, vol. 4, bks. 7 and 8 (Oxford: Clarendon Press, 1973), 188–89. Two recent discussions brought this passage to my attention: Sharon Farmer, "Persuasive Voices: Clerical Images of Medieval Wives," *Speculum* 61 (1986): 517–43; and Brian Stock, *The Implications of Literacy* (Princeton, N.J.: Princeton Univ. Press, 1983), 481–82.

6. Ibid. In *Christianity, Social Tolerance, and Homosexuality* (Chicago: Univ. of Chicago Press, 1980), John Boswell repeatedly points out that homosexuality and effeminacy were not necessarily connected in classical or medieval thinking. "The use of femininity as a measure of undesirability or weakness more properly belongs in a study of misogyny," he notes (24 n. 43).

7. Toril Moi, "Desire in Language: Andreas Capellanus and the Controversy of Courtly Love," in *Medieval Literature: Criticism, Ideology and History*, ed. David Aers (New York: St. Martin's, 1986), 19.

8. Eugene Vance, "Chretien's *Yvain* and the Ideologies of Change and Exchange," *Yale French Studies* 70 (1986): 42–62.

9. R. Howard Bloch, "Silence and Holes: the *Roman du Silence* and the Art of the Trouvère," *Yale French Studies* 70 (1986): 81–99.

10. Richard F. Green, *Poets and Princepleasers* (Toronto: Univ. of Toronto Press, 1980), 99–134.

11. "Irony and the Antifeminist Narrator," especially 26ff.

12. *Between Men* (New York: Columbia Univ. Press, 1985).

13. Ibid., 17.

14. All Chaucer quotations are from *The Works of Geoffrey Chaucer*, 2nd ed., ed. F. N. Robinson (Boston: Houghton Mifflin, 1957).

15. St. Augustine, for example, links the discussion of whether a man's lust can pollute a Christian woman (i.e., if she is raped) with the discussion of suicide, with much consideration of Lucrece, whom he pronounces guilty. In carefully explaining, in his version of the story, that Lucrece fainted *before* she was raped, Chaucer seems to be vindicating her of the suspicion Augustine raises, the suspicion held against all raped women: what if she enjoyed it? "Quid si enim (quod ipsa tantummodo nosse poterat), quamvis juveni violenter irruenti, etiam sua libidine; illecta consensit, idque in se puniens ita doluit, ut morte putaret expiandum?" (*De Civitate Dei*, I. xix, *Patrologia Latina* 41, p. 33).

16. For an earlier and important discussion of Chaucer's critique as a "bourgeois poet" of the literary conventions of Love poetry in the Legends and elsewhere, for instance, see Dorothy Bethurum, "Chaucer's Point of View as Narrator in the Love Poems," *PMLA* 74 (1959): 511–20.

17. On the displacement of the actual lady as object of medieval love poetry, see Green, *Poets and Princepleasers*, 99–134. As noted earlier, Green's discussion of the relative lack of social importance of the court poet informs my argument about the poet's anxieties and strategies in the *Legend of Good Women*.

18. Omitted from my argument here but worthy of fuller consideration as part of the historical context of the poem is the notion thoroughly explored in early twentieth-century scholarship that the *Legend of Good Women* was an occasional poem commissioned by (or presented to) a royal female patron—either Queen Anne, or possibly Joan of Kent, wife of the Black Prince and mother of Richard II. For an overview and bibliography of the historical argument, see John H. Fisher's review in *Companion to Chaucer Studies*, rev. ed., ed. Beryl Rowland (New York and Oxford: Oxford Univ. Press, 1979), 464–76.

19. It would be impractical to annotate here the many attempts to discover Chaucer's "attitude toward women" in the past decade or two; for a fair sampling of the major efforts, see my "Irony and the Antifeminist Narrator in Chaucer's *Legend of Good Women*," 11, nn. 1, 2.

20. *Chaucer Review* 4 (1970): 73.

21. See, for example: R. M. Garrett, "Cleopatra the Martyr and Hir Sisters," *Journal of English and Germanic Philology* 22 (1923): 64–74; Robert M. Estrich, "Chaucer's Maturing Art in the *Legend of Good Women*," *Journal of English and Germanic Philology* 36 (1937): 326–37; Eleanor Leach, "The Sources and Rhetoric of Chaucer's 'Legend of Good Women' and Ovid's 'Heroides,' " Ph.D. diss., Yale University, 1963; Mary P. Smagola, " 'Spek Wel of Love': The Role of Women in Chaucer's *Legend of Good Women*," Ph.D. diss., Case Western Reserve University, 1972; R. W. Frank, *Chaucer and Legend of Good Women* (Cambridge: Harvard Univ. Press, 1972); Robert O. Payne, "Making His Own Myth," *Chaucer Review* 9 (1975): 197–211.

22. A point I develop in "The Powers of Silence: The Case of the Clerk's Griselda," in *Women and Power in Medieval and Early Modern Europe*, ed. Mary Erler and Maryanne Kowaleski (Athens: Univ. of Georgia Press, 1988), 230–49.

Taken Men and Token Women in *Sir Gawain and the Green Knight*

Sheila Fisher

I. The Problem of Morgan

In Fitt IV of *Sir Gawain and the Green Knight*, after Bertilak de Haut-desert has explained the events of Gawain's testing to him, he concludes by revealing that Morgan la Faye has instigated the whole scheme. Until this point, about a hundred lines from the end of the poem, Morgan's name has never been mentioned, nor, when Gawain returns to Camelot, will it be mentioned again. In our first reading of *Sir Gawain and the Green Knight*, we are put in the position of Gawain himself—not one of innocence, surely, but of ignorance—as we suddenly come upon Morgan at the end of the poem. Her agency appears to be the trick, one might say the cheap trick, that provides a seemingly *dea ex machina* ending for this intricately structured romance. In our subsequent rereadings of the poem, however, we do not remain as ignorant as Gawain always will, for we know that Morgan is responsible for the events of the narrative. Yet most critics of the poem persist in treating Morgan (when they treat her at all) as a surprise that they need not make much of since the poem does not make much of her, either.[1] By ignoring Morgan's agency in order to concentrate on Gawain's moral dilemma and Bertilak's attempts to resolve it, these critics implicitly align themselves with and therefore read from Gawain's perspective. The assumption of this perspective amounts to a feigned ignorance that replicates, in the critical tradition, the deliberate marginalization of Morgan in the text.[2]

If we remove Morgan from the margins and reread *Sir Gawain and the Green Knight* in light of her agency, we take the poem at its word, for, by Bertilak's admission, Morgan has generated the plot of Gawain's adventure and of this romance. Not only did she send Bertilak as the Green Knight to Arthur's court, but she is at the narrative and thematic center of the poem, since the Lady, as her intermediary, accomplishes the hero's testing. Indeed, if we reread the romance from the perspective of Morgan's agency, it might seem that Morgan and the Lady exercise a function and a power that their historical counterparts did not often enjoy: they either participate in or are ultimately responsible for all of the many contracts made throughout the poem.[3] They generate the plot by functioning as the central generators of systems of exchange.

Unpacking the trick ending of the narrative works to clarify both the power of the poem's female characters and the nature of Gawain's testing. Most importantly, however, focusing on Morgan's responsibility for the narrative explains the reasons why she had to be marginalized in the first place. The poem assigns such power to the Lady and finally to Morgan in order to invert and deny it by figuring them as the disrupters of male homosocial bonds.[4] Once the poem has demonstrated that women constitute a threat to the chivalric code that is simultaneously sexual, political, and economic, it attempts to erase that threat by reasserting the values of Christian chivalry and of feudalism and by marginalizing Morgan.

The poem's inscriptions of its female characters imply an agenda for displacing women that both replicates and constitutes the dominant ideologies of feudalism and Christian chivalry.[5] By the end of the poem, the Lady and Morgan are converted from the generators of exchange into tokens that men can use in their own literary and political exchanges. Reading *Sir Gawain and the Green Knight* in light of Morgan's agency, then, alerts us not only to the nature and function of the power assigned to female characters, but also to the process by which that power is denied so that women can be converted into the tokens of men and specifically of the feudal economic structures reified by this poem.

II. Token Women: The Portraits
of Guenevere and Mary

In preparation for the disruptive activities of the Lady and Morgan, the poem, in Fitt I and early in Fitt II, presents two important images of "good girls," static portraits that emblematize women's proper placement as tokens within the aristocratic world of romance. The first, ironically, is of Queen Guenevere, but then, as many critics have pointed out, the poem presents a youthful, almost prelapsarian Camelot.[6] While Arthur's youthfulness makes him "sumquat childgered" and "wylde" of "brayn" ("rather boyish" and "restless" of "brain"),[7] his queen's youthfulness means that she is still "unfallen," and therefore still a fit symbol of her king:

> Whene Guenore, ful gay, grayþed in þe myddes,
> Dressed on þe dere des, dubbed al aboute,
> Smal sendal bisides, a selure hir ouer
> Of tryed tolouse, of tars tapites innoghe,
> Þat were enbrawded and beten wyth þe best gemmes
> *Þat my3t be preued of prys wyth penyes to bye,*
> > *in daye.*
> > Þe comlokest to discrye
> > Þer glent with y3en gray,
> > A semloker þat euer he sy3e
> > Soth mo3t no mon say.

> > > (74–84, emphasis mine)

[Queen Guenevere, brilliantly dressed, was set in the midst, placed on a dais of honour, all about her richly decorated, fine silk around her, a canopy above her of choice fabric of Toulouse, many hangings of Tharsian stuff, which were embroidered and set with the best gems that ever money could buy; most beautiful to look upon, she glanced around with her gray eyes; no man could truthfully say that he ever saw a lovelier lady (32; 34).]

Guenevere is mentioned only four other times in the poem: when we are told that she sits near Gawain at the Yuletide feast (109); when Arthur bids her not to be bothered by the Green Knight's talking head (470–73); when she suffers by comparison to the Lady and her beauty (945); and last, but not least, when she is named as one of the motivations for Morgan's scheme. Among other things, according to Bertilak, Morgan sent him on his errand

> "For to haf greued Gaynour and gart hir to dyȝe
> With glopnyng of þat ilke gome þat gostlych speked
> With his hede in his honde bifore þe hyȝe table."
>
> (2460–62)

[in order to shock Guenevere and cause her to die of terror at that man who, like a phantom, stood talking before the high table with his head in his hand (159).]

I will return to this part of Morgan's plot later in the essay. Suffice it here to say that, if Morgan wanted to scare Guenevere literally to death, her effort would have been redundant. As the poem depicts Arthur's queen, Guenevere could hardly be more dead than she already is. Morgan's marginalization is delayed until the end of the poem; Guenevere's has already occurred by the time the poem opens. Her static portrait inscribes her as the portrait of stasis. She never speaks, and she never responds. The poem, then, makes certain that at least part of Morgan's plan backfires because Guenevere has already been "killed into art" before Morgan can scare her to death.[8]

The silencing of Guenevere appears to be the poem's own radical revision of Arthurian romance and of Guenevere's place within it.[9] Static, beautiful, and silent, she can be "dished up"[10] at table as the ideal queen, whose function is to represent the king, and specifically, within the syntax of her description, to represent his purchasing power. She and the rich silks and canopy framing her "myȝt be preued of prys with penyes to bye" (79) [might be proved of worth to buy with pennies (my translation)]. Purchased with "penyes," exchanged for tokens, Guenevere becomes the token of young Arthur's power, wealth, and privilege, placed as she is within the economies of sexual exchange that constitute feudal marriage.[11]

The poem's second portrait of a lady as token within masculine systems of valuation occurs when, at Camelot, Gawain arms himself for his encounter at the Green Chapel. This scene is justifiably famous within the critical literature on *Sir Gawain and the Green Knight* because it is here that the poem introduces the symbol of the pentangle in order simultaneously to explicate its own values and to challenge the hero to live up to them.[12] At the beginning of his adventure, Gawain takes up a shield that, like his surcoat, is marked with the pentangle. And the poem devotes two stanzas (619–69) to explaining the virtues signified by the pentangle with specific reference to Gawain and his character.

> Forþy hit acordez to þis kny3t and to his cler armez,
> For ay faythful in fyue and sere fyue syþez
> Gawan watz for gode knawen, and as golde pured.
>
> (631–33)

> [And so it is appropriate to this knight and to his unblemished arms; because he was always trustworthy in five respects and fivefold in each, Gawain was known to be a good knight, and like refined gold (61).]

Although Gawain is like "golde pured," these stanzas deliberately beg the question of the pentangle's referentiality by informing us that it is "nwe" (636), that is, newly emblazoned on Gawain's equipment. If the pentangle is "a syngne þat Salamon set sumquyle / In bytoknyng of trawþe" (625–26) [a symbol that Solomon devised once upon a time as a token of fidelity (61)], it is for Gawain to prove whether the pentangle refers to the refined gold of his moral substance or only to his reputation for it.[13]

While the poem raises the question of Gawain's right to wear the pentangle, it leaves no question as to its affirmation of the values that the pentangle signifies. Four of its five sets of five put forth the values and virtues that form the substance of Christian chivalry: the right use of the body and of the senses; the belief in Christ's wounds; and the five courtly/Christian virtus of generosity, fellowship, cleanness, courtesy, and compassion. Moreover, as the poem's language asserts, the pentangle's very form implies stability, interconnectedness, and completeness: "vche lyne vmbelappez and loukez in oþer" (628) [each line overlaps and interlocks with another (61)]; "Englych hit callen / . . . þe endeles knot" (629–30) [and all over England . . . it is called the endless knot (61)]. These lines can be read as presenting a wish-fulfillment fantasy of the ideal feudal fellowship: endless, interdependent, and incapable of rupture. They assert belief in the stability, the eternality, the perfection, and the fundamental interconnectedness of masculine, aristocratic, Christian values.

Christian virtue, then, as it is defined by the pentangle, is exclusively the province of the knight, that is, of the male. One of its five points, however, *is* associated with the Virgin Mary: "alle his [Gawain's] forsnes he feng at þe fyue joyez / þat þe hende heuene-quene had of hir chylde" (646–47) [he should draw all his fortitude from the five joys which the gracious Queen of Heaven had in her child (61, 63)]. It seems that Gawain refers, as it were, to Mary in his times of need; she goes with Gawain to his testing. And it might seem too that if she is part of the endless knot of virtues signified by the pentangle, then she is included within the structure forming the ideals of Arthur's court.

But the way in which Mary is tied up in the pentangle's endless knot is telling when considered in light of Morgan's marginalization and of Guenevere's virtual annihilation in this poem. Mary is included in the pentangle explicitly through connection with her son and through the five joys that she derived from him. It is only through and because of this connection that the pentangle makes a token reference to Mary, the token woman of Christianity, who refers not to herself, but to the Holy Ghost who inseminated her and to God the Son whom she bore.[14] In the poem as in Christian orthodoxy, she is defined solely through relationship with the male. Moreover, as Mary Daly has pointed out, within the inversions or *metalepses* performed by Christian orthodoxy, the Virgin's virtues are determined more by what she lacks than by what she has: she lacks female sexuality, and therefore sin, and therefore volition.[15] Her identity is so inextricably bound up with figurations of absence that she can serve as the prototype for the particular version of the eternal feminine that neo-Freudian theory would define as absence itself.[16]

In this poem, then, Mary, like Guenevere, has the right references to admit her into Christianity and into chivalry. Along with Gringolet, the horse, she can accompany Gawain on his dangerous quest, but only—and this too is telling—when her image itself has effectively been made absent by being hidden on the back of Gawain's shield:

> At þis cause þe kny3t comlyche hade
> In þe inore half of his schelde hir ymage depaynted,
> Þat quen he blusched þerto his belde neuer payred.
>
> (648–50)

[For this reason the knight appropriately had her image depicted on the inner side of his shield, so that when he looked at it his courage never failed (63).]

The portrait of Guenevere gives us one (con)version of women in the poem; the portrait of the Virgin Mary gives us another. The former presents the female as public, the latter as private token.

III. Defining Women's Power:
The World of Morgan and the Lady

Gawain seldom remembers to call upon Mary in his times of need. He does not, for instance, pray to her when the Green Knight holds the axe over his head in Fitt IV. It is perhaps not altogether ironic, then, that one of his few prayers to Mary (736–39) brings him to the castle in which he will be tested by the Lady and by Morgan la Faye. This indirect association between Mary and Morgan suggests that Mary is not particularly good at protecting her knight. But it may also suggest that Mary and Morgan are two sides of the same female coin, for, when we reread the poem in light of Morgan's agency, we see that Mary has led Gawain straight into a world of women.[17]

The multifarious nature and consequences of women's power, which will become explicit in the Lady's later negotiations with Gawain, are implicit throughout this section of the poem. When Gawain enters this world of women, he is disarmed and dressed in flowing, furred robes. Throughout courtly literature, of course, the knight who lays aside arms in a foreign place makes himself vulnerable, literally and politically, because he has divested himself of the accoutrements that signify his protected, privileged position within feudal and chivalric codes. The language of *Sir Gawain and the Green Knight*, however, takes this conventional fear of vulnerability one step further, because the threatened loss of chivalric identity for Gawain is figured initially as an implied loss of masculinity. Not only does he put aside the pentangle, but he is "dispoyled" (860) [stripped (73)] of his arms; the poem employs the same sexually ambiguous term for this process that Chaucer applies to the undressing of the passive Griselda in *The Clerk's Tale*.[18]

As Gawain settles down in this world of women, the poem begins to assign to him the language that has earlier been associated with token-ized women in Arthur's court. Significantly, when the Lady of the castle is first introduced, she and her retinue enter the "closet" (934) [enclosed pew (77)] from which they hear Mass and in which Morgan, the "auncian" (948) [elderly woman (77)], must already be hidden, since she emerges with the Lady when the Mass is over. This closet is, however, the proverbial "room with a view," for, from this vantage, "Þenne lyst þe lady to loke on þe knyȝt" (941) [Then the lady liked to look on the knight (my translation)]. Like Guenevere in Fitt I (83–84), the richly attired Gawain has become a spectacle. The pentangle knight, formerly the object of male admiration, is now diminished to the object of the female gaze. It is no wonder, then, that four lines later, the poem makes one of its few references to Guenevere, for the Lady is "wener þen Wenore, as þe wyȝe þoȝt" (945) [lovelier than Guenevere, so the knight thought (77)]. For Gawain is here in a Gueneverian, that is, a feminized position.

There are, of course, crucial differences between the earlier marginalization and objectification of Guenevere and this displacement of Gawain's masculinity, what indeed we might call here the "objectification" of Gawain. Not the least of these differences, of course, is the fact that, within the sexual politics of feudal society, Guenevere is fixed right where she ought to be. Arguably the only "public" female character in the poem, Guenevere can be publicized specifically because she is the token of the male. But Gawain, within this world of women, has exchanged his public identity as Arthur's knight for private comfort and private desire. Dressed in flowing, furred robes, he moves through the castle's many private rooms and finally into the bedroom, which is described in the same language of opulence (853–59) as is Guenevere's setup at Arthur's table. Unwittingly under Morgan's power, Gawain is in a dangerous position because, as he circulates through this world of women, he runs the risk of referring to them, of becoming the token of the woman and of the privacy that is woman in this poem.

Women in *Sir Gawain and the Green Knight* are repeatedly associated with privacy, but the poem does not feminize privacy simply because this is medieval women's historical place. It does so primarily to conflate the dangerousness of privacy with the dangerousness of women themselves. The two are one and the same. *Sir Gawain and the Green Knight* conflates the political with the sexual in order to construct a sexual politics that inscribes women's (dis)placement within the exchange systems of Christian feudalism. That the Lady and Morgan seem placed at the poem's narrative center only underscores the dangerous power of women and their privacy.

What constitutes the danger that women are and that they represent in this poem? The most obvious place to locate the answer is in the otherness and privacy of female sexuality itself. Certainly, the medieval Christian misogynist tradition had much to say on this score.[19] Above all, the nature of Gawain's testing in Fitt III—naked, passive, entrapped in the bedroom by the seemingly seductive overtures of the Lady—would indicate that, whatever meanings accumulate around the threat of women in this romance, female sexuality is the source, if not the essence, of them all.[20] But the poem goes further. It presents female sexuality not only as cause of, but as trope for a specific cluster of threats to Christian chivalry and to feudalism.

We can begin to unpack this trope by looking at the phenomenon of the Lady's namelessness. For in a poem that names everyone and everything from the individual knights of the Round Table to Gawain's horse, the fact that a major character goes unnamed seems rather peculiar. The Lady is simply the Lady because she comes to represent essentialized womanhood; as such, she is so private that she needs no public token by which to identify herself. What is more, in her bedroom testings of Gawain, she is not acting on behalf of a man. Rather, she refers to Morgan and to Morgan's power. Unlike Guenevere, who is Arthur's token, the Lady acts as a woman on behalf of a (similarly unnamed) woman, and, in this capacity, she cannot be named or publicized. For these reasons, she is not named Lady Bertilak (except by some critics); in the middle fitts of the poem, she does not refer to her husband.

Rereading this section of the poem in light of Morgan's agency both clarifies the nature of women's dangerousness and prepares for the Lady's enactment of that specific dangerousness in Fitt III. A lady without a name is a lady without a lord, and that is dangerous enough. But there's more. If, at Camelot's Christmas Feast, Gawain is seated beside Guenevere at a table which Bishop Bawdewyn heads (109–12), then, in the second Christmas feast, the Lady has replaced Guenevere as Gawain's dinner companion, and Morgan has, significantly, taken the bishop's seat of preeminence at the head of the table: "þe olde auncian wyf heȝest ho syttez" (1001) [The venerable old lady sat in the seat of honor (81)]. Morgan's displacement of the highest ranking Christian churchman within Arthur's court anticipates what Bertilak's later designation of her as " 'Morgne þe goddes' " (2452) [Morgan the goddess (159)] confirms: Morgan and her power pose a fundamental threat to the Christian chivalric code.

The absence of a figure like Bishop Bawdewyn from the castle would be enough to suggest the nature of Morgan's profound subversiveness. But if we are to believe Bertilak's claim that the whole scheme to test Arthur's court originated with Morgan, then she displaces more than a bishop. Critics have been accustomed to write of Bertilak as Gawain's "host" and even to define Gawain's error in terms of a breach of the time-honored relationship between guest and host.[21] But despite Bertilak's assertion that Morgan " 'in *my* hous lenges' " (2446; emphasis mine) [dwells in my house (159)], the host either owns nothing himself, or owns all he has, " 'þur myȝt' " (2446) [through the power (159)] of his recalcitrant tenant. In the context of Morgan's agency, Bertilak becomes the host in name alone, just as, it might be argued, he is only nominally the husband of the Lady who does not refer to him. If he inhabits the castle through Morgan's might, if he magically changes forms and grows new heads to do her bidding, then Bertilak is, effectively, the taken man who is Morgan's token—feminized, as Gawain is, within this world of women.

Proprietor of her castle, generator of the contracts and exchanges forming the poem's plot, Morgan has the power to displace both Bishop Bawdewyn and Bertilak, ecclesiastical and secular authority. In her powers of displacement lies the danger the narrative needs to displace. For this poem's particular construction of female sexuality and subjectivity inscribes a threatening otherness that is not only, and perhaps not primarily sexual. It is also and specifically political and economic. To displace Bawdewyn as bishop and Bertilak as host and husband would be to subvert the exchange systems of Christian feudalism.

IV. Trafficking with Women:
Gawain's Perilous Negotiations with the Lady

Gawain, in the private world of the bedroom, squarely confronts the unmediated presence of the woman and the threat that she and the privateness associated with her pose to his knighthood. Even if the dalliance between the Lady and Gawain were no more (serious) than an extended exercise in courtly love conversation, the Lady's initiation of it would still be dangerous. For here, courtly love talk no longer represents the verbal game devised by aristocratic men to distance and define women's sexuality in reference to masculine desire.[22] Instead, the Lady's love language, if it does not literally refer to her own sexual desire for Gawain (an insult, perhaps, in and of itself), does refer to—indeed constitutes —Morgan's plan for testing him.

But, in *Sir Gawain and the Green Knight*, the danger of dalliance, of course, has far-reaching consequences. In her appropriation of the male language of courtly love, the Lady is shown tempting Gawain into an alliance with her that would threaten his chastity, to be sure, but Gawain's chastity is not the point. The point is that Gawain has made a previous commitment to Bertilak to exchange in the evening whatever each has won in the course of the day (1105–25). Gawain's contract with his "host," the man of the house and thus the putative repository of power, checks his actions in the bedroom. Otherwise, given Gawain's reputation as a notorious womanizer throughout Arthurian literature, we can be sure that this particular knight of the Round Table would not have been so scrupulous.[23] In cleaning up Gawain's act, the poem has revised Gawain's career as radically as it did Guenevere's and for the same purpose: in order to underline the primacy of contracts between men. To break the bond of loyalty to Bertilak and thus to deny the authority of the lord would rupture the endless knot of the pentangle.

As R. A. Shoaf argues in *The Poem as Green Girdle*, what is at stake in the bedroom scenes, and indeed, throughout *Sir Gawain and the Green Knight*, is the "pricing" of the hero, that is, the determination of what Gawain is worth.[24] I would like to take Shoaf's well-defined argument one step further by asking: what Gawain is worth *to whom*?[25] For it becomes clear, as the poem progresses, that Gawain runs the risk of becoming devalued when he trades in a different economic system, the one which, within the poem's narrative, is inextricably associated with women.

When the Lady begins her temptation of Gawain, the knight tries to squirm out of a tight place by resorting to the courtly convention of the lover's unworthiness. He invokes cliché in the attempt to save his skin:

> "In god fayth," quoþ Gawayn, "gayn hit me þynkkez,
> Paȝ I be not now he þat ȝe of speken;
> To reche to such reuerence as ȝe reherce here
> I am wyȝe unworþy, I wot wel myseluen."
>
> (1241–44)

> ["Really and truly," said Gawain, "this seems to me very agreeable, even though I may not be now the man you speak of; I am unworthy to attain such an honour as you have just mentioned, I know myself very well" (93).]

Within the systems of value affirmed by the poem, of course, Gawain's value is on the point of fluctuating because, as Shoaf points out, the knight disclaims his own identity (1242).[26] What is more, the Lady here takes Gawain at his word, for she proceeds to "price" him by translating his definition of *prys* into her own terms.[27]

Those terms are, as Shoaf demonstrates, blatantly commercial.[28] The poem builds gradually to this commercialism by working first through a more sexualized and thus more generalized notion of female possession. According to the Lady,

> "Bot hit ar ladyes innoȝe þat leuer wer nowþe
> Haf þe, hende, in hor holde, as I habbe here,
> To daly with derely your daynté wordez,
> Keuer hem comfort and colen her carez,
> Þen much of þe garysoun oþer golde þat þay hauen."
>
> (1251–55)

> [For there are many ladies who would have you, dear sir, in their power now, as I have you here, to exchange agreeable pleasantries in delightful conversation with you, find solace for themselves and assuage their longings, than much of the treasure or gold they possess (95).]

These women (in whose company Morgan, doubtless, belongs) would trade all their " 'garysoun oþer golde' " [treasure or gold] for the "golde pured" (633) [the refined gold] of Gawain himself. When the Lady states that women would trade all their material wealth for Gawain, she clearly implies that women, and not only the goddess Morgan, actually have their own material wealth to spend. The Lady's purchasing power, however, becomes diminished rather quickly, for her next speech is more hypothetical, and, interestingly enough, more historically accurate:

> "For were I worth al þe wone of wymmen alyue,
> And al þe wele of þe worlde were in my honde,
> And I schulde chepen and chose to cheue me a lorde,
> . . . .
> Þer schulde no freke vpon folde bifore yow be chosen."
>
> (1269–75)

> [for were I the equal of all the multitude of mortal women, and all the wealth of the world were in my hands, and I could bargain and select in finding a husband for myself, . . . no man on earth would be chosen in preference to you (95).]

Aristocratic women, of course, had neither material wealth that was legally their own nor the right to arrange their own marriages, to choose whom they would.[29] That the Lady's speech acknowledges as much is significant, for it is here that the poem's language simultaneously defines the precise nature of women's dangerousness and brackets that dangerousness through reference to historical reality. Women do not have this power, in reality, and what is more, this female character in a fantastic romance knows it. Her admission begins her displacement according to the model historically established for the poem by the economies of feudal marriage. And the Lady says something more: the combined worth of all the women in the world might just be equal to that of one Gawain. Within the values of *Sir Gawain and the Green Knight*, this is the closest the Lady comes to speaking the truth.

The Lady would buy Gawain, if she could, that is, if he and history would allow her to. She would buy Gawain, *if she could,* and it is that potentiality that the poem both explores and diffuses. If, within the context of Gawain's contract with Bertilak, she could succeed in negotiating her own transaction with him, she would explode the homosocial bonds signified by the pentangle in an act that would radically subvert the economies of Christian feudalism.

The hypothetical cast of this passage shows, however, that the Lady cannot accomplish so complete an act of terrorism, at the same time that it suggests how she gets as far as she does. Caught, as it were, between the economies of male feudalism and of female commercialism, Gawain thinks he speaks neutrally and, above all, diplomatically, when he replies, " 'Bot I am proude of þe prys þat ȝe put on me' " (1277) [but I am proud of the value which you set on me (95)].[30] While the predominantly male, aristocratic audience would rest assured that the Lady's price could never approximate Gawain's full value, the fact that she can begin to price him at all begins to discount him.

On the third day, the Lady levels her most dangerous assault by suggesting that she and Gawain exchange love gifts. Gawain initially refuses all she offers, because before his confrontation with the Green Knight, "he nay þat he nolde neghe in no wyse / Nauþer golde ne gary-soun" (1836–37) [he said that he would not touch either gold or treasure (my translation)]. The language here is significant. Echoing the Lady's earlier speech in her attempt to buy Gawain, the poem makes clear that, although Gawain may have gone on sale through his transactions with the Lady, he is ultimately not for sale, at least not to her.

As an emissary of Morgan, the Lady knows that Gawain will reject her girdle if it is a love token referring to her and to her sexuality. In a strategy of revaluation that Bertilak and Gawain will later appropriate and invert, the Lady redefines the girdle as token so that it refers not to her, but to Gawain, not to the female, but to the male:

> "Bot who-so knew þe costes þat knit ar þerinne,
> He wolde hit prayse at more prys, parauenture;
> For quat gome so is gorde with þis grene lace,
> While he hit hade hemely halched aboute,
> Þer is no haþel vnder heuen tohewe hym þat myȝt,
> For he myȝt not be slayn for slyȝt vpon erþe."
>
> (1849–54)

[But anyone who knew the powers that were associated with it would esteem it of more worth, perhaps; for anyone who is girt with this green girdle, while he has it closely wrapped about him, there is no mortal man who could cut him down, for he could not be killed by any stratagem whatsoever (127).]

The Lady has Gawain here, for protection against mortal injury in the confrontation to come would be, as Gawain himself ruminates, useful indeed: "Hit were a juel for þe jopardé þat hym iugged were" (1856) [it would be a jewel for the adventure that was judged to him (my translation)]. But here, as the commercial language in the Lady's speech makes clear,[31] the poem also has the Lady. The girdle, as she presents it at the beginning of her speech, is a metaphor for her. Like the Lady, the girdle has hidden powers, but as she offers it to an unnamed and generalized male recipient, she offers it up, and herself in the bargain, as a commodity which would be given a higher price if its properties were known. In the process, the girdle and the Lady of the girdle become the objects of the evaluating masculine subjectivity. And so Gawain can give in to the Lady, and to her demand that he keep the girdle hidden from her husband (1862–65), not for "hir sake" (1862), as she bids, but for his own. He will bear a token of the Lady not to remember her, but to save his neck.

But this reason, as Gawain learns in Fitt IV, is not good enough. In the private and therefore feminized space of the bedroom, he confronts not only the multivalent threat of the Lady. He also confronts the private desires of his private self, and these he must deny because they are associated, in the ideology of this poem, with the Lady and her privacy. These private desires are, in part, sexual, but as the third day of the testing makes clear, they are also much more, and therefore even more dangerous than sexual desire.

If female sexuality is associated with privacy and—explicitly through the girdle—with life and regeneration, all three are fundamentally antithetical to the purposes of Christian chivalry and feudal society. Throughout the three days of his testing, Gawain fails to uphold the terms of his contract with Bertilak and ultimately the ideals of Christian chivalry because he has betrayed a fundamental economic principle of feudal society. Rather than trafficking in women, he has traffic with them.[32] Rather than circulating women as tokens, according to their earlier designation in the poem, he actually bargains with the Lady, negotiates with her and, in so doing, accords her the status of an independent, evaluating subjectivity whose system of values and whose valuation of him are strikingly different from his own.

This is why, when the Lady initiates her own negotiations, the language of exchange is translated from that of a gift economy, the putative basis of idealized feudal bonding, to that of a money economy, of a commercial marketplace. As medieval economic theorists constantly warned, the dynamic of the marketplace and the temptations of commerce gave all too much power and self-determination to the individual subject.[33] Within a commercial economy, ownership could pass all too easily into the wrong hands. Tokens could be exchanged so freely that they would no longer refer. By associating this commercial idiom with the Lady, the poem underlines the fundamentally political and economic subversiveness inherent in her sexual threat. And when Bertilak himself later speaks in this language, we can see how far the threat contained within the world of women might actually go. Bertilak's use of a commercial idiom to articulate his contract with Gawain on the three days of the exchange shows that Gawain has already been priced within the marketplace of the bedroom through his traffic with the Lady.

The cost of traffic with the Lady would, in one sense, be the end of the exchange systems of feudalism, which are dependent upon the patronage and privilege that the lord has the power to dispense. In another sense, fully consummated sexual traffic with the Lady would be the end of Gawain; it would cost him his life at the Green Chapel. If the bedroom scenes suggest the time-honored but ever-interesting equation of (hetero)sex and death, they also raise and elide a more interesting possibility: what if Gawain had slept with the Lady and honored the terms of his contract with Bertilak? What if he had repaid Bertilak in kind?

There is no doubt that, in its use of incremental repetition, the poem poses this question and implies an answer: the only way to avoid the death guaranteed by sex with the Lady is to have sex with the Lord. Trafficking with her brings death; trafficking with him brings life. The poem raises this possibility and then swerves in order to forefront not the homosexual, but rather the homosocial, and within this poem, lifegiving and life-assuring bonds of feudal chivalry. The veiled possibility of a homosexual act suggests the intensity of these homosocial bonds. In his commitment to Bertilak or Arthur or Christ, Gawain must be willing, as it were, to go all the way. En route, he must traffic in the Lady and not with her in order to enact and construct the economies of feudalism.

V. Bertilak's Blows: The Father Confessor,
the Sinful Son, and the New Girdle

When Gawain chooses to wear the girdle over the pentangle as he goes to meet the Green Knight, he demonstrates his decision to gratify private desires at the expense of his contract with Bertilak. In Fitt IV, the poem is oblique in its articulation of the ways in which the girdle may actually obscure the pentangle on Gawain's surcoat:[34]

Whyle þe wlonkest wedes he warp on hymseluen—
His cote wyth þe *conysaunce of þe clere werkes*
Ennurned vpon veluet, vertuus stonez
Aboute beten and bounden, enbrauded semez,
And fayre furred withinne wyth fayre pelures—
Ʒet laft he not þe lace, þe ladiez gifte,
Þat forgat not Gawayn *for gode of hymseluen.*

(2025–31, emphasis mine)

[While he was putting on his noblest garment—his surcoat with the bright embroidered badge, emblazoned upon velvet, set about and adorned with potent gems, embroidered at the seams, and finely furred inside with good pelts—he nevertheless did not omit the belt, the lady's gift; for his own good, Gawain did not forget that (137).]

In this passage, the meaning of the pentangle has been obscured into a *conysaunce;*[35] the Lady's token has replaced the tokenized woman, the Virgin Mary; and it is clear that Gawain will make this exchange for his own good, rather than from his commitment to an abstract set of ideals.

Because of his choice of the woman and her token, Gawain is punished. Because he has trafficked with women, he has been sold into valuing his own life over his commitment to the code. But Gawain, worthy knight that he is, "golde pured" (633) within the economies of feudalism and Christian chivalry, must be redeemed, that is, bought back from the female who has, temporarily, bought him.[36] To redeem Gawain, the poem ends with its series of inversions and reversals that outline a program for displacing, marginalizing, and thereby denying women's power within the ideologies of Christian feudalism.[37] Such reversals work, finally, to "frame" women within the intricately structured plot of this narrative.[38]

The poem accomplishes the numerous reversals necessary to redeem Gawain through two major reversals that structure all the others. The role assigned to the Green Knight must be reversed so that, once outside Morgan's castle, he can publicly assert his identity as Bertilak, that is, as host and lord. And the meaning that the green girdle had carried out of the bedroom and into the woods must be reversed in order to redefine the nature of Gawain's testing. Taken together, these two reversals and their implications marginalize the women in the poem and prepare Gawain to return to Arthur's court.

In order to reassert masculine control over the systems of exchange that Morgan and the Lady have owned and operated at the center of the narrative, the poem transforms the Green Knight, Gawain's life-threatening enemy, into his moral instructor and father-confessor.[39] Bertilak can chasten Gawain and show him the error of his ways. As male, Bertilak can *inform Gawain* (and I mean this phrase in both its senses), as he clarifies the mystery generated by Morgan's plot. Bertilak immediately connects the nick on the neck that Gawain has received with Gawain's failure; his language, significantly, implies that this failure is associated with Gawain's traffic with the Lady:

> "Trwe mon trwe restore,
> Þenne þar mon drede no waþe.
> At þe þrid þou fayled þore,
> And þerfor þat tappe ta þe."
>
> (2354–57)

[The true man must truly repay, and then a man needs to dread no harm. On the third day, you failed then, and therefore, you take that tap (my translation).]

In the short, rhyming lines of the bob-and-wheel, the poem neatly summarizes the point that it will elaborate upon throughout the fourth fitt, a point so central that it can be compressed into a two-line axiom: " 'Trwe mon trwe restore, / þenne þar mon drede no waþe.' " As the repetition of *trwe* implies, there is no danger when the true man truly restores, returns, repays, exchanges with another (true) man. Then the exchanges of feudalism are sound. To do otherwise is to fail; to fail resoundingly enough is death. A small failure is just worth a nick on the neck.[40]

The inversions and reversals wrought upon women's power begin here in this bob-and-wheel. To choose the Lady and life would actually constitute physical death, or the threat of it, as well as the death of the perfected public self that could have been signified by the pentangle. Bertilak here begins to show Gawain that death comes from women's power, and not from the dictates of the chivalric code. In a piece of blatantly false political propaganda, he suggests that only adherence to the code can ensure life. It is significant indeed that Bertilak is authorized by the poem as the explicator of the dangers associated with women. He is allowed to publicize the women in the castle, for he has experienced their dangers firsthand. The errand boy of Morgan, he is periodically transformed into a green giant running around the countryside to perform her bidding.

Read in light of Morgan's agency, Bertilak's informative absolutions of Gawain strain not only the narrative's credibility, but also the moral agenda that the poem has set for itself. In order to assume the role of father-confessor, Bertilak, the tenant of Morgan's castle, must linguistically reappropriate all property (including the events of the second and third fitts) that is associated with women:

"For hit is my wede þat þou werez, þat ilke wouen girdel,
Myn owen wyf hit þe weued, I wot wel for soþe.
Now know I wel þy cosses, and þy costes als,
And þe wowyng of my wyf: I wroȝt hit myseluen.
I sende hir to asay þe."

(2358–62)

[For it is my garment you are wearing, that woven girdle there; I know for certain my own wife gave it to you. Moreover, I know all about your kisses and your conduct too, and my wife's wooing of you; I myself brought it about (153).]

The girdle is his; the wife is his; the testing is his. He has set the Lady to the seduction. In order to deny Morgan's power, Bertilak reasserts his feudal property rights, the chief of which is the right to traffick in women. In so doing, he becomes cast—theoretically if not practically—as the pimp for his wife in order to test another man's virtue. In a poem allegedly concerned with the ability to uphold the Christian virtues of the pentangle, this is a role hardly appropriate for Gawain's moral instructor.

In this passage, too, the Green Knight begins a process of redefining the girdle that enables Gawain ultimately to bring the token back to Camelot as an emblem referring to himself and to his reinstatement in feudal society, and not to the Lady's shopping spree. To begin, through the very act of claiming ownership of the girdle (let alone the wife), Bertilak makes it a sign referring to the male. His wife may have woven it (although even the syntax of the passage quoted above calls this into question), but it belongs to the male as surely as does the headgear that women embroidered for Gawain to wear into battle against the Green Knight (609–14).

Bertilak then goes on to reprice Gawain, effectively removing him from the previous (de)valuation incurred during his commerce with the Lady; he takes Gawain off the market. Gawain, for Bertilak, is one of the most faultless knights alive (2363): " 'As perle bi þe quite pese is of prys more, / So is Gawayn, in god fayth, bi oþer gay kny3tez' " (2364–65) [as a pearl in comparison with a dried pea is of greater value, so, truthfully is Gawain beside other gallant knights (153)]. This act of revaluation returns Gawain to his place within the economies of feudalism and recontextualizes his acceptance of the girdle within that system.

Gawain's failure can now be named: " 'yow lakked a lyttel, sir, and lewté yow wonted' " (2366) [Yet in this you were a little at fault, sir, and lacking in fidelity (153)]. Through this very specific use of the language of Christian chivalry, Bertilak simultaneously displaces the Lady from the token that she made and that belongs to her, and connects the femaleness of that sign with lack or absence—here, significantly, with the absence of loyalty. Through this transformation of the girdle's meaning, the Lady is implicitly positioned as the force rupturing bonds of homosociality. This recontextualization accomplished, Bertilak can forgive Gawain for taking the girdle in the first place, " 'for 3e lufed your lyf; þe lasse I yow blame' " (2368) [because you loved your life; I blame you less for that (153)]. Bertilak can now afford to forgive Gawain for loving his life because Bertilak has squarely revalued that life in relation to the masculine codes of chivalry.

Gawain, however, is too humiliated to accept forgiveness gracefully or to allow the girdle its relatively positive signification. Before he throws the girdle to Bertilak, he says, " 'Corsed worth cowarddyse and couetyse boþe! / In yow is vylany and vyse þat vertue disstryez' " (2374–75) [A curse upon cowardice and avarice too! In you is ill-breeding and vice which destroy knightly virtue (155)]. Although Gawain goes on to attribute these failings to himself, it is significant that he assigns them first to the girdle.[41] In Gawain's first reading of Bertilak's information, he associates with the girdle, and, by extension, with women, both the absence of courage belonging to men and the presence of a commercialized cupidity associated with the mercantile language of the Lady's negotiations in Fitt III. Fear for his life, he declaims, caused him " 'To acorde me with couetyse, my kynde to forsake, / Þat is larges and lewté þat longez to kny3tez' " (2380–81) [to have to do with covetousness, to forsake my true nature, that generosity and fidelity which is proper to knights (155)]. Gawain's covetousness is here implicitly linked to the desire, sexual and economic, of the Lady. And while her desire prompted a similar response in Gawain, he now interprets it (and her) as betraying his nature, his *kynde,* and, in effect, his masculinity itself.

By naming the girdle and his own actions according to the categories of cowardice and covetousness, Gawain displaces the Lady yet further, and, in so doing, he is led to the accomplished confession for which Bertilak congratulates him in the next stanza. The absence of virtue that Bertilak's earlier speech had associated with the absence that is woman here becomes named in terms of and linked explicitly with the presence of sin, a concept embedded in the values of Christianity. In this process, then, the transforming magic of Morgan and the life-assuring interests of the Lady are themselves transformed into the absence that is woman in this poem, into the threat of physical and spiritual death, a kind of absence in and of itself. Gawain's use of Christian terminology allegorizes the events of Fitt III and abstracts the Lady's presence into nothingness.

Critics have been eager to point out the generosity and forgiveness with which Bertilak, the older and wiser man, meets the youthful Gawain's exuberant overreaction to his not-so-bad sin.[42] What they have not noticed are the ways in which Bertilak's generosity acts to obliterate the Lady from the girdle, from the scene in the forest, and from the poem. Bertilak wants Gawain to keep the girdle, and according to Bertilak's description of it, Gawain could do so with some safety:

> "And I gif þe, sir, þe gurdel þat is gold-hemmed,
> For hit is grene as my goune. Sir Gawayn, 3e maye
> Þenk vpon þis ilke þrepe, þer þou forth þryngez
> Among prynces of prys, and þis a *pure token*
> Of þe chaunce of þe grene chapel at cheualrous kny3tez."
>
> (2395–99, emphasis mine)

[And I will give you, sir, the girdle edged with gold; because it is green like my tunic, Sir Gawain, you may remember this contest of ours when you have made your way back among noble princes, and this will be a perfect token, in the company of chivalrous knights, of the adventure at the Green Chapel (155).]

Here, the girdle is fully back in the realm of male signification. Gawain should keep it because it is as green as Bertilak's attire. As such, in its varied references to the male, the girdle will have meaning when Gawain circulates through the homosocial world of " 'prynces of prys' " because it is now a pure token, cleansed as Gawain himself is, of association with the female. Moreover, the girdle will have meaning to men because, as a cleansed token it refers to men, to the escapade in the forest (and not in the bedroom), to the doings that go on among " 'cheualrous kny3tez.' " Gawain, the "golde pured" of feudal economies, will wear a "pure token" of the male back to Camelot, a token given to him in a gift-exchange, not a feminized mercantile exchange, by his male mentor. Once the male has reappropriated the sign, he can fully assume the role of host, as he promptly does by inviting Gawain back to the castle to be reconciled with " 'my wyf' " (2404). If this is hospitality, it sounds pretty salacious.

Gawain, however, will have none of it. The last thing he wants is proximity to the Lady, as he proves by launching into his famous anti-feminist diatribe. This speech has caused critics much worry, because, coming from Gawain, the knight of courtesy, it seems so out of character.[43] But it should be clear that the diatribe is not only in character, but actually constitutes character, the character of the fully reintegrated knight.

> "Bot hit is no ferly þa3 a fole madde,
> And þur3 wyles of wymmen be wonen to sor3e,
> For so watz Adam in erde with one bygyled,
> And Salamon with fele sere."
>
> (2414–17)

[But it is no wonder if a fool behaves foolishly and is brought to grief through the wiles of women, for Adam while on earth was thus beguiled by one, and Solomon by many different women (157).]

If Gawain was beguiled, then, according to Gawain himself, he ought to be excused (2427–28). It is in the very nature of men, especially of very great men like Solomon of pentangle fame, to fall prey to women's powers, just as it is in the very nature of women to be beguilers. In ex-

cusing himself, Gawain positions himself as the heir of a noble tradition
of Old Testament figures, purveyors of an Old Order, as it were, just as
he himself is the purveyor of the Old Order of Feudalism, in contradis-
tinction to the new order of commercialism offered forth by the Lady.
By excusing himself according to the sins of the fathers, Gawain gives
himself license to claim both the sin and the fathers.

Gawain's final movement toward reintegration comes when he accepts Bertilak's offer of the girdle and places his final signification upon
it. In so doing, he ensures that the girdle no longer refers to the Lady,
but to himself, to the reintegrated Gawain who has been brought back to
chivalric life through the midwifery of Bertilak. He accepts the girdle as
the

> "syngne of my surfet I schal se hit ofte,
> When I ride in renoun, remorde to myseluen
> Þe faut and þe fayntyse of þe flesche crabbed,
> How tender hit is to entyse teches of fylþe;
> And þus, quen pryde schal me pryk for prowes of armes,
> Þe loke to þis luf-lace schal leþe my hert."

> (2433–38)

> [sign of my transgression I shall often look at it, when I ride in honour, to
> remind myself with remorse of the sinfulness and the frailty of the erring
> flesh, how liable it is to catch the plague spots of sin; and so, when pride of
> my prowess in arms shall stir in me, one glance at this love-lace will humble
> my heart (157).]

Except for the fact that the girdle is called a "luf-lace"—an epithet
that can be admitted because of the successful displacing of the woman
—the Lady has vanished from that article of clothing that she wove,
wore, and gave to Gawain. For Gawain, now, it is a sign of "surfet," of
transgression, of sin, and, oddly enough, of his place in the tradition of
noble sinners articulated in his misogynist diatribe. Moreover, if it is a
sign of "surfet," of transgression, it is a sign naming this poem's final
definition of the woman whom it has displaced.

At this point, as the revelation of Morgan's agency lies just around the
narrative corner, the *metalepses* in the text come fast and furious. If the
girdle is a sign of sin, that sin is specifically " 'þe faut and þe fayntyse of
þe flesche crabbed, / How tender hit is to entyse teches of fylþe.' " This
is significantly strong language. The Lady's gift of a life-preserver has

been converted into a sign of the corruption and death of the flesh. And, since the girdle came from the Lady, since Gawain was "beguiled" by her, that filth is associated specifically with female flesh. As in Gawain's diatribe against woman the beguiler, we find ourselves in the realm of garden-variety misogyny here. But the language of this passage encodes that misogyny in specific reference to the two women characters at the center of this poem. Because " 'crabbed' " and " 'tender' " modify the same flesh, the two ladies in the castle, the old and the young, have been fused to suggest an icon of the filth and decay imputed by Christianity to all female physicality and sexuality.

VI. Morgan's Unveiling:
"In Camelot, I know it sounds a bit bizarre"

At this point in the poem, with about a hundred lines left to go, Morgan's agency can be admitted to Gawain, because, at this point, it does not matter. The disenfranchising and displacing of women have been accomplished successfully enough to admit Morgan where she belongs, on the margins of the poem. Because the poem has converted the Lady into the token of the male through Bertilak's speeches and Gawain's responses, it can afford to name Morgan, and, for the first time, it can afford to tell the truth about itself and its narrative.

The syntactical construction of Bertilak's revelation is, in and of itself, significant, for, once he names Morgan, it takes him ten lines of preamble to admit her agency, to name her in a subject-verb construction that actually defines her activity in the poem:

> "Þurȝ myȝt of Morgne la Faye, þat in my hous lenges,
> And koyntyse of clergye, bi craftes wel lerned,
> Þe maystrés of Merlyn mony hatz taken—
> For ho hatz dalt drwry ful dere sumtyme
> With þat conable klerk, þat knowes alle your knyȝtez
>   at hame;
>   Morgne þe goddes
> Þerfore hit is hir name:
>   Weldez non so hyȝe hawtesse
> Þat ho ne con make ful tame—

"Ho wayned me vpon þis wyse to you wynne halle
For to assay þe surquidré."

(2446–57)

[Through the power of Morgan le Fay, who dwells in my house, and by
her wiles has learned much skill in magic lore, has acquired many of the
miraculous powers of Merlin—for she once had very intimate love–dealings
with that accomplished wizard, as all your knights at home will know; and so
Morgan the goddess is her name; there is no one so arrogantly proud whom
she cannot humble utterly—

it was she who sent me to your splendid hall in this guise to put your presumption to the test (159).]

I quote this passage at length not only to demonstrate how long it takes
Bertilak to assign a verb to Morgan (significantly, when she does get a
verb, Bertilak is the object of it), but also to demonstrate that Bertilak has
constructed his preamble carefully in order to diffuse Morgan's power
yet further.

Bertilak's description of Morgan and her agency is, in and of itself, a
fitting conclusion to the program of displacing the female that the poem
has outlined. Morgan, according to Bertilak, is one of those girls who
sleeps her way to the top. She may be called Morgan the Goddess, but
even then she refers to a preeminent male deity, to Merlin. Her magic is
not her own. Rather, she has come by it, rather underhandedly, because
of her love affair with the magician. Even if Morgan is dangerous, the
threat of her power is undermined, not only because Gawain himself
has escaped in one piece, but also because that power is secondary,
ultimately male-defined and -originated.

If women have been the objects of varied and various meanings in
this poem, it is not surprising that the testing generated by Morgan is
presented as variously motivated. Because she can tame anyone's pride,
she has sent Bertilak on his errand to test the pride of the Round Table,
a fairly conventional and thus legitimate motivation and one that has in-
spired assorted enemies, including Morgan herself, throughout Arthurian
legend. Morgan's subsequent motivations, however, become increasingly dubious and increasingly trivial, because they are represented as
increasingly dissociated from the values intrinsic to feudal, Christian
ideology. According to Bertilak, Morgan sent him to Camelot to scare

Guenevere to death (2459–62). If Morgan was actually interested in testing the pride of the Round Table, then Gawain can leave the Green Chapel believing that he has risked his life in a worthy, that is, a chivalric and masculine cause. If not, he has been duped—made, almost, into another Green Knight who can be sent scurrying around the winter landscape at Morgan's whim. He has been taken by Morgan's power and put to severe inconvenience in the name of a contest, not between men, but between women.

The poem, at this point, may be reasserting the Yuletide humor for which it has been critically famous. If so, it reasserts levity by changing the terms of the romance from a testing of chivalric valor into a sort of medieval catfight. In the process, the poem completes both its marginalization of Morgan and the conversions of women into the tokens of masculine economies. Bertilak's reference to Guenevere, the young and beautiful queen who is the wife of the young and beautiful Arthur, suggests that the suspiciously old Morgan wants to punish the beautiful young woman precisely for her youth and beauty. The old Morgan, goddess or not, wants what(ever it is that) the static Guenevere has. Arthur's half-sister thus becomes unnaturally aged in this poem to underline the *metalepsis* at the center of the poem's figuration of women.[44] As the " 'auncian lady' " (2463), with her withered flesh, she becomes associated not with life or with regeneration, but with death: the death of the flesh and the spirit for men, and for women, with the death of the flesh that will make them as repugnant as old Morgan and that will work toward their devaluation within feudal economies. Or perhaps here the poem finally projects onto Morgan herself its own desire to obliterate Guenevere from Camelot.

Morgan's motivations revealed, Bertilak can now present Gawain with a fact that must surely be no news to anyone. Morgan, alas, is Gawain's aunt: " 'Ho is euen þyn aunt, Arþurez half-suster' " (2464) (she is actually your aunt, Arthur's half-sister [159]). This revelation of what is already known is significant. In Fitt I, Gawain has claimed the right to take up the challenge because of his relationship to Arthur: " 'Bot for as much as 3e ar myn em I am only to prayse, / No bounté bot your blod I in my bodé knowe' " (356–57) [I am only to be esteemed in as much as you are my uncle; I acknowledge no virtue in myself except your blood (47)]. Within the values of chivalric society, Gawain is not only being modest, he is being downright accurate when he states that his only claim to worth derives from his relationship to the king. And now that Gawain has reasserted his allegiance to the fathers, he can be told that he also bears Morgan within him.

Gawain has been punished for yielding to the Morgan within himself. In other words, he has been punished at the Green Chapel for yielding to the private self and to private desires, to the privacy associated with the female in the figurations of this poem. In his pricing, he has been taught the cost of bearing Morgan within him. And, because Morgan is in Gawain, just as women will always be lurking somewhere within or around the aristocratic court, the threat of the woman's power is always there. Women are always at court, but, if they can be converted into appropriate tokens, they can be managed within the economies of Christianity and of feudalism.

The fate of the green girdle and its ultimate definition within the society of Arthur's court work to complete the tokenization of women. Riding back to Camelot, Gawain wears the girdle "[i]n tokenyng he watz tane in tech of a faute" (2488) [in order to signify that he had been detected in a guilty fault (161)]. But if Gawain is not ready to forgive himself, the poem is. As his nick on the neck heals, his transgression fades, and with it, the traces of the Lady and of Morgan. In the end, if the pentangle exists "[i]n bytoknyng of trawþe" (626), the girdle, according to Gawain himself, is " 'þe token of vntrawþe' " (2509). The meaning of the Lady is reduced to one word, significantly the antonym of the word encoding the agenda of values at the center of Christian chivalry and of this poem.

Happy to have Gawain home in one piece, the court makes a magnanimous move that completes the erasure of the Lady and her meaning(s) from the girdle. In order to relieve Gawain of his apparently morbid obsession with a rather small sin, the members of the court agree to wear the girdle, to take it as a collective symbol.[45] In the process, they not only convert the token of Gawain's dishonor into a sign of honor and take the "un" off the "vntrawþe." They also make the private public, as the girdle moves into the domain of public currency and public signification. In this way, the privacy of the Lady and the privateness associated with her are erased, as is her relation to Gawain as the source of his dishonor. In one respect, then, the court's appropriation of the girdle suggests a way to rehabilitate the Lady and, by extension, the privateness, the power, and the sexuality of women. When women are made the public tokens of aristocratic honor (that is, of aristocratic men), then they can be admitted to the court; they can be the "ladis" that with their "lordes" "longed to þe Table" (2515).

When Gawain learns that his testing has come not at the Green Chapel and at the hands of the Green Knight, but in the bedroom and at the hands of the Lady, his extreme reaction and his excess of humility suggest that he feels taken. What Arthur's nephew thought was a quest romance turned out to be a bedroom farce; and Arthur's nephew has been taken because he is Morgan's nephew, too. But if Gawain feels taken, so should the feminist critic who refuses to reread the poem from Gawain's perspective. For, in order to diffuse and marginalize women's power, the poem risks the credibility of its narrative in its *dea ex machina* ending. What is more, the poem that presents young Arthur as "childgered" for demanding marvels as appetizers asks us to swallow the greatest marvel of all: that the purpose of this intricate and meticulously wrought narrative is only to describe a Christmas game conjured for the entertainment of a hyperkinetic young king. In making this leap, however, the poem can fulfill its ideological agenda, for, in its association of women's power with the Christmas game, it can turn a serious threat into sport.

But as even the most lenient critics of *Sir Gawain and the Green Knight* know, this humorous poem has a serious moral as it explores the dialectic between what Chaucer would have called "ernest" and "game." The poem's last stanza, while it leaves Arthur's court in a state of laughter, stability, and self-congratulatory integrity, holds out a foreboding message to feminist readers. The Lady's girdle has been appropriated as a token within the realm of public, masculine signification. At the same time, however, this token is made to serve as a warning against women's presence in the masculine, feudal establishment. Regardless of the inversions and the redefinitions that the girdle has undergone, regardless of the marginalization of women in the poem, Morgan is still Arthur's half-sister and Gawain's aunt. Her blood is still current in the court, just as the girdle cannot ever entirely escape its association with the Lady. And now that the girdle is *de rigeur* courtly attire, women's presence in the court is even more obvious, even if its meaning has been diminished by appropriation. Morgan is in this court, much as the court would like to ignore it. And if the now reintegrated court blithely wears the green girdle as a sign of its own honor, the poem may well be lamenting its youthful shortsightedness.

The romance ends, as it began, with references to the cycle of prowess and betrayal at the center of its configuration of British history: "After þe segge and þe asaute watz sesed at Troye" (2525) [after the siege and the assault had ended at Troy (163)]. The juxtaposition of all the green girdles at Arthur's court with this historical reference to a civilization destroyed because of "love" for a woman points to the reasons why women must be marginalized within Arthur's court. Guenevere may be the portrait of stasis, the purchased queen, the token woman in Fitt I, but the conclusion deliberately points us back to the poem's beginning. If Guenevere is now a queen "preued of prys with penyes to bye" (79), the course of Arthurian romance will prove her price quite differently. Her stasis is deceptive, for, as she ruptures the bonds of the Round Table, she will prove herself a counterfeit token within the feudal economy of Arthur's world.

The poem concludes by linking the green girdle with betrayal, and specifically with the betrayal generated by women. The green girdle stands, then, as a warning against women and the currency of their tokens and even of their tokenism within the court. Ironically, had Morgan been allowed to succeed in scaring Guenevere to death, she would have performed a signal service to her half-brother. Instead, both Morgan and Guenevere survive, and the poem must rest content with presenting a proleptic cure for Arthurian history. For if Morgan could be effectively marginalized and if Guenevere could be reduced to permanent absence, the Round Table would not fall. The successful absenting of women from the homosocial world of Christian chivalry is, then, indeed a marvel, the stuff of romance and of Christmas games.

NOTES

I would like to thank the National Endowment for the Humanities, which allowed me to be a participant in Robert Hanning's summer seminar on *The Canterbury Tales* when I was preparing my initial work on this essay. I would also like to thank Dana Brand for the astute reading and criticism he gave to this piece.

1. The exception to this neglect of Morgan occurs in the few articles published on her in the 1950s and 1960s: Denver Ewing Baughan, "The Role of Morgan la Faye in *Sir Gawain and the Green Knight*," *ELH* 17 (1950): 241–51; Albert B. Friedman, "Morgan le Fay in *Sir Gawain and the Green Knight*," *Speculum* 35 (1960): 260–74; Mother Angela Carson, O.S.U., "Morgain la Fée as the Principle of Unity in *Gawain and the Green Knight*," *Modern Language Quarterly* 23 (1962): 3–16; Douglas Moon, "The Role of Morgan la Faye in *Gawain and the Green Knight*," *Neuphilologische Mitteilungen* 67 (1966): 31–57; and a more recent article, Edith Whitehurst Williams, "Morgan La Fée as Trickster in *Sir Gawain and the Green Knight*," *Folklore* 96 (1985): 38–56. Most book-length studies of the poem, however, give relatively little emphasis to Morgan's significance to the poem. J. A. Burrow's summary of Morgan's function is typical of the critical treatment of her; see his *A Reading of Sir Gawain and the Green Knight* (London: Routledge & Kegan Paul, 1966), 64. Larry D. Benson offers a detailed treatment of the poem's sources and Morgan's counterparts within them, but he ends by finding her inclusion in the poem one of its least successful adaptations of sources; see his *Art and Tradition in Sir Gawain and the Green Knight* (New Brunswick, N.J.: Rutgers Univ. Press, 1965), 32–35. Morgan's traditional enmity toward the Round Table stands as the most frequent justification for her presence in the poem. To date, there has been no comprehensive feminist study of the placement of women in this poem.

2. J. A. Burrow, for example, argues that, because the poem was delivered orally, it should be read as a linear narrative (3). This insistence on linearity enforces the marginalization of Morgan by giving priority to the circumstances of oral performance at the expense of those surrounding private reading. For an interpretation of the process of rereading that comes to much different conclusions from my own, see Victor Y. Haines, *The Fortunate Fall of Sir Gawain: The Typology of Sir Gawain and the Green Knight* (Washington, D. C.: University Press of America, 1982), 145ff.

3. For a discussion of medieval women's legal and political rights, and specifically their abilities to make contracts, see Shulamith Shahar, *The Fourth Estate: A History of Women in the Middle Ages*, trans. Chaya Galai (New York: Methuen, 1983), 11–21. See also Shahar's chapter on aristocratic women in *The Fourth Estate*, 126–73. Most critics do not see either Morgan la Faye or the Lady as the generators of contracts and exchanges, except in the case of the Lady's bedroom testing in Fitt III. Rather, they attribute most of the poem's significant

exchanges to Bertilak. See Benson, 55, and Peter L. Rudnytsky, "*Sir Gawain and the Green Knight*: Oedipal Temptation," *American Imago* 40 (1983): 377. Carson was the first to acknowledge Morgan's responsibility for the plot and Bertilak's role as *her* agent (13).

4. Many of my ideas about the configurations of male homosociality in literary texts are indebted to the introduction and first two chapters of Eve Kosofsky Sedgwick's book, *Between Men: English Literature and Male Homosocial Desire* (New York: Columbia Univ. Press, 1985). While Sedgwick's book primarily discusses later literature, these opening sections are relevant to the study of medieval and early modern texts.

5. Throughout this essay, I have chosen, for scholarly and ideological reasons, to address *Sir Gawain and the Green Knight* as "the poem" or "the romance." The author of this text has still not been identified, although scholarly efforts are constantly trying to name him. Rather than attempting to attribute intention to an anonymous author, I have preferred to concentrate on patterns and images that manifest themselves in the text. Any attempt to fix authorial intention, but especially in an anonymous poem, is a problematic enterprise. To quote Gayle Greene and Coppélia Kahn quoting Barthes on the issue of the author and/in the text: " 'To give the text an Author is to impose a limit on that text' " [Barthes: *Image-Music-Text*, trans. Stephen Heath (London: Fontana, 1977), 147], and they continue: "Feminist criticism can gain from a practice that does not privilege the author's intentions, for such a practice . . . '. . . puts into question the authority of authors, that is to say the propriety of paternity,' " in "Feminist Scholarship and the Social Construction of Woman," *Making A Difference: Feminist Literary Criticism*, ed. Greene and Kahn (New York: Methuen, 1985), 27.

6. See, for example, Benson, 97–98; A. C. Spearing, *The Gawain-Poet: A Critical Study* (Cambridge: Cambridge Univ. Press, 1970), 181 and 222; John Eadie, "Morgain la Fée and the Conclusion of *Sir Gawain and the Green Knight*," *Neophilologus* 52 (1968): 300–1; Robert W. Hanning, "Sir Gawain and the Red Herring: The Perils of Interpretation," *Acts of Interpretation: The Text in Its Contexts 700–1600: Essays on Medieval and Renaissance Literature in Honor of E. Talbot Donaldson*, ed. Mary J. Carruthers and Elizabeth D. Kirk (Norman: Pilgrim Books, 1982), 11.

7. *Sir Gawain and the Green Knight*, ed. J. R. R. Tolkien and E. V. Gordon, 2nd ed., rev. Norman Davis (Oxford: The Clarendon Press, 1972), ll. 86 and 89. All quotations from *Sir Gawain and the Green Knight* are taken from the Tolkien-Gordon-Davis edition and will be cited by line number within the body of the essay. Modern English translations are quoted from W. R. J. Barron's dual-language edition of *Sir Gawain and the Green Knight* (Manchester: Manchester Univ. Press; New York: Barnes and Noble, 1979), 33. They will be cited by page number within the body of the text. When Barron's translations are not faithful to the original text, I have supplied my own translations.

8. I take this idea of "killing women into art" from Sandra M. Gilbert and Susan Gubar's chapter, "The Queen's Looking Glass," in *Madwoman in the Attic: The Woman Writer and the Nineteenth-Century Literary Imagination* (New Haven: Yale Univ. Press, 1984), 3–44, esp. 20–27. In this section, Gilbert and Gubar also present an interesting discussion of the authority of texts and of authors, which, like Greene's and Kahn's essay, "Feminist Scholarship," examines the problem of privileging authorial intention. Robert Hanning also notes that Guenevere in this scene is an "elegant courtly artifact" (11).

9. For a discussion of the revision of Arthurian legend in this poem, see my essay, "Leaving Morgan Aside: Women, History, and Revisionism in *Sir Gawain and the Green Knight*," in *The Passing of Arthur: New Essays in Arthurian Tradition*, ed. Christopher Baswell and William Sharpe (New York: Garland, 1988).

10. The significance of Guenevere's placement at Arthur's table was suggested to me by Susan Gubar's comment about the dual meaning of Judy Chicago's *Dinner Party*: "But *The Dinner Party* plates also imply that women, who have served, have been served up and consumed." In " 'The Blank Page' and the Issues of Female Creativity," *Critical Inquiry* 8 (Winter 1981); reprinted in *The New Feminist Criticism: Essays on Women, Literature, and Theory*, ed. Elaine Showalter (New York: Pantheon, 1985), 300.

11. For a discussion of medieval women's marital position and rights, see Shahar, 65–125. Throughout my analysis of women's placement within the economies of marriage, I am of course indebted to Gayle Rubin's important feminist revision of Claude Lévi-Strauss's *The Elementary Structures of Kinship* in "The Traffic in Women: Notes on the 'Political Economy' of Sex," in *Toward an Anthropology of Women*, ed. Rayna R. Reiter (New York: Monthly Review Press, 1975), 157–210.

12. Spearing (175, 196–98) and Burrow (50, 105) offer representative interpretations of the criticism on the pentangle. In *The Poem as Green Girdle: "Commercium" in Sir Gawain and the Green Knight*, Humanities Monograph Series, no. 55 (Gainesville: Univ. of Florida Press, 1984), R. A. Shoaf gives a new reading of the pentangle, which is based in medieval and postmodern sign theory and which gives full weight to the problematics of referentiality in the poem. See, esp. 71–75.

13. Shoaf, 71–75; Hanning, 17–18.

14. Mary Daly's radical feminist theology has made important contributions to a revisionist understanding of the Virgin Mary's placement within the Christian tradition. See, for example, "Dismemberment by Christian and Postchristian Myth," in *Gyn/Ecology* (Boston: Beacon Press, 1978), 73–105.

15. Mary Daly, in *Gyn/Ecology*, defines "patriarchy" as "the Religion of Reversals" (79), and she locates the ways in which these reversals operate within Christian orthodoxy in order to displace the Virgin Mary (75–79). While Adrienne Munich differs with Daly on the degree to which power and language

have been stolen from women by patriarchy, she presents a relevant analysis of the ways in which Genesis is structured according to *metalepsis*, "the trope of reversal" in her essay, "Notorious Signs, Feminist Criticism, and Literary Tradition," *Making A Difference*, ed. Greene and Kahn, 239–41.

16. This idea is, of course, prevalent throughout Lacan's writings. Lacan's "God and the *Jouissance* of The [*sic*] Woman" provides a formulation of the absence (actually the erasure) of the woman that is particularly interesting in light of the concerns of this essay. See *Feminine Sexuality: Jacques Lacan and the école freudienne*, ed. Juliet Mitchell and Jacqueline Rose, trans. Jacqueline Rose (New York: Norton, 1985), 137–48.

17. I am grateful to Sonia Lee of the Department of Modern Languages at Trinity College for the suggestion that the poem may be obliquely positing a connection between Morgan and Mary.

18. In *The Clerk's Tale*, Chaucer writes of Griselda: "And for that no thyng of hir olde geere/ She sholde brynge into his [Walter's] hous, he bad/ That wommen sholde dispoillen hire right theere." *The Canterbury Tales*, IV (E), 372–74, in *The Works of Geoffrey Chaucer*, 2nd ed., ed. F. N. Robinson (Boston: Houghton Mifflin, 1957). See also Burrow, 56.

19. One cogent discussion of the threat of female sexuality and its various implications can be found in Gilbert's and Gubar's "Toward a Feminist Poetics," *The Madwoman in the Attic*, 3–104. Elizabeth Robertson summarizes the dualities that structured medieval misogynist attitudes toward female sexuality in "The Rule of the Body: The Feminine Spirituality of *The Ancrene Wisse*," the next essay in this volume.

20. For representative interpretations of the Lady as seductress, see Benson, 38–40 and 49–50, and W. A. Davenport, *The Art of the Gawain-Poet* (London: Athlone Press, 1978), 137, 167–68, and 187. Carson argues, on the basis of the poem's sources, that Morgan and the Lady are one and the same because of the dual nature of Morgan (5 and 13). For an interpretation linking the Lady and Mary, see Haines, 131, 138–42, 148.

21. See, for example, Davenport, 164; Edward Wilson, *The Gawain-Poet* (Leiden: E. J. Brill, 1976), 122; and W. R. J. Barron, *Trawthe and Treason: The Sin of Sir Gawain Reconsidered* (Manchester: Manchester Univ. Press, 1980), 43–44.

22. Important feminist contributions to the debate over women's relationship to the structures of courtly love include Joan M. Ferrante, *Woman as Image in Medieval Literature: From the Twelfth Century through Dante* (New York: Columbia Univ. Press, 1975); Shulamith Shahar, *The Fourth Estate*; and E. Jane Burns and Roberta L. Krueger, "Introduction," *Courtly Ideology and Woman's Place in Medieval French Literature*, ed. Burns and Krueger, spec. issue of *Romance Notes* 25 (Spring 1985): 205–19.

23. For discussions of Gawain's traditional reputation as a "lady's man," see Benson, 95, 103; Spearing, 198–99; and Barron, 21. In a chapter on *Sir Gawain*

and the Green Knight in her dissertation, "Mordred's Hidden Presence: The Skeleton in the Arthurian Closet" (Yale University, 1985), M. Victoria Guerin offers a thorough analysis of Gawain's past history. I am grateful to Professor Guerin for sharing the manuscript of this chapter with me.

24. Throughout my discussion of Gawain's activities in the bedroom and of the poem's definition of the girdle, I am particularly indebted to R. A. Shoaf's *The Poem as Green Girdle* and to the bibliography on the poem that he generously shared with me before his monograph appeared in print. While Shoaf's conclusions are different from my own, his extensive discussion of the poem's commercial language and his appendix to its commercial vocabulary have greatly influenced and clarified my own thinking about Gawain's exchanges and their significance. Shoaf, however, sees Morgan primarily as God's emissary and places God in control of the poem's exchanges (41). For an earlier discussion of the poem's commercial idiom, see Paul B. Taylor, "Commerce and Comedy in *Sir Gawain and the Green Knight*," *Philological Quarterly* 50 (1971): 1–15.

25. Shoaf, *The Poem as Green Girdle*, especially the section, "What *Prys* Gawain?" (34–46).

26. Ibid., 37–39. Shoaf writes of these transactions: "Ever more certainly if also subtly the Lady is convincing Gawain that he has a *price* and that he is marketable. Soon it will be easy to convince him that he is for sale" (39).

27. Ibid., 34–46.

28. See Shoaf's appendix to *The Poem as Green Girdle* for an indication of the density of commercial images in this section (77–80). See also Burrow, 76–77 and 88–89.

29. Shahar, 126–73.

30. Cf. Shoaf, 55–65.

31. Ibid., 42–46.

32. I am indebted here, as elsewhere in this essay, to Gayle Rubin's formulations in "The Traffic in Women." Cf. Shoaf, 46–47.

33. In the large body of literature on the "commercial revolution" in the late Middle Ages, the following works specifically address the issue of the effect of mercantilism on social relations of the period: F. R. H. DuBoulay, *The Age of Ambition: English Society in the Late Middle Ages* (London: Nelson, 1970); Lester Little, *Religious Poverty and the Profit Economy in Medieval Europe* (Ithaca, N.Y.: Cornell Univ. Press, 1978); and Alexander Murray, *Reason and Society in the Middle Ages* (Oxford: Clarendon Press, 1978). Burrow emphasizes the ways in which the exchanges between Gawain and Bertilak replicate the patterns of a gift economy and imply "a still more primitive 'act of fraternisation' —the shared or lent wife" (95–96).

34. Paul F. Reichardt has written that the girdle is "concealed under his armor," in "Gawain and the Image of the Wound," *PMLA* 99 (1984): 157, but nowhere does the text of the poem support this concealment. See Barron, 135, who argues that the girdle is placed across the pentangle.

35. Cf. Shoaf, 71–72; Burrow, 115–16; and Barron, 135.

36. For a cogent discussion of the connection between *commercium* and redemption within Christian sacramentality, see Shoaf, 9 and 53: esp. 53 on the subject of the wages of Gawain's sin and the grace that the Green Knight extends to Gawain.

37. Adrienne Munich, "Notorious Signs, Feminist Criticism, and Literary Tradition," in *Making a Difference*, 238–59.

38. I borrow this phrase from Gilbert's and Gubar's discussion of the placement of women in narrative in *The Madwoman in the Attic*, 36.

39. For representative interpretations of Bertilak's role in Fitt IV, see Burrow, 137 and 169; Davenport, 168–73; Spearing, 31 and 221; and Barron, 132.

40. Both Rudnystsky and Shoaf see the nick on the neck as an emblem of circumscision, Shoaf, within a Christian sacramental context (15–30), and Rudnystsky within a Freudian interpretative framework (375).

41. Shoaf, 66.

42. Critical disagreement about the poem is sharpest in the divergent interpretations of the seriousness of Gawain's sin. For two recent examples of this divergence of opinion, see Thomas D. Hill, "Gawain's Jesting Lie: Towards an Interpretation of the Confessional Scene in *Gawain and the Green Knight*," *Studia Neophilologica* 52 (1980), 279–86, and Shoaf, 66–76. But by arguing that Gawain is either excused for his humanity or accused for his sinfulness, and by focusing critical debate on this argument, critics contribute to the significant erasure of the Lady and Morgan from this scene of the poem, or else they reincorporate them in terms authorized by the poem.

43. The reaction to Gawain's antifeminist diatribe is one of the most interesting interludes in the history of the critical tradition on this poem. Benson calls the diatribe a "diverting spectacle" (240). Burrow thinks the poem goes off course here because "*Sir Gawain* is concerned with women's wiles no more than it is with chastity: each has a place, but a very subordinate one" (148). Spearing believes that the speech shows a salutary rejection of women on Gawain's part (223–24), while Haines sees the diatribe as an example of Gawain's politeness to let the individual Lady off the hook (94–95 and 122–23). Mary Dove cannot explain precisely why Gawain gives this speech, but she locates one possibility in his traditional failure to attain the Grail, in "Gawain and the *Blasme des Femmes* Tradition," *Medium Aevum* 41 (1972), 20–26.

44. Tolkien's footnote on Morgan's advanced age (130) has been consistently accepted by most critics who have raised this issue. See, for example, Burrow, 145–46; Haines, 147; and Barron, 9 and 131. Others, like Benson (32), associate Morgan's aging with the filth of the flesh whose presence within him Gawain must acknowledge as the wages of his sin.

45. For a representative sampling of the disagreement over the poem's ending, see Burrow, 158–59; Spearing, 222 and 230; Benson, 241–42; and Wilson, 130–31.

Part Two

Informing Women: Medieval,
Early Modern, and Postmodern

The Rule of the Body: The Feminine Spirituality of the *Ancrene Wisse*

Elizabeth Robertson

The ways in which gender informs reading and writing have been a major interest of feminist studies.[1] Uncovering the ideological assumptions inscribed in a text, these studies have addressed primarily nineteenth- and twentieth-century writing, giving little attention to texts written in earlier periods. Early medieval works have been especially neglected in such critical evaluations partly because of the shortage of specific information available about female readers and writers. Yet the thirteenth-century Middle English religious guide, the *Ancrene Wisse* ("Guide for Anchoresses"), offers us an unusual opportunity for such an investigation because, unlike many other medieval works, it tells us of its intended audience: the *Wisse* author, a male cleric, originally wrote his work at the request of three female recluses in Herefordshire and it was later revised to address larger groups of women.[2] One of the work's special features —its pragmatic spirituality—therefore derives in part from the author's concern for the precise material circumstances of his female audience. Yet more than material circumstances inform this work. The *Ancrene Wisse*'s peculiar style, we shall see, is also shaped by its author's culturally determined assumptions about women. This apparently gender-neutral text, I shall argue, is governed by its male author's view of women as daughters of Eve, inescapably rooted in their bodies.

Characteristic of the *Ancrene Wisse* is its quotidian psychological realism, a realism that includes consideration of such varied problems as the anchoress's thoughtless anger at her cook's boy and the spiritual dangers of excessive asceticism. Both Linda Georgianna and Janet Grayson have praised the text's literary and psychological sophistication in its investigation of such problems.[3] As Georgianna has explained, the author takes a radically new approach to the idea of a religious rule, by emphasizing an inner rule—the right ruling of the unruly heart—over an outer rule focused on instructions about dress, prayer routines, and other external circumstances. Janet Grayson has shown how the *Wisse* interweaves its discussions of external rules with analyses of inner experience through the use of imagery which links Christian precepts with illustrations drawn from everyday life. Grayson also notes that the work is structurally innovative in that it urges the reader to dip into the text at random and to use it only in so far as it applies to everyday experience. This psychologically sophisticated integration of everyday experience with abstract religious precepts permeates the work.

While Georgianna and Grayson have recognized the psychological and literary sophistication of the *Wisse*, they have overlooked the ways in which its psychological specificity is especially tailored for women and, further, the ways in which its spirituality reflects a circumscribed view of women's spiritual potential. The *Ancrene Wisse* is clearly a response first and foremost to the highly specialized needs of the female recluse. Although little is known about the particular women to whom the work is addressed, Dobson has at least been able to identify them conclusively as the three unnamed anchoresses who lived in the anchorhold of the Deerfold near Wigmore Abbey.[4] From the *Wisse* itself, we learn that they were women deeply committed to their profession. That they did not know Latin can be assumed from the fact that not only is the book in English, but also every reference and biblical quotation is translated. Accordingly, they were probably not able to read Bernard or Hugh of St. Victor, although, given the popularity of these authors in England, it is likely that they knew of them. It might be argued, then, that the author's repeated emphasis on daily life rather than books may simply be the result of his belief that the anchoresses were unfamiliar with books. Surely an anchoress, isolated in a room far from the French centers of scholasticism, would not find the abstract and abstruse discussions of the continent particularly meaningful to her experience. She probably never visited a continental religious house or engaged in theological debate. (In these respects, the anchoress shares the restrictions of many English audiences.)

The fact that the audience was female as well as distanced from Latin learning placed further limitations on the author who wrote for the anchoress. Unlike the anchorite, her male counterpart in England, the anchoress was especially restricted in terms of place and sphere of influence. Her problems and interests were confined to the room into which she was bricked for life. The anchorhold, a space that historical records imply was especially attractive to women in England, offered women unusual opportunities for intellectual independence but also posed particular problems.[5] Although the anchorhold was a place of seclusion, it nonetheless contained several windows through which the anchoress received food, clothing, and the sacraments. These windows afforded the anchoress distracting and potentially dangerous contact with the outside world. Whereas men were allowed to choose anchorholds or hermitages far removed from town life, the anchoress had to choose an anchorhold in the center of town because, as a woman, she was considered in need of protection. She was, therefore, subject to the distractions and temptations of a constant flow of townspeople. Furthermore, as a woman she lacked the authority to conduct her own spiritual life and therefore also had to succumb to the constant supervision and visits of male authorities, from the priest who administered her sacraments to the bishop who was held responsible for her anchoritic vocation. Her experience offered peculiar enticements of the flesh and challenges of socialization. Consequently, she needed a guide appropriate to her circumstances, one that focused with psychological astuteness on the pressures and distractions of everyday life. The author's pragmatic treatment of anchoritic life thus derives in part from his sensitivity to the restrictions that life imposed upon women.

More than external circumstances, however, shape the author's investigation of female anchoritic experience. Clearly the author's understanding of the anchoress's situation, and indeed, the anchoress's understanding of herself as well, was influenced by contemporary views of female sexuality, views ultimately derived from Aristotle. Aristotelian categories define the differences between men and women in terms that equate such linked contraries as male/female, form/matter, completion/incompletion, active/passive, and possession/deprivation. These categories, in turn, informed subsequent Christian commentaries on women in which Eve is repeatedly associated with the will and the body, Adam with wit and the mind.[6] As daughters of Eve, then, women are alleged to inherit Eve's rootedness in the body, her incapacity for theory, her dependence on the senses, and her fundamental willfulness. Moreover, because Eve's desire for the apple is attributed to her sensuality, Eve comes to be blamed for illicit sexual desire. Male writers assume that all women, even the most holy—with the sole exception of Mary—inherit Eve's sexual guilt. Although medieval commentators sometimes considered a woman's soul as having the potential to transcend such sexual guilt, Aristotelian concepts of the inferior and limited nature of the female soul so predominate in discussions of the nature of a woman's soul that a woman's spiritual life was inevitably bound up in her guilt by association with Eve. From a medieval perspective, therefore, a woman's spiritual nature was defined by her inescapable corporeality, and so it is presumed that she can understand spiritual ideals only through the body.

The style of the *Ancrene Wisse* reflects its male author's assumption that the spiritual potential of the women for whom he wrote was circumscribed and defined by their femininity. For example, the style of the work is accommodative, emphasizing the temporal and interactive rather than atemporal and static, focusing not on timeless Christian ideals, but on the exfoliation of those ideals in daily life. The work also focuses on the personal and the contemporary rather than the universal and the historical; it is nonteleological and is concrete rather than abstract, and practical rather than theoretical. Such stylistic techniques, we shall see, reflect the author's organization of his discussion around his underlying belief that female sexuality leads to the downfall of mankind and that a woman can achieve union with God only by recognizing her body to be responsible for that *poena damni*.

In identifying the *Wisse*'s distinctive features, critics have not fully taken into account these medieval attitudes toward women. By neglecting what is particular to women, those who have studied the *Wisse* have read the book as if it were written for the general reader. This dismissal of the text's particularities leads critics to study the *Wisse* primarily in terms of its indebtedness to the continental affective movement. Clearly, the psychological sophistication of its exploration of the inner life does reflect the new interest in the self found in works by such writers as Anselm, Abelard, and Bernard. In the English work, the emphasis on feeling falls in line with the Latin affective movement in general.[7] Indeed, Bernardine mysticism, especially the lyricism of the *sponsa Christi* motif developed by Bernard in his commentary on the Song of Songs, pervades the text.

Nevertheless, it is a mistake to characterize the mysticism of these works simply as an outgrowth of the affective movement. Despite affinities with continental mysticism, the *Ancrene Wisse* shows, interestingly enough, as Geoffrey Shepherd notes, a fundamental "aversion to mysticism."[8] Like continental contemplatives, the anchoresses who read the *Wisse* presumably believed that their ultimate goal was union with God. Yet these women were taught that they could achieve such union only through a full awareness of the pressures and demands of the world, rather than through a traditional dismissal or denial of such worldliness. Because the *Wisse* focuses so insistently on the boundary between inner and outer experience (as Grayson and Georgianna have discussed), the outside world is as important as the inner life in the meditative sphere of this English work. Continental affective texts, on the other hand, are primarily concerned with inner meditation. In addition, whereas continental texts take the contemplative from the earth to mystical union with God, the imagery of the *Wisse* constantly draws the attention of the contemplative back to earth. We must look away from the continent for a source of this unusual and particular spirituality.

It might be argued that the pragmatic focus of the *Ancrene Wisse* has more in common with the English tradition—that is, with works written for audiences similarly removed from continental centers of Latin learning—than with continental sources. Like other lay audiences, the anchoresses needed a work that explained Christian precepts in the terms of everyday experience. Indeed, the work's essential "Englishness" has been praised by early critics of the work, although what is particular to its Englishness has never been investigated in any depth.[9] It is possible that part of the *Ancrene Wisse*'s representation of a spirituality that emphasizes the integration of the everyday with spiritual goals may reflect a characteristically English emphasis. Indeed, Wolfgang Riehle in *The Middle English Mystics* has shown how English mystical works characteristically employ concrete imagery to communicate theological concepts.[10] Yet comparisons of the *Ancrene Wisse* with other English mystical works written for men suggest that there are further aspects of the author's representation of spirituality that cannot be accounted for by its English context. *The Cloud of Unknowing*, for example, asserts the male mystic's hierarchical ascent to union with God, a progressive ascent that is conspicuously absent from the *Wisse* author's account of spirituality. While the exact relationship of the *Ancrene Wisse* to other English works is outside the concerns of this essay, it is important to recognize that its characteristic pragmatism can be accounted for in part by its English context.

The worldly focus of the *Wisse* could also be said to be derived from other continental theological developments rather than from medieval theories about women. Indeed, the text's discussion of the outside world as an appropriate focus for meditation does reflect the Chartrian investigation of God's presence in all things.[11] And the Victorine exploration of the literal interpretation of the Bible also influences the text's emphasis on the physical world.[12] There are indeed many reasons for finding in Victorine thought a hitherto unnoticed, yet major, influence on the *Ancrene Wisse*. After all, Wigmore Abbey, the abbey associated with the *Wisse*, was led by Andrew of St. Victor, an abbot who wrote extensively about the need to recover the literal sense of the Bible. Smalley describes Andrew as a "rationalist explaining scripture in terms of everyday life."[13] His concerns, therefore, may have had an indirect influence on the *Wisse* author. Another Victorine whose work is quoted frequently in the *Ancrene Wisse* is Hugh of St. Victor, whose effect on exegesis in general was profound, for his philosophy encouraged exploration of history, archeology, and literary criticism—all necessary disciplines for the understanding of the literal sense of the Bible. Because his exegetical techniques suggest that the world itself is particularly worthy of the contemplative's attention, Hugh's emphasis may have had an effect on the attitudes of the *Wisse* author. Clearly both the Victorines and Bernard figured in the *Wisse*'s rendering of spiritual goals, but, as we shall see, theoretical assumptions about women ultimately inform the work's rhetoric and imagery and account for its particular character that makes it so very different from mystical works written for men.

The relationship of the *Ancrene Wisse* to both its Anglo-Saxon and its continental contexts is complex, yet, if we look closely at the *Wisse* author's use of continental sources with his consideration of his female audience in mind, we find there are significant differences between his work and that of continental writers—differences suggesting that his views of female spiritual potential were foremost in his mind. To see some of the ways in which the *Wisse* author's attitudes towards women affect his use of continental sources, let us compare a well-known passage of the *Wisse*—the discussion of the dangers of sight in section II, "The Custody of the Senses"—to two of its sources: (1) Bernard's exegesis of the dangers of curiosity in chapter 10 of *De Gradibus Humilitatis Superbiae* and (2) Hugh of St. Victor's commentary on Noah's ark, *De Arca Noe Morali*.[14] All three texts discuss the dangers of sight with reference to biblical exempla. Although the English passage closely follows both Bernard and Hugh, the differences between the *Wisse* and its sources, which have previously been considered small and insignificant, point to a major difference in the English author's understanding of spirituality. This major difference originates in his view of his audience, in his belief that his women readers, as daughters of Eve, must guard constantly against their sensual willfulness. This willfulness, the English text implies, can be controlled only through confrontation and analysis of the female contemplative's sensual experience of the world. Books and the theories that spring from them—essential as guides for the male contemplative—are peripheral to the female contemplative's meditative frame, both because women have little experience with books and because women's alleged descent from Eve dissociates them from the theoretical realm.

Before considering the *Wisse* author's direct quotation of Bernard, it is important to recognize that Bernard was not unaware of audience need, that is, of his male monastic audience's needs. At the beginning of chapter nine of his commentary on the Song of Songs, for example, Bernard justifies his exegesis:

Accedamus iam ad librum, verbisque sponsae rationem demus et consequentiam. Pendent enim, et praerupta nutant absque principio. Ideoque praemittendum cui competentur cohaereant.

[It is time for us to return to the book (the Bible) and attempt an explanation of the words of the bride and their consequence. For there they are swinging precipitately out of nowhere suspended before us. But we must see if there is something antecedent to them to which we may suitably connect them up.] [15]

The diversity and sophistication of Bernard's explanations provide his monks with that which they can use to save themselves from what he calls

> animi arentis languore atque hebetudine stolidae mentis, quod Dei scilicet alta atque subtilia penetrare nequirent.
>
> [The langor and dryness of the soul, an ineptitude and dullness of mind devoid of the power to penetrate the profound and subtle truths of God.] [16]

The *Wisse* author clearly adopted some of Bernard's concerns; he, too, recognized the dangers of routine and dullness of mind. Yet Bernard's different audience, monks well trained in both the Bible and in a wide range of biblical commentaries, allows him to provide references to such works. When Bernard looks for antecedents to connect things to, those antecedents come from the intellectual world of the monks: he links his words to words of other writers. As we shall see in his changes to Bernard's commentaries, the *Wisse* author, when writing for women, also looks for things to connect words to, and sometimes he, too, connects words to the words of other commentators. More often than not, however, he connects words to things—objects or events taken from the everyday experience of the anchoress. The *Wisse* author also tries to save the anchoress from staleness of mind. For her, however, staleness arises not from familiarity with biblical texts, but rather from the stark and restricted routine of the anchorhold, a routine devoid of so many of the books known to men. Dullness of mind can lead the anchoress to sin because she will be drawn paradoxically out into the world rather than into herself; this self-absorption will lead to unease of conscience, an impediment to meditation, and eventually to despair. In order to guide the anchoress to proper meditation, the writer must draw the outside world safely into the meditative frame, reinterpreted for her by the male author who has the critical tools to do so. Thus, instead of providing the anchoress with antecedents and contexts for words as Bernard does, the author of the *Wisse* provides spiritual contexts for physical objects and actions. Whereas Bernard leaves the outer world far behind, the *Wisse* author redefines the outer world as part of the inner world. The ultimate meditative goal of the two authors may be the same, but the different audiences dictate radically different methods for reaching that goal.

These general differences in purpose affect the two authors' otherwise similar exegeses of the dangers of curiosity. The *Wisse* author bases much of his discussion of the anchorhold and its dangers on chapter 10 of *De Gradibus*, where Bernard discusses the dangers of sin that begins with the eyes. Both Bernard and the *Wisse* author examine this sin by discussing the circumstances, motivations and results of the actions of three biblical figures, Dinah, Eve, and Lucifer. The most extensive discussion in both is devoted to Dinah and the sin that resulted when Dinah went out to see the strange women. The *Wisse* author's shift from theory to practice is clear in his use of Bernard's exegesis. Lamenting Dinah's actions, Bernard writes:

> Dina namque dum ad pascendos haedos egreditur, ipsa patri, et sua sibi virginitas rapitur. O Dina, quid necesse est ut videas mulieres alienigenas? Qua necessitate? . . . Etsi tu otiose vides, sed non vitiose videris. Tu curiose spectas, sed curiosius spectarius: Quis crederet tunc illam tuam curiosam otiositatem, vel otiasam curiositatem, fore post sic non otiasam, sed tibi, tuis hostibusque tam perniciosam (PL, 958).

> [For when Dinah goes out to feed her kids, her father loses her and she loses her virginity. Oh Dinah, why is it necessary for you to see the daughters of the land? What is the need? Even though you see them idly, you are not idly seen. You look curiously, but you are seen curiously. Who would believe that this curious idleness or idle curiosity would not afterwards be idle to you but would be pernicious to you and your friends and enemies.]

The *Wisse* author begins his passage by quoting Bernard, but he continues by spelling out the dangers that will face the anchoress if she looks out of her anchorhold or allows anyone to visit her:

> Egressa est dyna filia iacob ut videret mulieres ali enigenas. ꝩcetera. A Meiden as dyna het iacobes dohter as hit teleð i Genesy. eode ut to bihalden uncuðe wummen. ȝet ne seið hit nawt þet ha biheold wepmen. Ant hwet come wenest tu of þ bihaldunge? ha leas hire meidenhad & wes imaket hore . . . þus eode ut hire sihðe . . . ant nim þer of ȝeme þ tis uvel of dyna com nawt of þ ha seh sichen emores sune þ ha sunegede wið. ah dude of þ ha lette him leggen ehnen on hire (Tolkien, 32).

> [Dina, the daughter of Jacob, went out to see the strange women. There is a story told in Genesis of a maiden called Dina, the daughter of Jacob, who went out to look at the strange women. It does not say that she looked at men. What happened, do you think, as a result of that looking? She lost her maidenhood and became a harlot. . . . That is what came of her looking. . . .

And observe that Dina's evil was not the result of seeing Sichem, the son of Hamor, with whom she sinned, but the result of her allowing him to look upon her (Salu, 23–24).]

Bernard uses the biblical reference to Dinah to support his theological argument that the first step of pride is curiosity. The *Wisse* author, on the other hand, has a concrete and immediate purpose, rather than a theological argument, in mind. He is warning the anchoress of the specific danger she faces of losing her virginity as a result of either looking out her window at men, or, alternatively, of allowing men to look at her. Dinah is invoked by the *Wisse* author not to provide a biblical context for a discussion of curiosity, but to provide a negative female model for the anchoress. In both the Latin and the English versions, women are blamed for enticing men to rape, but for the *Wisse* author this is a danger of which the anchoress must be immediately conscious, for her beauty could entice even a visiting priest. The example thus suggests that women are in peril whether they are the subjects or objects of action. In his reference to Bathsheeba which immediately follows this example, the sexual dangers facing women are made even more explicit:

> Alswa Bersabee þurh þ ha unwreah hire idaviðes sihðe. ha dude him sunegin on hire se hali king as he wes ⁊ godes prophete. Nu kimeð forð a feble mon. halt him þah ahelich ȝef he haveð a wid hod ⁊ a loke cape ⁊ wule iseon ȝunge ancres. ⁊ loki nede ase stan hire wlite him liki. þe naveð nawt hire leor forbearnd i þe sunne. ⁊ seið ha mei baldeliche iseon hali men (Tolkien, 33).

> [Bethsabee also, by unclothing herself before David's eyes, caused him to sin with her, even though he was so holy a king and a prophet of God. And after all this, a weak man comes forward, thinks himself formidable in his wide hood and closed cloak, and wishes to see some young anchoresses, and must needs look, as if he were made of stone, to see how the beauty of a woman whose face is not burned by the sun pleases him, saying that she may look without fear at holy men (Salu, 24).]

Although men, too, are implicated in the *Wisse* author's censure, women are blamed not only for being vulnerable to sexual sin, but are held responsible for inspiring it in men. Returning to Dinah, the author concludes his discussion with the following warning:

> ȝe mine leove sustren ȝef ei is anewil to seon ow. ne wene ȝe þer neaver god. ah leveð him þe leasse. Nulle ich þet nan iseo ow bute he habbe of

ower meistre spetiale leave. for alle þe þreo sunnen þ ich spec of least. ⁊ al
þ uvel of dina þ ich spec of herre (Tolkien, 33).

[Ah, my dear sisters, if anyone insists on seeing you, believe no good of it
and trust him the less for it. I do not want anyone to see you without the
special leave of your director, for all those three sins I have just spoken of,
and all the evil that came about through Dina, of which I spoke above (Salu,
24).]

The English author thus moves his discussion continually out of the
realm of the theoretical and historical into that of the practical and immediate. A subtle but significant difference in Bernard and the *Wisse*
author's versions is that whereas Bernard's argument progresses from a
biblical event to the general, abstract, and theoretical nature of curiosity,
the *Wisse* author avoids the general and returns continually to the immediate, practical concerns of daily life. Furthermore, whereas Bernard
asks a rhetorical question of a biblical figure, the *Wisse* author steps out
of the context of books by addressing his question directly to the contemporary anchoress, thereby giving his discussion a paternalistic rather
than an egalitarian tone. His reference to Dinah is in fact presented as an
answer to an hypothetical question posed earlier by the anchoress:

"Me leove sire seið sum ⁊ is hit nu se over uvel forte totin utwart?"
(Tolkien, 31).

[Someone may say, "But dear master, is it so excessively evil to peep out?"
(Salu, 22).]

The female voice that the author here constructs indicates his view of
women as naive and further belittles what could otherwise be viewed as
a legitimate question. Female logic is thus dismissed in favor of male
logic.

A similar shift from the theoretical to the practical occurs in the *Wisse*
author's use of Bernard's discussion of Eve. Of Eve's fascination with
the apple Bernard says:

Quid illo tam crebro vagantia lumina jacis! Quid spectare libet, quod
manducare non licet? Oculos, inquis, tendo, non manum. . . . Etsi culpa
non est, culpae tamen occasio est et indicium commissae et causa est
committendae (PL, 958–59).

[Why cast wandering glances so frequently hither? Why does sight of it
delight thee, when to bite is not allowed thee? It is my eyes, thou sayest,

not my hand which I reach out. . . . Though it be not a crime, yet it is the occasion of crime, the mark of one committed and the cause of one to be committed.]

The *Wisse* author, on the other hand, allies Eve's experience directly with that of the anchoress, Eve's daughter:

> Of eve ure alde moder is iwriten on alre earst in hire sunne inʒong of hire ehsihðe. . . . Eve biheold o þe forboden eapple. ⁊ seh hine feier ⁊ feng to deliten iþe bihaldunge. ⁊ toc hire lust þer toward. ⁊ nom ⁊ et prof. ⁊ ʒef hire lauerd. low hu hali writ spekeð. ⁊ hu inwardliche hit teleð hu sunne bigon. þus eode sunne bivoren ⁊ makede wei to uvel lust. ⁊ com þe dede þrefter þ al moncun ifeleð. Þes eappel leove suster bitacneð alle þe wa þ lust falleð to ⁊ delit of sunne. Hwen þu bihaldest te mon. þu art in eve point (Tolkien, 31).

> [Of Eve, our first mother, it is recorded that at the very beginning of her sin its entry was through her eyes; . . . Eve looked upon the forbidden apple and saw that it was fair, and she began to take delight in looking at it, and to desire it, and she plucked some of it and ate it, and gave it to her lord. Observe how Holy Writ speaks of this, telling how sin began in an inward manner; this inward sin went before and made way for evil desire, and the deed followed, the consequences of which are felt by all mankind. The apple, my dear sister, symbolizes all those things towards which desire and sinful delight turn (Salu, 23).]

As in the Dinah sequence, the *Wisse* author places the anchoress in a long line of sinful women. Once again, instead of leading into a discussion of the abstract nature of sin, the biblical example leads directly back to the experiential and an emphasis upon the temporal and interactive rather than the atemporal and static. His discussion of Eve thus reinforces the immediate concern raised in his discussion of Dinah—a concern about the anchoress's susceptibility to the temptation of visiting priests.

Although both authors consider temptation from Eve's point of view, for the *Wisse* author the relationship between Eve and his readers is real rather than theoretical, literal rather than figurative. He presents this hypothetical response of the anchoress:

> hwerof chalengest tu me. þe eapple þ ich loki on · is forbode me to eoten ⁊ nawt to bihalden. þus walde Eve inohreaðe habben iondsweret. O mine leove sustren as eve haveð monie dehtren þe folhið hare moder þe ondswerieð o þisse wise (Tolkien, 32).

["Of what are you accusing me? I am forbidden to eat the apple at which I am looking; I am not forbidden to look at it." Thus Eve would have answered readily enough, my dear sisters and she has many daughters who, following their mother, answer in the same way (Salu, 23).]

Although the *Wisse* author draws the reader into the experience of sin by recreating a scene of Eve's temptations—much like Bernard's exegesis—he applies his reference to Eve specifically to the daily life of the anchoress by warning her not to look upon a man. Later in the passage, the *Wisse* author makes this connection even clearer by framing another hypothetical question from the anchoress:

"Me wenest tu seið sum þ ich wulle leapen on him þah ich loki on him?" (Tolkien, 32).

["But do you think someone will say that I shall leap upon him because I look at him?" (Salu, 23).]

The author's hypothetical response indicates his assumption that women are unlikely to formulate consequences outside of the immediate and circumstantial; once again, the hypothetical response of the anchoress contains a strong point that is being denied and ruled out of legitimate consideration. Whereas Bernard's discussion of Eve's curiosity is rooted firmly within a biblical context, the *Wisse* author's discussion moves in and out of the Bible and the everyday world of the anchoress.

Both authors also refer to Lucifer as another example of the dangers of curiosity, but, whereas the *Wisse* author mentions him only in passing, Bernard saves the fallen angel for the culmination of his argument. Bernard urges his monks:

Sta in te, ne cadas a te (PL, 959)

[Stay in yourself lest you fall from yourself]

and continues,

per curiositatem a veritate ceciderit quia prius speravit curiose quod affectavit illicite speravit praesumptuose (PL, 963).

[Through curiosity he (Lucifer) fell from the truth because he first curiously observed what he then unlawfully coveted and boldly aspired to.]

The *Wisse* author, however, makes only one reference to Lucifer:

Lucifer þurh þ he seh ⁊ biheold on him seolf his ahne feiernesse. leop in to prude. ⁊ bicom of angel eatel ich deovel (Tolkien, 31).

[Lucifer, because he looked upon himself and saw his own beauty, leapt into pride and from being an angel he became a loathsome devil (Salu, 22–23).]

Both authors refer to Lucifer as part of their argument that it is necessary to guard the heart, but the *Wisse* author's primary concern is to remind the anchoress of the relationship of an abstract example to her daily experience. His substitution of the word "beauty" for Bernard's word "truth" further suggests his assumption that a woman's sphere of sin is more narrowly circumscribed. Whereas male spirituality includes the moral, philosophical, and intellectual realm conveyed by the abstract word "truth," female spirituality is circumscribed in the word "beauty" which, although also abstract, is realized sensorily. Her experience of sin is thus determined by and confined to her essential corporeality. The *Wisse* author uses Lucifer as an example primarily to turn the female reader's attention yet again to contemplation of her own sinful body, warning her to beware of pride in physical asceticism—a virtue of the anchoresses he had earlier praised—and reasserting again her culpability in the dangers her physical beauty poses for men.

The placement of this example illustrates differences between the authors' meditative plans. Bernard's argument follows an ascending progression, moving back through scriptural time from Dinah to Eve to Lucifer and from historical example to eternal archetype. The examples the *Wisse* author employs—first Lucifer, then Eve, Dinah, and Bathsheeba—move in the opposite direction, from the otherworldly to the worldly. Interestingly, Lucifer becomes a less direct negative example than do the examples of wayward women. But even without Lucifer as the pinnacle of a series of negative exempla, the order of the author's discussion of women is not hierarchical. Although it might be argued that his discussion charts the historical progress of women's victimization—although in each story it is female rather than male guilt that is emphasized—the *Wisse* author's discussion does not suggest that any one incident is worse than another, for each example in his discussion contains the whole argument. Bernard, on the other hand, for whom sexual sin is less important than the sin of pride, arranges his examples so as to suggest an ascending order of temptation. Indeed, this order is a rhetorical device that reinforces his stated overall purpose, a discussion of the steps of humility that lead to truth. The *Wisse* author's nonprogressive, and apparently random, order is typical of his overall design. He is not interested in logical progression to higher truths but rather in the fluctuating process of spiritual education in which the female contemplative must always be reminded of the spiritual as she falls from her path.

The *Wisse* author's overriding concern for the practical, quotidian realization of religious ideals underlies his alteration of Bernard's conclusion. Bernard writes:

> utquid audes oculos levare ad coelum qui peccasti in coelum? Terram intuere, ut cognoscas teipsum. Ipsa te tibi repraesentabit quia terras es et in terram ibis (PL, 957).

> [How do you dare lift your eyes to heaven, when you have sinned against heaven? Look at the earth in order to know yourself. Only it will show you an image of yourself: for dust thou art, and unto dust shalt thou return.]

The *Wisse* author, on the other hand, concludes:

> ha schulden schrapien euche dei þe eorðe up of hare put þ ha schulien rotien in. Godd hit wat þ put deð muche god moni ancre. for as Solomon seið. Me morare novissima tua & in eternum non peccabis. þeo þe haveð eaver hire deað as bivoren hire ehnen þ te put munegeð (Tolkien, 62–63).

> [They should scrape up earth every day out of the grave in which they shall rot. God knows, the sight of her grave near her does many an anchoress much good, for as Solomon says: Remember thy last end and thou shalt not sin. She who keeps her death as it were before her eyes, her open grave reminding her of it (Salu, 51).]

Bernard's advice is much less literal and concrete than that of the English author. His words are the culmination of an argument designed to facilitate meditation. The *Wisse* author's advice will also lead to meditation, but his words are not the key; for his female audience, a literal, physical contact with the earth by digging a grave is a more effective key to understanding. Although Bernard's reference to the earth is also to a physical thing, his concept is general and impersonal, whereas the *Wisse* author's concept is specific and personal.

Clearly, the *Wisse* author's attitudes towards women govern his use of Bernard. What, then, of his use of Hugh of St. Victor? The ways in which the English author discusses the dangers of looking out of the anchorhold's window could perhaps derive from Hugh's exegesis of the ark's window and door in his *De Arce Morali*, which has a similar emphasis on the connection between physical things of this world and spiritual meditation. Hugh argues that through contemplation of the outside world, the contemplative gains inner understanding:

> Plena est omnis terra majestate ejus per terram omnis corporea creatura significatur quae plena est majestate Dei (PL, 622).

> [The whole earth is full of His Glory which means that every corporeal creature on earth is full of the glory of God.]

Earthly experience is significant to Hugh as a meditative focus, just as it is to the *Wisse* author.

Hugh's meditation on every aspect of a physical object—the ark—leads the contemplative to an understanding of the human heart, a psychological application of external reality shared by the author of the *Wisse*. It is in his discussion of the door of the ark that Hugh's exegesis most resembles that of the *Wisse* author, since both authors use a physical boundary as the starting point for inner meditation:

> Ostium significat exitum per operationem, fenestra exitum qui fit per cogitationem ostium deorsum est, fenestra sursum quia actiones ad corpus pertinent cogitationes ad animam. Hinc est quod per fenestram aves exierunt, per ostium bestiae et homines. Quod autem per avem anima significetur, et per hominem corpus. . . . Quod vero ostium in latere positum dicitur hoc significat quod nunquam a secreto cordis nostri per operationem exire debemus ex proposito intentionis sed ex accidenti occasione necessitatis (PL, 636).

> [The door denotes the way out through action, the window the way out through thought. The door is below the window because action pertains to the body, and thought to the soul. That is why the birds went out through the window and the beasts through the door. The bird denotes the soul and the man the body. But the fact that the door is situated in the side denotes that we must never leave the secret chamber of the heart through our own deliberate choice, but only as necessity demands it.]

Like Bernard and the *Wisse* author, Hugh employs the example of Dinah in discussing the dangers of going out:

> Hunc igitur exitum caveamus, ne egrediamur temere. Nemo de conscientia sua confidat. Dina intus virgo, intus casta, intus columba fuit, sed quia

columba seducta fuit non habens cor, egressa foras colorem pariter cum nomine mutavit (PL, 639).

[Let us beware then of our going out. Let none be too sure of his own moral sense. Dina was a virgin within, she was pure within, she was a dove within. But because the dove being heartless was seduced, when once it had gone out, it altered both its color and its name.]

Like the *Wisse* author, but unlike Bernard, Hugh refers to Dinah in the context of a discussion of a physical boundary. While Hugh discusses the dangers of going out through a door, the *Wisse* author treats those of going out—both literally and symbolically—through a window, in his case, through the window of the anchorhold. But although the *Wisse* author, like Hugh, considers the window a crucial boundary for the contemplative, he deliberately combines the function of the door and the window so that the window represents the boundary through which the soul and the body can escape.

What this conflation suggests is that, for women, the soul and the body are inextricably bound. While a man can purify his meditation by concentrating on the mind, a woman must always consider both. Although the bird traditionally represents the soul as it aspires to heaven, a woman's soul is inevitably earthbound. As the *Wisse* author says later, the contemplative must consider herself like the sparrow who spirals towards heaven but inevitably falls back to earth (Tolkien, 74). Given the fact that the eagle is traditionally associated with the soul in works written for men, the association of the female soul with the sparrow indicates that her spiritual role is limited to the domestic and quotidian. Also, whereas the male image charts the ascent of the bird as soul, because sparrows ascend only a short distance and return frequently to the earth and the eagle's descent is rarely seen, the image for women emphasizes not only the ascent but the inevitable descent of the soul. This extended image implicitly suggests that female mysticism can never maintain the heights of transcendence found in male mysticism. Moreover, because Hugh's discussion is based on a sacred and historical object, his interest in the outside world differs considerably from the *Wisse*'s emphasis on objects common to contemporary experience. Ultimately, the idea of a door and a window in Hugh's account is a metaphorical and biblical one. The male contemplative is thus taken in meditation from a theological precept to a biblical context that reinforces an abstract meditative ideal. The female contemplative, on the other hand, is given access to that biblical context only insofar as it relates to her body—that is, to the dangers that could follow if she puts her hands outside, not a sacred and metaphorical window, but the very real window of her anchorhold.

We have seen that the *Ancrene Wisse* is permeated with references to biblical commentaries of the day. We have also seen that, as a guide for women, it differs from those commentaries in its continual emphasis on the integration of the pressures of everyday life with spiritual goals. I propose that the English work's distinctive spirituality is primarily the result of the male author's very different interpretations of the places of men and women in religion. The comparison of the *Wisse* to its sources suggests that male contemplatives in the Middle Ages were trained to see themselves as part of an abstract hierarchy through which they progressed in stages to God, whereas female contemplatives were expected to perceive that hierarchy only insofar as it related to their everyday experience and their bodies. Whereas the texts written for men use biblical or sacramental objects or events to direct the contemplative to God's order, this work written for women introduces sacred exempla to direct their attention to daily experience as it should be ordered. Male contemplatives are encouraged to leave earthly experience behind, whereas female contemplatives are to be made always conscious of their rootedness in inherently sinful bodies. Not only that, the very examples that have given the *Wisse* author a reputation for psychological realism and acumen can also be seen as misogynist, for through these images women are taught they can never maintain the mystical heights men can. Instead, they are constantly reminded of their inferior status as women, in their present bodies and historically as well. In the end, a man writing for women, and responding to his tradition's construction of them, alters literary precedents in order to emphasize the concrete, personal, and contemporary, rather than the abstract and historical.

The English author's attitude to women influences not merely his discussion of curiosity, but indeed the entire theme, structure, and imagery of the work. The stated theme of the *Wisse* is the need to control the unruly heart. This theme is meaningful for both men and women; but because women are presumed to be by nature willful, they have to give special consideration to controlling their unruly hearts. For women, the

heart is finally governed by sexual desire. They should beware of behaving like Eve, the first woman who let her heart "leap out" (Tolkien,
31), much less Dinah, Bathsheeba, and other women who sinned sexually. It scarcely matters that the sexual sin is not even their own; they are
blamed for the sin they inspire in men. The face of a woman, writes the
author, is the pit into which falls the animal, that part of man that is not
controlled by reason (from the Nero text; see Salu, 25). Yet the woman
is not urged to control this unruly heart through reason. Rather she is to
control it through her heart again—this time, by redirecting her heart
to a more appropriate object, Christ. But even a woman's relationship
to Christ is defined finally in terms of her body.

The author's view that a woman is governed by her sexuality underlies
even the most apparently conventional section of the *Wisse*, the opening
list of prayers known as Devotions. At the center of this section is the
twin celebration of the five joys of Mary and of the Eucharist. Grayson
outlines how the text moves from outer concerns to inner ones and back
out again, mimicking the overt theme of the work.[17] What Grayson has
not remarked upon is that this movement depends upon and reflects the
idea of a woman's sexual guilt. The center of the passage celebrates the
Eucharist, which exemplifies the transcendence of sinful flesh through
Christ, an idea that has meaning for both men and women. For the anchoress, however, this redemption occurs only through her recognition
of her sinfulness, not as a soul in flesh, but rather as a soul in female
flesh. As a daughter of Eve, the anchoress inherits Eve's sexual fault and
thus can never fully mimic Mary, who was praised for her lack of sexuality. The anchoress must, therefore, first admit her inherent sinfulness,
and then imitate Mary by denying her sexuality. The five joys of Mary
specifically celebrate Mary's transcendence of her sexuality: for example, she conceives without intercourse and gives birth without breach.
Although a denial of flesh is central to all Christianity, for the woman
it is specifically female sexuality that must be overcome. For a man, on
the other hand, a denial of his sexuality is part of a hierarchical set of
denials including such other sins as pride. Furthermore, for a man, the
process of overcoming sin does not mean denying his maleness, whereas
the process for a woman involves overcoming what is considered to be
her femaleness, her corporeality. For a woman, all sins, even pride,
are associated with her body. Through her experience of the host, and

through her transformation of herself from Eve to Mary, the woman's flesh is redeemed because her gender is denied.

The anchoress's need to use her body as a guide to contemplation governs the structure of the entire work. The author divides his work into eight parts: (1) devotions; (2) the custody of the senses; (3) regulation of inward feelings; (4) temptations; (5) confession; (6) penance; (7) love; and (8) daily rules. Parts 2 to 7 follow an apparently conventional meditative plan, leading the anchoress from contemplation of earthly things to love of God. Underlying this progression, however, is the anchoress's inescapable attachment to her sinful body. Thus, parts 2 and 3 teach the anchoress to control her senses, those that lead specifically to sexual sin. She can overcome this sinfulness only through her body. Inherently "wounded" as a biologically incomplete man, she can especially identify with Christ's wounded body. Because the Bible defines woman as a handmaiden to men, it is natural that she meditate on comforting Christ in his passion and caring for his wounds. After overcoming the rule of her senses, the anchoress can progress through parts 4, 5, and 6—temptation, confession, and penance. While some early critics of the *Wisse* viewed temptation as an inappropriate subject for a devout audience, when the author's view of women is taken into consideration, failure is inherent to women, and temptation, therefore, is a necessary part of the work.[18]

Cleansed by penance, the anchoress is then ready to contemplate her love of Christ. Even this love, however, is ultimately defined in terms of her body. The Bernardine marriage of the soul to Christ is here literalized, where for a male audience it is allegorized.[19] The *Wisse* culminates in a Christ-Knight allegory in which the female contemplative's relationship is defined as if she were literally Christ's wife. For example, Christ addresses the anchoress as a suitor:

Nam ich þinge feherest. nam ich kinge richest. nam ich hest icunnet. nam ich weolie wisest. nam ich monne hendest . . . wult tu castles. kinedomes. wult tu wealden al þe world? Ich chulle do þe betere. makie þe wið al þis cwen of heoveriche (Tolkien, 202–3).

[Am I not fairer than any other? Am I not the richest of kings? Am I not of the noblest kindred? . . . Would you have castles, kingdoms? Would you have the whole world in your power? I will provide more for you, make you with all the queen of heaven (Salu, 175–76).]

Even at the height of contemplation, a woman is assumed to be rooted in earthly, bodily, and domestic desires.

The necessity of continuous contemplation of the body may also be behind the unusual reading plan of the work. The work interweaves inner and outer meditation; the one can never escape the other. The author's concern with will rather than wit leads him to abandon conventional views of progressive structure. He initially follows standard scholastic technique of division, whereby the book is divided into eight parts and many subdivisions, and tells his reader that this structure has a cumulative design. Finally, however, he urges the anchoress to abandon this hierarchical structure and read at random instead. Each part of the work contains the whole. He tells the anchoress to read as little or as much as holds her attention, and to dip into the book whenever she needs to. The discipline of the heart is to be achieved whether the anchoress reads a single line or one from the beginning followed by one from the end or vice versa. The author often abandons a logical progression. His discussion of the dangers of sight, for example, is filled with references to all the other senses. Underlying this random structure is the author's view that the anchoress needs a guide that will cause her daily experience to be filled with religious meaning. Rather than focusing her mind on abstract, hierarchical discussion, reading exists for her only in order to affect her responses through the day. Implied in this structure is the inherent willfulness of women; their thoughts are randomly dictated by willful impulse rather than reason.

The theoretical concept of women as associated with matter, will, and imperfection also affects the imagery of the text. As we have seen, the imagery of the *Wisse* directs the reader to everyday experience rather than providing her with verbal or intellectual contexts. This is so not only because the woman does not have access to books, but also because she must teach the senses through the senses. What references to books there are in the text do not provide a context of abstract argument, but rather reinforce the anchoress's sense of herself as committed to Christ in daily life. Should she contemplate putting her hand out the window, for example, she is taught to perceive this potential desire not as part of a hierarchy that leads to sin, but rather as an event rooted in her body, a movement that she can finally prohibit only by identifying it with driving nails into Christ's hands. She must control her desire both by thinking of her own sexual guilt and by identifying with Christ's suffering. (It is possible that the prominence of stigmata among female mystics may be related to this issue.[20]) To emphasize further her connection with her body, she is told to dig her grave daily. The everyday images of the text, the earth of her garden, the sparrow outside her window, and the like thus remind the anchoress of her inevitable association with earthly experience because of the embodiment of her soul in female flesh.

The idea of a female audience guides the author's choice of structure, theme, and imagery. Furthermore, although the *Ancrene Wisse* is psychologically innovative, it is actually just as prescriptive as the Benedictine rule. Women are taught to control their bodies. They are to be silent and to repress anger, and, most of all, to control their senses. The cackling Eve must be transformed into the passive, silent Mary rather than into an active, abstract thinker. If women have a voice, it is the constructed querulous female voice the author uses in his text. More often, women are denied any voice at all because of their sexuality.

By examining the male author's representation of female spirituality in the *Ancrene Wisse*, I am also raising questions about the legitimacy of the female mystic's voice celebrated by Luce Irigaray and to some extent by Simone de Beauvoir.[21] At the basis of feminist analyses of female mysticism is a recognition of the centrality of a woman's sexuality to her mystical vision. Blood and tears, for example, considered to be physiologically prominent in women's experience, occur frequently in female mystical visions. The possible physiological basis of female mystical imagery raises a fundamental interpretive problem for feminists: is the focus on the body redemptive for women or not? De Beauvoir, for example, suggested that a mystical vision, as the logical expression of a woman's sociological condition "on her knees," redeems her body, but ultimately denies her a sphere of action in the world. Irigiray, taking this point to an opposite conclusion, argues that a woman associates her vagina with Christ's wounds. This association allows her access to a distinctively feminine voice unavailable to men; the lips of her vagina, Christ's wounds, and her mouth are all linked symbolically. I suggest that the elements that Irigaray and de Beauvoir identify as distinctively feminine features occur in women's texts because male theories about women encourage women to think in such terms. But Irigaray and de Beauvoir have not focused enough attention on the ways in which women's own images of themselves have been encouraged, if not defined, by men's views of women. Caroline Bynum's recent book, *Holy Feast and Holy Fast*, has done much to enhance our appreciation of the historical circumstances that shape female spirituality. Yet her study does not consider works written by men for women, and consequently some of her suggestions about the positive implications for humanity evoked by women's symbols may need to be qualified in the light of issues raised by texts like the *Ancrene Wisse*.[22]

An examination of the role gender plays in the creation of the *Ancrene Wisse* is fundamental to an understanding of that text. The distinctive features of that text—a focus on the heart rather than the mind, on the concrete rather than the abstract, on the practical rather than the theoretical—are the result of the interaction of historical circumstances, those that denied women access to other modes of thinking, with theories that reinforced that denial. The work's method is double-edged. The failure to universalize and abstract also unwittingly undermines much of the force of the conservative male ideological position and method. Of course, the focus on the concrete and experiential is underpinned by a basic abstract equation: the concrete equals women's bodies, and women's bodies equal sin. Even though women may not have been conscious of this abstraction, they doubtless often had absorbed as self-contempt prevailing male attitudes. The equation of women's bodies with sin could be maintained psychologically if not theologically. However, a method which avoids abstraction is itself risky, for if the abstract equation is removed (which the work's method unwittingly encourages one to do), one has a celebration of the immediate, the physical, the coordination of body and soul, God and the world. Rather than viewing her body as a locus of sin, the anchoress can celebrate her own physicality. However, although a direct address to a woman's experience does give a woman's voice legitimacy and potential power, that voice is finally bound by categories that define woman as mindless. The female anchorhold therefore ultimately has the limitations and strengths of "a room of one's own," a room one recent critic has defined ultimately as the grave.[23]

By overlooking the role of gender in the production of texts, critics also misassess literary movements and literary developments. As we have seen in comparisons of the *Wisse* to continental texts, the failure to recognize the importance of the feminine audience of the *Wisse* has led to a misunderstanding of its relationship to the twelfth-century affective movement. It has also led to a misunderstanding of the role women played in the development of the English vernacular. The special focus of the *Ancrene Wisse* on what seems unique to the nature of women has the effect of redefining a person's relationship to spirituality. Later, the psychologically realistic focus on the integration of the spiritual and the everyday becomes increasingly prominent in English literature. Anchoresses, a small but significant group, created a demand for a new body of literature explaining religious goals in terms of personalized daily experience. Such a demand is met in later Middle English literature as it turns to address a wider audience of laypeople. As Bynum has pointed out, in some respects women were the quintessential laypeople; it might also be argued, however, that laypeople were also viewed as women.[24] The pressures such laypeople placed on the development of the resources of English prose not only alters our understanding of the *Ancrene Wisse*, but may also alter our understanding of the development of the late medieval English tradition as a whole. The impetus to explain spiritual goals to women in concrete rather than abstract terms is the first instance of a development that becomes central to the flourishing of later English literature. Influenced and encouraged by the Franciscan movement, this literature becomes increasingly concerned with explaining religious goals to every person—an impetus that culminates in the Ricardian poets, Chaucer, Langland and the *Pearl*-Poet.

NOTES

I would like to thank Gerda Norvig and Elihu Pearlman for their helpful comments on this manuscript.

1. For a summary of feminist theory, see Elaine Showalter, "Feminist Criticism in the Wilderness," and Elizabeth Abel's introduction to her book, *Women Writers and Sexual Difference* (Chicago: Univ. of Chicago Press, 1980), Jonathan Culler's chapter, "Reading as a Woman," in *On Deconstruction, Theory and Criticism after Structuralism* (Ithaca, N.Y.: Cornell Univ. Press, 1982), 43–64, and Toril Moi, *Sexual/Textual Politics: Feminist Literary Theory* (London: Methuen, 1985).

2. E. J. Dobson locates the *Ancrene Wisse* in *The Origins of Ancrene Wisse*

(Oxford: Clarendon Press, 1976). My discussion of this work is based on the edition by J. R. R. Tolkien, *The Ancrene Wisse*, MS Corpus Christi College Cambridge 402, Early English Text Society, no. 249 (London: Oxford Univ. Press, 1962). I have followed Tolkien's transcription of the work except that where Tolkien's edition prints the letter *v* as *u*, I have used *v* for the sake of clarity; I have also omitted unnecessary manuscript marks. The modern English is that of M. D. Salu's very accurate translation, *The Ancrene Riwle* (Notre Dame, Ind.: Indiana Univ. Press, 1956). All subsequent references are to these editions and will be cited in the text by page number.

3. Linda Georgianna, *The Solitary Self: Individuality in the Ancrene Wisse* (Cambridge: Harvard Univ. Press, 1981); Janet Grayson, *Structure and Imagery in the Ancrene Wisse* (New Hampshire: Univ. Press of New England, 1974).

4. See Dobson, 174–311.

5. For a more detailed study of the nature of anchoritic life, see Ann Warren, *Anchorites and Their Patrons in Medieval England* (Berkeley: Univ. of California Press, 1985); Elizabeth Robertson, *An Anchorhold of Her Own: The Role of the Female Audience in the Development of Middle English Literature* (Knoxville: Univ. of Tennessee Press, forthcoming), title tentative.

6. See Ian Maclean's discussion of these categories as well as his superb discussion of the nature of the female soul in *The Renaissance Notion of Woman: A Study of the Fortunes of Scholasticism and Medical Science in European Intellectual Life* (Cambridge: Cambridge Monographs on the History of Medicine, 1980), 6–27.

7. For a general discussion of the affective movement, see R. W. Southern, *The Making of the Middle Ages* (New Haven: Yale Univ. Press, 1970).

8. Geoffrey Shepherd, *The Ancrene Wisse: Parts Six and Seven* (New York: Barnes and Noble, 1959), xxiii.

9. See, for example, R. W. Chambers, "The Continuity of English Prose from Alfred to More and His School," in Nicholas Harpsfield, *The Life of Thomas More*, Early English Text Society, o.s., 186 (1932; rpt. London: Oxford Univ. Press, 1963), xlv–clxxiv. For a recent challenge to such views, see Bella Millett, "Hali Meiðhad, Sawles Warde and the Continuity of English Prose," in *Five Hundred Years of Words and Sounds*, ed. E. G. Stanley and Douglas Gray (Cambridge: D. S. Brewer, 1983), 100–8; Elizabeth Robertson, "The Triumph of Feminine Spirituality: The Katherine Group and Its Contexts" (Ph.D. diss., Columbia University, 1982), and *An Anchorhold of Her Own* (forthcoming).

10. Wolfgang Riehle, *The Middle English Mystics* (London: Routledge & Kegan Paul, 1981).

11. See M. D. Chenu, *Nature, Man and Society in the Twelfth Century* (Chicago: Univ. of Chicago Press, 1957).

12. For a discussion of the Victorines, see Beryl Smalley, *The Study of the Bible in the Middle Ages* (Oxford, 1952; rpt. Notre Dame, Ind.: Univ. of Notre Dame Press, 1978).

13. Ibid., 147.

14. My comparisons will be based on St. Bernard, "De Gradibus Humilitatis et Superbiae," *Patrologia Latina*, 182, cc. 942–72, and Hugh of St. Victor, "De Arca Noe Morali," *PL*, 176, cc. 618–81. All subsequent quotations will be taken from these editions and will be cited in the text by column number.

15. St. Bernard, "Sermones super Cantica Canticorum," in *S. Bernardi Opera: Volume I*, ed. J. Leclercq, H. M. Rochais and C. H. Talbot (Rome: Editiones Cistercienses, 1957), Sermo 9, 42. The translation is taken from *On the Song of Songs I*, trans. Kilian Walsh, in *The Works of Bernard of Clairvaux, Volume Two* (Spencer, Mass.: Cistercian Publications, 1971), 53.

16. St. Bernard, Sermo 9, 43–44; Walsh, 55.

17. Grayson, 17–37.

18. See Georgianna's discussion of the author's interest in temptation, 69ff.

19. John Bugge pointed out this very important use of the *sponsa Christi* motif in the AB texts in his *Virginitas: An Essay in the History of a Medieval Ideal*, *Archives Internationales d'histoire des idées*, Series Minor 17 (The Hague: Martinus Nijhoff, 1975).

20. See Simone de Beauvoir, "La Mystique," in *Le Deuxième Sexe* (Paris: Librarie Gallimard, 1949), 508–17.

21. See de Beauvoir's discussion of the mystic (cited in n. 20, above) and Luce Irigaray, "La Mysterique," in *Speculum de L'Autre Femme* (Paris: Les Editions de Minuit, 1974), 238–52.

22. Caroline Bynum, *Holy Feast and Holy Fast: The Religious Significance of Food to Medieval Women* (Berkeley: Univ. of California Press, 1987).

23. Elaine Showalter, *A Literature of Their Own* (Princeton: Princeton Univ. Press, 1982), 297. Many of my comments in this paragraph were the result of a conversation with James Kincaid.

24. See Bynum, 286.

Sexual Enclosure, Textual Escape:
The *Pícara* as Prostitute in the
Spanish Female Picaresque Novel

Anne J. Cruz

> De cuantas coimas tuve—toledanas,
> de Valencia, Sevilla y otras tierras;
> Izas, rabizas y colipoterras,
> Hurgamanderas y putarazanas.
>   De cuantas siestas, noches y mañanas
> me venían a buscar, dando de zerras
> las Vargas, las Leonas y las Guerras,
> las Méndez, las Correas y Gaitanas.
>   Me veo morir agora de penuria
> en esta desleal isla maldita
> pues más a punto estoy que San Hilario.
>   Tanto que no se iguala mi lujuria—
> ni la de fray Alonso el Carmelita,
> ni aquella de fray Trece el Trinitario.[1]

The Spanish picaresque novels are noted for their gallery of rogues, from the central character of the *pícaro* to his low-life entourage of beggars, thieves, and whores. The *pícaro* in particular is presented as a marginalized antihero who functions in the text as a scapegoat for the social ills of sixteenth- and seventeenth-century Spain. Both as historical figure and as literary persona, he is an outsider—the end result of the economic and political failures of the Hapsburg monarchs and of society's inability to resolve the pressing issues of poverty, vagrancy, and criminality.[2] The female picaresque, with its *pícara* as main protagonist, is generally taken to have been conceived in the image of the male, a literary *segundona* ancillary to the traditional canon.

Most literary studies subsume the female picaresque novels under their male counterparts and view the presentation of the *pícara* as similar criticism of societal problems.[3] Yet, while both types of picaresque novels were written by male authors, those with female protagonists share neither the origins of the male picaresque tradition nor its purpose. Although *La vida de Lazarillo de Tormes*—whose anonymous author was most certainly a man—has long been recognized as the progenitor of the male picaresque, the female picaresque derives from Fernando de Rojas' *Tragicomedia de Calisto y Melibea*, which became known by the name of its most famous character, the old go-between, Celestina. Published in its expanded version in 1500, this novel in dialogue form dwells as much on the picaresque lives of the servants as on the ill-starred lovers of its title. It is this lower-class stratum of the text, inhabited by the lascivious servants and the old bawd, that the female picaresque novels reconstruct as their milieu.

The *Lazarillo* and subsequent picaresque novels parody the exploits of the knights-errant of chivalric novels by inverting the image of their archetypal heroes into the amoral *pícaro*. The female picaresque, on the other hand, models its literary antiheroines on the already debased female characters of the *Celestina*. The picaresque thus becomes a gender-oriented genre, separated by the sex of the protagonists and differentiated by its distinct literary parentage. The female picaresque novels *La Lozana andaluza* (1527), *La pícara Justina* (1605), *La hija de la Celestina* (1614), and even *La niña de los embustes, Teresa de Manzanares* (1632), and *La Garduña de Sevilla y anzuelo de las bolsas* (1642) all descend from a matriarchy which delimits the heroine's role solely to her sexual function. Alonso de Castillo Solórzano's last two tales focus more on the *pícaras'* confidence tricks than on their overtly immoral conduct; nevertheless, both narratives rely on the women's willingness to entice their suitors sexually in order to rob them. Peter N. Dunn rightly comments that "women, in Castillo's novels, are 'el flaco sexo', 'the weaker sex', with due emphasis on the 'sex'."[4] What is clearly evident is that, in nearly all the picaresque novels, the *pícara* is portrayed either explicitly or ironically as a prostitute.[5]

Such a depiction distinguishes her from her male counterpart, since her marginalized role in society is far more complex and deeply embedded than the *pícaro*'s: the prostitute historically holds an important place in society and her treatment reflects the prevailing consciousness about women and sexuality in general.[6] From the Middle Ages on, the moral ambivalence toward prostitution created an atmosphere of oppression that encouraged society to punish the prostitute while it ignored the reasons for her behavior—principally, the dreadful poverty and mistreatment suffered by these lower-class women. Historians Angel Galán Sánchez and María Teresa López Beltrán have noted that the times were conditioned by a triple exigency: on the one hand, the total repression of prostitution; on the other, the acceptance of its inevitability and the need to control it as much as possible; and finally, the fact, no less obvious, that prostitution could bring in substantial revenues.[7] Thus, despite the moral urgency of the issue, prostitution was allowed to remain a practical means of support for many women.

Yet, although the clergy were permitted their concubines and the *scorta erratica* followed the military expeditions, most prostitution remained illegal in much of medieval Spain. Ironically, clandestine houses of prostitution were often called monasteries, with the madams in charge correspondingly known as abbesses. Penalties for acts of prostitution committed by the "sisters" consisted of fifty lashes for the first offense, one hundred for the second; a prostitute's nose was cut off for the third. Justice was generally much more lax towards the owners of the houses, who were usually rich noblemen. When such a "monastery" was discovered, the confiscated property was sold to the highest bidder, only to be reopened by a new owner when the pressure subsided. Despite the many laws, inns frequently harbored prostitutes, as it was quite easy to bribe a judge with the favors of the very prostitutes accused.[8] While the municipal charters (*fueros*) of the sixteenth and seventeenth centuries in part liberated the third estate from the abuses of the nobility, protecting women from the accustomed *droit du seigneur,* they also severely punished the prostitute. The Sepúlveda *fuero* 235, for example, which governed the whole of the Extremaduran province, provided for the injury and even death of a prostitute who insulted an honest man or woman.[9] Alfonso el Sabio's *Siete Partidas* permitted concubinage, but ruled that procurers and their whores should be driven out of town. In

an attempt to effect a restitution of sorts, the seventh *partida* also speci-
fied that where procurers had lured women to a life of sin, they were
responsible for the prostitutes' rehabilitation under penalty of death, and
should provide for their dowries and marriage.[10]

Although prohibited within the cities, prostitution outside the city
gates was legally allowed. As early as 1321, the city of Valencia decreed
that a series of small houses outside of the city—rented by procurers
or *hostalers* who then furnished supplies to their wards at outrageous
prices—should be turned into a public brothel. To protect the prostitutes
from exploitation by these procurers, the city fathers imposed several
laws forbidding the *hostalers* to live among the women or to hire them
for immoral acts. Their treatment under this system, while decidedly
more humane than the punishment meted out under the various *fueros,*
nonetheless reveals the moral condemnation implicit in their segregation.
All prostitutes found practicing within the city were relegated to the
brothel and, in order to distinguish them from "decent" women, were
forbidden to enter the city wearing a cape. They were also forbidden
to enter dancing or to dance while in the city, activities deemed too
seductive to engage in outside the brothel.[11]

From 1470 through 1473, any prostitute caught working outside the
designated brothels was heavily fined by the town council of Seville,
which served as model for many of the town councils in the recently incorporated kingdom of Granada. After the kingdom's conquest in 1492,
the Catholic Monarchs granted the monopoly of all houses of prostitution
in the area to Alonso Yáñez Fajardo, a local noble known, disparagingly
enough, as "*el putero,*" the "whoremonger." All prostitutes were legally
required to work only in Yáñez's brothels, or *mancebías,* which he in
turn rented to third parties called *padres,* who looked after the prostitutes
and established the rates to be charged.[12] Although the desired outcome
of the Monarchs' organizing efforts was to restrict and control the prostitutes' activity, there remained a considerable number of unregulated
prostitutes who acted as free agents.[13]

Throughout the sixteenth century, Seville was to continue its attempts
to regulate prostitution. The 1568 syphilis epidemic forced city government to redouble its efforts to control the spread of the disease. Historian
Mary Elizabeth Perry has aptly described the circumstances:

Rumors of an epidemic so frightened city residents that they were willing to accept greatly expanded government regulations. These regulations were directed particularly against prostitutes, who were commonly suspected of passing on plagues. Clients of prostitutes, after all, often entered the city from a ship that had arrived in port, and prostitutes could easily contract any diseases they carried and pass them on into the city. Prostitutes were more susceptible to illness, too, if they were the poorer women who were undernourished and used secondhand clothing and bedding, both of which frequently carried disease in this period.[14]

Legalized prostitution not only prevented diseases by ensuring routine medical examinations, it also provided for those young girls who were unable to find employment and who were too poor to marry. If prostitution was an evil, it was one accepted by society as necessary in order to respond pragmatically to the economic hardships suffered by so many women. As Perry points out, not only was it profitable for city officials and churchmen, many of whom owned the property leased to the brothels, it was "even a form of public assistance, providing jobs for women who would otherwise starve. It strengthened the moral attitudes that supported the city's hierarchy of authority, and it permitted the city oligarchy to demonstrate its authority to define and confine evil." [15]

Spanish society attempted to circumscribe both the libertine actions of its prostitutes and the everyday lives of its "decent" women. Juan Luis Vives, in his *Instrucción de la mujer cristiana* (1527), urged young girls to remain indoors as much as possible. However, if they had good reason to venture out, they were to protect their reputations by covering their breasts, throat, and face, looking straight ahead with only one eye exposed, and avoiding all eye contact so as not to see nor be seen by anyone. Although "decent" women followed his precepts by covering their faces with a cloak when going outdoors, it was not long before prostitutes and other women of questionable virtue began to take advantage of the anonymity afforded by such a garment. The two groups were finally differentiated by the public's naming the first group of women *cubiertas,* and calling the second group *tapadas*—both synonyms meaning "covered," but establishing a moral distinction between them. To end the prostitutes' abuse of the cloak, which permitted them to mingle freely in society, its use by all women was finally prohibited in 1639.[16]

Comments by several contemporary foreign travelers to Spain attest

to the enforced confinement of most Spanish women by their male relatives in order to protect the family honor—a reclusion which condemned
them besides to a life of ignorance and childish frivolity.[17] The zealous
overprotection of wives by their husbands had the ironic effect of allowing the prostitutes far greater freedom on the streets, creating a division
of internal and external space for women along behavioral lines—the
"good" women were literally locked indoors, while the "bad" had the
run of the outdoors. The prostitutes' relative mobility also resulted in
their easy availability as companions to the majority of men who valued
their wives mainly for their domestic and maternal functions.

Increasingly, the role of prostitution in society extended beyond its
marginalization in the criminal underworld to its larger significance for
all women within the social order. The literary characterization of the
pícara as a prostitute thus provides a means of understanding the social
and historical attitudes toward women held by the male authors of the
female picaresque. By portraying the character as a whore, the novels
allow us to view her as transgressor, freely moving within a society
whose moral and legal boundaries no longer deter or confine her. This
release from the hypocritical constraints of Spanish society affords the
pícara an apparent honesty in her actions and thoughts: just as she is free
to behave as she wishes, she is able to state openly what she thinks, with
no regard for the consequences, since she has already violated the strict
social standards required of women. The freedom with which the *pícara*
expresses herself is most evident in the narratives that are structured
autobiographically, such as *La pícara Justina* and, at least partially, *La
hija de la Celestina*. Here, the male author not only creates a female
character, but by narrating her life in the first person, he also assumes a
feminine voice. Given the freedom he ostensibly allows her, the author
would seem to partake of the character's unfettered outlook. Instead,
the *pícara*'s discourse serves to reveal his manipulation and control,
disclosing a relationship of repression between author and narrator.[18]

The female picaresque novels thus expose their authors' perceptions
of prostitutes and prostitution, but even more importantly, they illustrate
the manner in which the male authors themselves are created by their
texts, speaking to other men from their privileged place in a society separated by gender and delimited by their own definitions of virtue and vice.
Thus, a homologous situation arises between the prostitutes of Renais-

sance Spain and their literary counterparts. As the prostitutes become socialized by royal decree and their activities increasingly regulated for the benefit of the male population, so the language of the female picaresque is both generated and controlled by the male point of view. The licentiousness of the *pícara* does not give her license to break away from authorial control: the protagonist remains at the service of the author, a seductive figure of speech ready to lure the reader into a male-dominated and male-oriented discourse.

As I shall argue, the female picaresque differs from its literary siblings such as the *Lazarillo*, the *Guzmán de Alfarache*, and the *Buscón* by seldom aiming at social subversion. Instead, by restricting the *pícaras* to their role as prostitutes, the texts are in collusion with a society that views the *pícaras* as performing a necessary and vital service. Since female sexuality historically has been deemed threatening to the social order, its containment guarantees the health and morality of the existing society, thereby contributing to its preservation.[19] The constant attempts to enclose the prostitute are thus a means of protecting society, inasmuch as confinement of prostitution within approved urban zones neutralizes the dangers its practitioners pose to the social order. Ironically, then, in their description of the *pícaras* as wanderers and pilgrims, generally free to cross the different social class boundaries, the female picaresque novels ultimately disclose a severe critique of those prostitutes who remain unconstrained.

The criticism implicit in the female picaresque reveals a polarized view of woman as either entirely "good" or "bad" held by its male authors—a view that helped to shape social reality for all women. The male perception of women's morality in turn reflects the symbiotic relations between purity and pollution delineated by anthropologist Mary Douglas:

> Where sexual purity is concerned it is obvious that if it [sexual purity] is to imply no contact between the sexes it is not only a denial of sex, but must be literally barren. It also leads to contradiction. To wish all women to be chaste at all times goes contrary to other wishes and if followed consistently leads to inconveniences.[20]

In Spain, this contradiction was resolved through the purity of those young women who would remain chaste until marriage. As Perry has noted, for the *Siete Partidas* marriage was a means "to avoid quarrels, homicides, insolence, violence, and many other very wrongful acts which would take place on account of women if marriage did not exist."[21] Yet those who did not marry also contributed to the social order. By servicing the sexual demands of men, regulated prostitutes protected the purity of marriageable women and the morality of the matriarchs:

> Women who did not marry ran the risk of losing their respectability, but even "bad women" could be tolerated if they were carefully distinguished from "good women."[22]

In fact, prostitution was not only tolerated by Spanish society—it was considered necessary to its welfare. The polarization of virgins and whores was based on a social infrastructure that required both, so long as each remained readily identifiable. The rampant poverty among women contributed to the maintenance of the status quo. While the religious life was an alternative to marriage for women with dowries, poor women who did not marry could enter relatively few nunneries, and by the middle of the sixteenth century even these were further restricted by royal decree. By 1700, there were only half the number of mendicant houses for women as for men.[23] For an increasingly large number of poor women, then, the sole option remaining required a different form of social enclosure—the public brothel.

There is no doubt that the protagonists of the female picaresque belong to the category of "bad women." The poor, lower-class origins of the *pícara,* her early promiscuity and her social marginalization are literary commonplaces that help to interpret the female picaresque in terms broader than those of the male picaresque, which traditionally has been defined by the pseudo-autobiographical narrative of a poor rogue, its episodic structure, and its social criticism. In particular, it is the female picaresque's separation of the *pícara* from "decent" society which underscores its male-authored critique of women's sexual freedom. By doing so, the female picaresque fully acknowledges its debt to the *Celestina* as the novel that first redirected the focus of the picaresque genre from its male protagonists to the *pícara.*

Indeed, the dangers of the wicked intermingling with the virtuous are spelled out clearly in the *Celestina.* Here, servants and masters come into contact with each other with easy familiarity. Areúsa and Elicia, the servants of the young noblewoman Melibea who is courted by Calisto, lead carefree lifestyles markedly different from the other servants' cloistered dependency on their vigilant mistresses. Because their actions have yet to be socially constrained, Areúsa and Elicia not only work for Melibea, they also function interchangeably as lovers of Calisto's manservants, as the old bawd Celestina's young relatives and wards, and as whores in her employ. This interaction, marked in the text by the servants' many comings and goings from Melibea's residence to Celestina's shack, creates a network of relationships which ultimately leads to Melibea's seduction and consequent downfall. Since the servants have followed Celestina's lead in preferring their own economic interest to their mistress's honor, critics have viewed Melibea's fall as symbolic of the destabilization of the closed, structured society. José Antonio Maravall has rightfully attributed the breakdown of *Celestina*'s feudal world to the substitution of money for the mutual respect that had previously existed between the servants and Calisto and Melibea.[24] Alan Deyermond has recently noted that the exchange of money for respect has caused the rupture of the social order, thereby permitting Calisto's servant Sempronio to fall in love with Melibea, and Lucrecia, Melibea's most trusted servant, with Calisto. He asks:

> ¿Cómo interpretar estos nexos sexuales entre miembros de clases distintas? Seguramente indican que la lujuria es contagiosa, y que el deseo obsesionado de Calisto por el cuerpo de Melibea influye en los criados de ambos.[25]

> [How must we interpret these sexual connections between members of differing social classes? They surely indicate that lust is contagious, and that Calisto's obsessive desire for Melibea's body influences both their servants.]

While it is true that Calisto and Melibea's furtive trysts have served as an incentive to the immoral desires of their servants, it is also evident that the constant interrelationship of Melibea with Celestina and the servants has precipitated their loss of respect for her, to the extent that Lucrecia can now emulate her mistress's desire for Calisto, and Sempronio fantasize about possessing Melibea, his own master's lover.

The *Celestina* exposes the dangers faced by young women who are insufficiently protected from the immorality which surrounds them. The novel's dramatic irony is evident in its choice of punishment for the two lovers' illicit passion: leaving Melibea's side to investigate a noise outside, Calisto accidentally falls to his death from the garden wall; mourning his death, Melibea throws herself from a tower, dying at the feet of her bereaved father. Following the *Celestina*'s moral point, the female picaresque novels measure their heroines' moral downfall by the physical freedom the novels allow them yet are careful to restrict the *pícara* to her own social milieu. The *Celestina*'s tragic ending, as well as its portentous first act, in which Calisto meets Melibea when he rashly enters her walled garden while hawking, are vividly recalled in the first chapter of *La Lozana andaluza*. The sexual symbolism of the hunt and the lover's intrusion into the *hortus conclusus* are echoed in the later work by Lozana's literal—and symbolic—loss of blood when she scales a wall without her mother's consent:

> [S]altando una pared sin licencia de su madre, se le derramó la primera sangre que del natural tenía (*LA*: 37–38).
>
> [W]hile scaling a wall without her mother's permission, she spilled the first blood from her sex.]

Lozana's "escaped" menstrual blood, a metaphor for her early loss of virginity, signifies her own escape from the protection of her mother to the *Pozo Blanco* district in Rome, where she sets up housekeeping with Rampín, a *pícaro* who will act as her pimp, servant, and lover. Although Lozana is most successful in her new occupation, her social position has already been determined both by birth and by her loss of virginity. The blood spilled in the garden also symbolizes the social rupture she experiences in Rome: as a procuress and as a prostitute, she remains always with her own kind.

In *La Lozana andaluza*, the polarity between "good" women and those of little virtue is textually noted by the comparison between the two Roman matrons whom Lozana encounters during her first outing in the city:

> Lozana: ¡Oh qué lindas son aquellas dos mujeres! Por mi vida, que son como matronas; no he visto en mi vida cosa más honrada, ni más honesta.
> Rampín: Son romanas principales.
> Lozana: Pues ¿cómo van tan solas?
> Rampín: Porque ansí lo usan. Cuando van ellas fuera, unas a otras se acompañan, salvo cuando va una sola, que lleva una sierva, mas no

hombres, ni más mujeres, aunque sea la mejor de Roma. Y mirá que van sesgas; y aunque vean a uno que conozcan, no le hablan en la calle, sino que se apartan ellos y callan, y ellas no abajan cabeza ni hacen mudanza, aunque sea su padre ni su marido (*LA*: 92).

[Lozana: Oh, those two women are so beautiful! By my life, they look like matrons; I've never seen anything so honest, nor so decent.
Rampín: They are Roman nobles.
Lozana: Then why are they walking so alone?
Rampín: That is their custom. When they go out, they accompany each other, unless one goes out by herself, and then she takes a servant, but she never goes out with a man, nor with more than one woman, even though she is the noblest in Rome. And notice that they walk quietly, and although they might see someone they know, they do not speak to him on the street, but instead, the others become silent and move aside, and the matrons do not bow their heads or change their stride, even if the others are their fathers or husbands.]

The contrast between Lozana, recently arrived in Rome, and already walking the streets busily chatting with her future lover, and the aloof Roman matrons, silently going about their business, is striking. Unlike the rest of the characters who populate the novel, the noblewomen never interact with Lozana, and are only mentioned once. Treated with uncommon respect by the author, they signify his concern with maintaining order among the different social classes, and exemplify besides his own beliefs as to how matrons should behave.

In contrast, Delicado humorously relates Lozana's sexual encounters in scurrilous detail. *La pícara Justina* was to emphasize that the picaresque genre should be viewed solely as entertainment, and most of the female picaresque novels gloss over the weighty social issues of poverty and criminality central to the male picaresque tradition. Although Delicado had revised his earlier version of *La Lozana andaluza* to incorporate the sack of Rome in 1527 as divine punishment for the city's wickedness, he seemingly casts a benevolent eye on his protagonist's sinful business—so much so that the ending, which carries out the motif of separation first indicated by her literal and moral fall, is primarily a happy one. We find Lozana tired of her life as whore and procuress— "estoy harta de meter barboquejos a putas" [I'm tired of fixing whores to pass as virgins] (*LA*: 245)—wealthy and ready to isolate herself willingly from society by retiring with the faithful Rampín.

Yet Lozana's carefree life, which culminates with the couple on the island of Lípari—a well-known literary *locus* for lovers—barely conceals the many tensions within the text.[26] Delicado proudly proclaims the mimetic excellence of his novel, whose earthy language and vivid descriptions, he claims, accurately capture the amoral ambiance of the Roman underworld. Lozana's experiences as a whore fittingly take place in the Roman districts known for prostitution; indeed, while the text clearly exaggerates the numbers of prostitutes in Rome at the time as thirty thousand, the 1526 census attests to 4,900 prostitutes among a total population of 55,035 spread throughout the city's districts—an alarming ratio of one prostitute to every ten residents.[27] However, Lozana can hardly be considered a real woman, since her life is far too idealized to be taken as a realistic representation. Delicado's romantic depiction of the *pícara*'s adventures skillfully disguises the actual conditions in which she lives. A careful reading of the text, however, reveals that while Lozana appears to take advantage of her customers, it is she who must be constantly on her guard to protect herself from her customers, who would not hesitate to leave without paying for her services. Lozana cannot allow herself to trust anyone: her relations with Rampín disclose her need for human contact as much as they celebrate Lozana's voracious sexual appetite. And although she is insistently described as graceful and lovely, her small nose and the scars on her forehead are not physical manifestations of beauty, as she would have us believe, but the ravages of venereal disease. Lozana's beauty, her shrewd business sense, and her keen enjoyment of sex, then, are qualities willfully exaggerated by the author to delight his male audience.

Clearly overrating Lozana's qualities as a vivacious free spirit, Delicado restricts the *pícara* to her profession. Although the young Lozana ardently desires financial independence, she can obtain it only by moving up from whore to procuress; both occupations, however, require that she remain in the low-life milieu of Roman prostitution. When she is compared to the legendary pimp Zoppino, known for his corruption of young girls, Lozana retorts that she has never abused her expertise as a procuress for anyone evil enough to harm an innocent person. Showing her own version of thieves' honor, she proudly notes that she has limited her activities to those who have already joined the trade:

Yo puedo ir con mi cara descubierta por todo, que no hice jamás vileza, ni alcagüetería ni mensaje a persona vil. . . . Y esto se dirá de mí, si alguno me querrá poner en fábula: muncho supo la Lozana, más que no demostraba (*LA*: 166–67).

[I can go everywhere with my face uncovered, as I have not committed any vile deed, or acted as go-between or given a message to an evil person. . . . And if anyone wants to write about me, he may say this of me: Lozana had much more wisdom than she revealed.]

Lozana is further constrained by her Jewish origins. As she joins other *conversas* in the Pozo Blanco district, they recognize their common religious background and exclaim, "¡Por tu vida, que es *de nostris*!" [By your life, she's one of us!] (*LA*: 53). Yet Delicado does not attribute Lozana's lifestyle to religious persecution: she did not leave Spain for religious reasons, and her ties to Judaism are tenuous at best.[28] Since it is most unlikely that the percentage of Spanish prostitutes of either Moorish or Jewish descent was any higher than those of Old Christian stock, the author portrays Lozana as a *conversa* to reinforce her isolation from society. The text makes use of the literary archetype of the "dark woman" to highlight Lozana's sensual nature, thereby justifying her choice of profession. Both her social class and her inherent sensuality collude to separate her from "decent" society: though a Cordoban by birth, Lozana sets up trade in Rome, a city whose reputation as Babylon, as city of whores, reflects upon her own choice of action and confirms her segregation.

Neither does the female picaresque recognize the consequences to women of their restricted social roles; it signals instead the dangers that women pose to society as conceptualized by the genre's male authors. Writing before the Counter-Reformation, Delicado confirms his liberality in his apology, "Cómo se escusa el autor en la fin del Retrato de la Lozana, en laude de las mujeres" [How the author apologizes at the end of the Portrait of the Lozana, lauding women] (*LA*: 247) by recommending reasonable moderation to both men and women in their sexual relationships. Nevertheless, he should be taken at his word when he states that only the fear of God differentiates good women from wicked:

[Y] como las mujeres conocen ser solacio a los hombres y ser su recreación común, piensan y hacen lo que no harían si tuviesen el principio de la

> sapiencia, que es temer al Señor, y la que alcanza esta sapiencia o inteligencia es más preciosa que ningún diamante, y ansí por el contrario muy vil (*LA*: 248).

> [And since women know they are men's solace and their recreation, they think and do what they would not if only they had the principle of wisdom, which is to fear the Lord, and whoever achieves this wisdom or intelligence is more precious than any diamond, and therefore, whoever does not, is very wicked.]

Thomas Hanrahan points out that the antifeminism of the female picaresque stems more from the genre's role as an ascetic and didactic literature of the Counter-Reformation than from medieval misogynist writings. He rightly concludes that, while the medieval tradition and the female picaresque both ultimately view women as "seductive, lascivious, and avaricious," the female picaresque's antifeminism was meant to have a far more serious purpose than to censure women. It was directed instead toward the instruction and reformation of the most important member of society—the male.[29] In its warning against women, *La Lozana andaluza* anticipates the shift in focus from the medieval reprobation of women's moral weakness to the later female picaresque novels' emphasis on virtue as a uniquely male quality.

In seeming contradiction to the *Lozana* yet, as Bruno Damiani has suggested, surely influenced by it, López de Ubeda's heroine, the *pícara* Justina, plays to the reader's sympathies by relating her adventures as a virginal peasant girl who constantly foils her suitors' attempts to seduce her.[30] But all the puns and euphemisms she coyly uses when referring to herself belie her innocence and reveal her role as that of the prostitute she undoubtedly represents. Indeed, the author pointedly assigns Justina such picaresque characteristics as her probable *converso* origins, and her childhood experiences at her parents' inn, where she first learns to steal from the customers. The novel, which follows Justina's rise as a rogue, her travels to several Spanish towns, and her marriages, imitates the format of the *Guzmán de Alfarache* with its picaresque chapters followed by a moral coda, or *aprovechamiento,* of little relevance. Given its contrived plot, critics have long debated whether *La pícara Justina* should even be considered a picaresque novel, rather than a parody of the *Guzmán de Alfarache* or a roman à clef of the court of Philip III. Marcel Bataillón, for example, views the novel as a sarcastic reply to the seriousness of the picaresque, appropriating its format in order to satirize the concerns of the privileged classes.[31] Bataillón accurately points out that, in the chapter on Justina's so-called pilgrimage to León, López de Ubeda is less interested in realistically depicting the peasant girl's misadventures than in parodying Philip III's recent visit to that city, in which López de Ubeda most likely took part.[32] Yet, although López de Ubeda may not intend the novel to represent the realities of seventeenth-century Spain, his views of women must be seen in the context of its patriarchal system. By breaking with the male picaresque tradition and casting a woman as the protagonist, *La pícara Justina*'s author reveals his own concerns about women's role in society.

While Delicado blames Lozana's faults on her lowly social origins, López de Ubeda is quick to condemn Justina's feminine nature as well. In Justina's constant defense of her equivocal virtue, López de Ubeda establishes a parallel between all "good" women and the whore, since she argues that her weaknesses are common to all women, and openly warns the reader of their perfidy:

> Nota las falsas lágrimas de una mujer: la astucia de una doncella, la codicia de una mozuela, sus embustes y mentiras y todo te sirva de escarmiento y de aviso (*PJ* 2: 670).

> [Note the false tears of a woman; the astuteness of a virgin; the greed of a young girl, her deceptions and lies, and let everything be a lesson and a warning to you.]

López de Ubeda's ironic depiction of the poor, innocent Justina, therefore, results in a much stronger condemnation of women than Delicado's comparatively candid admission of a prostitute's experiences. Uneasily conflating the prostitute and the virgin, the author at times blames Justina's weaknesses on her legacy from Eve, as the first woman, and at other times on the direct picaresque inheritance from her mother, in both cases constantly undermining Justina's seeming virtuousness. Thus, while at the last, Justina refuses to continue the narrative ostensibly so as not to bore the reader with her virginal tale—"justo es que piense yo que la larga historia de mi virginal estado te dará fastidio" [I'm right in believing that the long story of my virginal state will bore you] (*PJ* 2: 739)—she has conveniently forgotten the double entendre at the beginning of her story, where she describes her dubious family origins:

> No te espantes, que tuve abuelo tamboritero a quien no le holgaba miembro; verásme echar muchas veces por lo flautado; no se te haga nuevo, que tuve abuelo flautista y parece nací con la flauta inserta en el cuerpo según gusto della (*PJ* I: 184).

> [Don't be horrified—I had a drummer grandfather whose members were never still; you'll see me tend toward the fluting many times; this shouldn't come as anything new, since I had a flutist grandfather and it seems like I was born with the flute inserted in me—I enjoy it so much.]

Justina's picaresque beginnings, her life as a whore, and her future as a go-between are all borne out in the various sexual meanings of the term *flute,* which represents not only the phallus and the sexual act arranged by a go-between, but the go-between herself. As a literary *pícara,* Justina cannot escape from her lowly origins; neither, as a woman, can she run away from masculine control. By blaming Justina's moral frailty on both her mother and Eve—on her social and natural conditions— the author reveals his own uncertain attitudes towards all women. But most importantly, by admitting his belief in man's "higher" nature, he attempts to justify the need for masculine control of the "weaker" sex not only to himself, but to society as well.

López de Ubeda discloses his perception of male superiority by continually ascribing Justina's talkative nature and her constant movement both to her maternal legacy and to her inherently feminine condition. As a *pícara,* Justina traces her lineage from a long line of *pícaros* on her mother's side whose dubious occupations of puppeteer, mask vendor, musician, and barber have all contributed to her gadabout and gossipy character:

> ¡Ay hermano lector! Iba a persuadirte que no te admires si en el discurso de mi historia me vieres, no sólo parlona, en cumplimiento de la herencia que viste en el número pasado, pero loca saltadera, brincadera, bailadera, gaitera, porque, como verás en el número presente, es también herencia de madre (*PJ* I: 183).

> [Oh, brother reader! I meant to persuade you not to be surprised if in the narrative you not only find me a gabber in keeping with the inheritance you saw in the previous chapter, but also a frenzied jumper, skipper, dancer, jigger, since, as you'll see in the present chapter, this too I inherited from my mother.]

To substantiate his claim that Justina, as a woman, comes to this inheritance naturally, López de Ubeda bases himself on Biblical authority. Slyly parodying Genesis, he insists that women owe their loudness and their footloose nature to Eve's having been created from Adam's rib. In her own version of the Biblical story, Justina assures us that, since Adam begged Eve not to rest until she found his missing rib, Eve's descendants are obliged to continue her futile search:

> Y de aquí les vino a las mujeres que, como la primera iba pregonando, ellas salen vocineras, y como nunca acaban de hallar quien tenga una costilla de más, nacen inclinadas a andar en busca de la costilla y viendo si hallan hombres con alguna costilla de sobra (*PJ* 1: 247)

> [And for this reason, since the first woman went about clamoring, all women sound their horns, and as they can never find anyone with a rib to spare, they are naturally inclined to wander about in search of Adam's rib, looking for men with an extra one.]

The burlesque tone of the narrative does nothing to conceal the text's seriousness; rather, it confirms an antifeminism so entrenched that it would allow a comical reading of the Bible, despite Justina's disclaimer that the anecdote is "blasphemy only for those who believe it" (*PJ* 1: 247).

La pícara Justina resolves the problem of woman's freedom through marriage; according to the author, her motivation, like all women's, is not love but greed. Since she marries only men of her own station, Justina does not represent all women: she maintains the social separation seen earlier in *La Lozana andaluza*. Justina's three marriages therefore underscore López de Ubeda's hesitation in unequivocally condemning all women, whether "decent" or not. However, by plotting these repeated marriages—the last to the infamous *pícaro* Guzmán de Alfarache—the author casts doubt on the effectiveness of marriage to reform the protagonist, and by implication, questions its power as a social institution to protect society fully from the moral weaknesses of all women.

Justina's several marriages may indeed restrain the *pícara* from her compulsive wandering, at least for a time. Her talkative and gossipy nature, however, appears uncontrollable and undiminished throughout the narrative. Since the power of language as a means of self-expression and self-determination is central to the issue of authorial control, *La pícara Justina* must somehow account for women's talkative nature while delimiting its use by Justina. Both Vives and Fray Luis de León had earlier stressed silence as a cardinal virtue of the Christian woman, with the latter cleverly drawing an analogy between her closed mouth and the enclosed state in which she should ideally remain.[33] Justina, however, is never at a loss for words; her loquacious nature becomes a part of the female condition which the author consciously parodies in his garrulous tale. He discounts Justina's extraordinary verbal ability by attributing it yet again to her legacy from Eve, in the process imputing man's fall to Eve's purported abuse of language: "[D]el cuerpo de Eva heredamos las mujeres . . . parlar de gana, aunque sea con serpientes" [From the body of Eve we women inherit our . . . incessant chatter, if only with serpents] (*PJ* 1: 181–2). Ironically, since the author speaks through Justina's persona, he cannot silence his heroine without rendering mute his own voice. López de Ubeda appropriates Justina's language by superimposing his own discourse upon the prostitute's unlearned speech. The author's control of his protagonist's language is demonstrated in the puns, amphibologies, and complex conceits Justina delights in, yet which are hardly consonant with her illiterate village background.

Thus, while appearing to celebrate Justina's freedom and her linguistic ability, *La pícara Justina* decries women's attempts to liberate themselves from male control. Whether by regulating women's voice or actions, the authors of the picaresque impose male standards upon women, using their female literary characters as illustrations of their own social prejudices. Like Lozana's, Justina's questionable ancestry may be "tainted" with Jewish blood, but her author is not so concerned with presenting Justina's dark sensuality as he is with satirizing the Spanish obsession with proving one's *limpieza de sangre*. The Counter-Reformation, with its insistence upon the determinism of sin and the moral frailty of all women, provides the backdrop for *La pícara Justina*. In the paranoid atmosphere of a Spain rigorously controlled by the Inquisition, Justina stands, not for a marginalized group of *conversos,* but for everyone's social fears.[34] Similarly, her assumed virginity is an invisible symbol whose precariousness marks all women; her freedom, a literary ruse by which the author again condemns them all. Yet, like *La Lozana andaluza*, *La pícara Justina* also maintains the separation of the *pícara* from the rest of society by setting her as an example of how women ought not to behave (and by pointing out the fate in store for the unmindful):

> En este libro hallará la doncella el conocimiento de su perdición, los peligros en que se pone una libre mujer que no se rinde al consejo de otros (*PJ* 1: 76).

> [In this book the virgin will come to know the cause of her perdition, the dangers a libertine woman exposes herself to when she does not accept the advice of others.]

The more liberated the protagonist of a female picaresque novel, therefore, the stronger the condemnation by its author of women in general, and the more insistent the warnings of the potential hazards in permitting both "decent" and "indecent" women to interact without any differentiation.

The hazards of unconstrained prostitution are illustrated most forcefully in *La hija de la Celestina* by Alonso Jerónimo de Salas Barbadillo. Narrated in the third person, the novel assumes the pretense of a woman's discourse only when Elena relates her genealogy. Otherwise, her story is told from its inception by a stern moralist who passes swift and certain judgment on his literary creation. The narrative begins with the wedding of a young and dissolute nobleman, don Sancho, hastily arranged by his rich uncle to put an end to the youth's scandalous behavior. Elena, the *pícara* of the story, together with her pimp and lover, Montúfar, proceeds to bilk the rich old man by accusing don Sancho of raping her, convincing his uncle by showing him a dagger Elena had previously taken from a servant, who in turn had stolen it from the nephew. The picaresque plot can unfold only when Elena flaunts her beauty in complete freedom and mobility, since she must pass herself off to the uncle as a virtuous, wronged noblewoman. Upon seeing Elena in Toledo, the young nobleman falls desperately in love with her, destroying the social stability sought by the uncle through the arranged marriage. Yet what at first seems a caveat against arranged marriages turns out to be a strongly-worded directive against prostitution:

> El otro suspiraba por la desposada, ella por el ingrato que tenía al lado—a quien amaba con verdad de corazón, y le había conocido la tibieza de la voluntad—y él por la fugitiva Elena; y entre los tres, quien justamente

merecía grave pena, era el triste, el infeliz don Sancho pues pudiendo
descansar en los honestos y hermosos brazos de su mujer, codiciaba los de
una vil ramera que había sido y era pasto común, entregándose por bajos
precios a todos aquellos que con medianas diligencias la pretendían
(*HC*: 70).

[The other [don Sancho's wife's previous suitor] pined for the new spouse,
she, for the ingrate by her side—whom she loved truly, and whose moral
weakness she had found out—and he, for the fleeing Elena; and of the three,
the one who truly deserved his grave suffering was the sad, the sorrowful don
Sancho since, although he lay in the decent and beautiful arms of his wife,
he desired those of a wicked whore, who had been and was common fodder
to all, giving herself cheaply to all those who showed the slightest interest.]

Don Sancho's untimely desire for Elena is clearly to blame for the disruption of a potentially happy marriage between two social equals. Yet,
while male desire sets the narrative in motion, it is Elena, as the untram-
meled prostitute fleeing with Montúfar through the countryside, who
propels the novel to its close. Although don Sancho at first chases after
Elena, he eventually returns repentant to his forgiving wife and wealthy
uncle. Elena, desirous of reaching Madrid, where she can earn more
money on her own, attempts to escape from Montúfar's control. He
catches her, ties her to a tree, beats her, and releases her only when he
is certain that she will not try to escape again. Significantly, the male
author shifts his focus from a critique of male desire as the cause of
social destabilization, to the condemnation of the prostitute.

The actions of the four main characters in the novel are to be read
normatively, since each character represents a particular social position.
Thus, the differences between don Sancho and Montúfar are mainly
of social class; their actions are eminently acceptable under the male
code of behavior for each social group. Don Sancho's lack of resolve
is presented as an unintentional slip brought about by Elena's diabolical
beauty, while Montúfar's violent behavior is a direct result of Elena's
treachery. The two women, don Sancho's wife and Elena, are also of
different social class, but don Sancho's wife conforms to her role of the
patiently suffering wife, whereas Elena undertakes to lead her own life.
While the wife is rewarded with her husband's love, Elena must endure
Montúfar's wrath as punishment for her short-lived independence. Despite the difference in their roles—the virtuous wife in opposition to the

wily whore—both are defined by male expectations of women, and their behavior is condoned or condemned accordingly.

The violent dénouement of the narrative is Salas Barbadillo's final and most devastating criticism of Elena's attempts to liberate herself from masculine control. Montúfar, after marrying Elena and pandering her to wealthy men in order to support the two in style, again beats her unmercifully when she refuses to ignore the attentions of a young street tough. When he realizes she has served him a dish of poisoned cherries in revenge, Montúfar threatens her with his sword but is stabbed through the heart instead by the young tough. The youth is hanged for his troubles, and Elena garrotted, placed in a wooden barrel and tossed into the river Manzanares. Elena's punishment is not only Salas Barbadillo's eloquent commentary on the picaresque life, but more specifically, on her endeavors to interact freely among all levels of society.

The female picaresque novels all acknowledge their debt to the *Celestina* by making repeated references to the primary text. Lozana's house is extolled as the place where "aquí adolatró Calisto, aquí no se estima Melibea, aquí poco vale Celestina" [here Calisto worshipped, here Melibea is not valued, here Celestina counts for nothing] (*LA*: 155). Justina, exhorting the reader to listen to her story, announces: "escucha y oyrás las hazañas de otra Celestina" [listen and you'll hear the exploits of another Celestina] (*PJ* 1: 208). *La hija de la Celestina* is most obvious in its title, which names Elena the "daughter" of Celestina. These three novels, however, have learned the social lesson taught by the older narrative. Despite the *desenfado* of their language, both *La Lozana andaluza* and *La pícara Justina* portray only the illusion of liberated discourse. The authors reveal their power by their implicit judgment of the circumstances in which they place the female protagonists. While *La hija de la Celestina* is the most explicitly punitive of the novels discussed, even *La Lozana andaluza* has the sack of Rome to pressure Lozana to flee from Rome and give up her sinful life. *La pícara Justina* ends with Justina's dubious marriage to another *pícaro*—Guzmán de Alfarache—a repentant sinner who, as Justina's author well knew, narrates his own life from a watchtower where he espies everyone's vices and foibles. All three *pícaras,* then, are forced to delimit their range of action in accordance with male-defined boundaries.

By taking the *Celestina* as their model, the authors of the female picaresque accept its premise that unrestrained immorality poses a serious threat to society. The solution they adopt not only illustrates their awareness of the social importance of legalized prostitution as a means of maintaining the status quo, but also reveals to the reader the authors' own historically conditioned prejudices against women, and the strategies through which these prejudices become ideology. The trajectory of the female picaresque moves from the dangerously interactive society of the *Celestina* to the enclosure of the prostitute and her separation from the rest of society, to the final erasure of differences between all women, whether virgins or whores. Whether pure or defiled, the woman is viewed by the male-dominated society as a necessary evil who must be controlled by the governing institutions. The sexual specificity of that control signifies the danger she presents to society—woman's sexuality threatens constantly to disrupt the male order.

As such, women's sexuality is a social factor to be repressed, bartered, and controlled by the male structures of power. In like manner, woman's voice is suppressed, dominated, and exchanged for the male's. In its mimicry of what the authors construe as female discourse, the female picaresque, while claiming to assume a feminine voice, in actuality bespeaks male prejudice, formulating a cultural strategy through which sexual and social reality is created and maintained. By implicitly condemning the purported freedom of the *pícara,* the genre sanctions only such legally constrained sexual behavior as benefits the social order—but it also succeeds in continually defining that order to male specifications. The authors of the female picaresque fabricate their own male identity as surely as they create the persona of the *pícara.*

NOTES

Research for this essay was funded in part by a grant from the Focused Research Project in Gender and Women's Studies, University of California, Irvine.

1. Anonymous sonnet included in the *Cancionero general*, Antwerp, 1557.

Thanks to all the whores I've slept with—Toledans,
from Valencia, Seville, and other lands,

sluts, strumpets, and streetwalkers,
bedqueens and mattressbacks;
   Thanks to all the noons, nights, and mornings
they'd come for me, clawing their way(?),
the Vargases, Leonas, and the Guerras,
the Méndezes, Correas, and Gaitanas.
   I now find myself completely penniless
in this damned, unfaithful island
since I'm more to the ready than Saint Hilaire,
   So much so that my lust's no less
than Friar Alonso the Carmelite's,
or that of Friar Trece the Trinitarian.

2. The origins of the picaresque genre should be considered within the social and historical contexts of sixteenth-century Spain. See my essay, "The Picaresque as Discourse of Poverty," *Ideologies & Literature* 1 (1985): 74–97.

3. Thomas Hanrahan, in *La mujer en la novela picaresca española*, 2 vols. (Madrid: Ediciones Porrúa Turanzas, 1967), and Harry Sieber, in *The Picaresque* (London: Methuen, 1977) both consider *La pícara Justina* the first female picaresque novel; the latter rejects Alonso de Salas Barbadillo's *La hija de la Celestina* for not conforming to the conventions of the male picaresque (Sieber, 32). To my knowledge, only Carlos Blanco Aguinaga addresses the issue of the female picaresque as separate from the male picaresque tradition. See his "Picaresca española, picaresca inglesa: Sobre las determinaciones del género," *Edad de Oro*, 2 (Madrid: Universidad Autónoma de Madrid, 1983), 49–65. See also Pablo J. Ronquillo, *Retrato de la pícara: La protagonista de la picaresca espanola del XVII* (Madrid: Editorial Playor, 1980), for a useful compendium of female picaresque tales. His study, however, ignores the genre's inherent irony when, for instance, it takes seriously the descriptions of the *pícaras* as great beauties (19). His characterization of the *pícara* as socially mobile and easily metamorphosed into a noble woman (13ff.) further overlooks the inglorious endings of the narratives and their condemnation—explicit and implicit—of the protagonists' so-called independent lives.

4. Peter N. Dunn, *Castillo Solórzano and the Decline of the Spanish Novel* (Oxford: Basil Blackwell, 1952), 55.

5. For all quotations, I have used the following editions: *La Lozana andaluza*, ed. Bruno Damiani (Madrid: Clásicos Castalia, 1969); *La pícara Justina*, ed. Antonio Rey Hazas, 2 vols. (Madrid: Editora Nacional, 1977); *La hija de la Celestina*, ed. José Fradejas Lebrero (Madrid: Instituto de Estudios Madrileños, 1983). All translations are my own.

6. See Mary Elizabeth Perry's excellent study, "Deviant Insiders: Legalized Prostitutes and a Consciousness of Women in Early Modern Seville," *Comparative Studies in Society and History* 27 (1985): 138–58; and her " 'Lost Women' in Early Modern Seville: The Politics of Prostitution," *Feminist Studies* 4 (1978):

195–214. I am grateful to Dr. Perry for her comments on an earlier version of this essay. My thanks, also, to Janet E. Halley and Sheila Fisher, whose judicious editing considerably improved the clarity of the essay's argument.

7. Angel Galán Sánchez and María Teresa López Beltrán, "El 'status' teórico de las prostitutas del Reino de Granada en la primera mitad del siglo XVI (Las Ordenanzas de 1538)," in *Las mujeres en las ciudades medievales: Actas de las Terceras Jornadas de Investigación Interdisciplinaria*, ed. Cristina Segura Graiño, Seminario de Estudios de la Mujer (Madrid: Universidad Autónoma de Madrid, 1984), 162.

8. Enrique Rodríguez Solís, *Historia de la prostitución en España y América* (Madrid: Biblioteca Nueva, 1921), 46–48.

9. Ibid., 50–51.

10. Law II, Title XXII, *Las Siete Partidas*, trans. Samuel Parsons Scott (The Comparative Law Bureau of the American Bar Association, New York: Commerce Clearing House, Inc., Loose Leaf Service Division of the Corporation Trust Company, 1931), 1429–30.

11. Manuel Carboneres, *Picaronas y alcahuetes o la mancebía en Valencia* (Valencia: Librería de Pascual Aguilar, 1876), 16ff. The Valencian brothel remained protected by law through the sixteenth century. Similar arrangements were allowed in other cities under Philip II's 1571 law, which regulated the brothels. See also Fernando Henríques, *Prostitution in Europe and the New World* (London: MacGibbon & Kee, 1963), pp. 52–53.

12. See Angel Caffarena, *Apuntes para la historia de las mancebías de Málaga* (Málaga: Juan Such, 1968), and María Teresa López Beltrán, *La prostitución en le Reino de Granada en época de los Reyes Católicos: El caso de Málaga* (Málaga: Biblioteca Popular Malagueña, 1985), 27–33.

13. Angel Galán Sánchez and María Teresa López Beltrán, 163.

14. Mary Elizabeth Perry, *Crime and Society in Early Modern Seville* (New Hampshire: Univ. Press of New England, 1980), pp. 227–28.

15. Ibid., *Crime and Society*, 233.

16. See José Deleito y Piñuela, *La mujer, la casa y la moda (en la España del Rey Poeta)* (Madrid: Espasa-Calpe, S.A., 1966), 64. He cites Antonio de León Pinelo, *Velos antiguos y modernos en los rostros de las mujeres. Sus conveniencias y daños. Ilustración de la Real Premática de las Tapadas* (Madrid, 1641).

17. See Deleito y Piñuela, 17ff.

18. See Edward H. Friedman, "Man's Space, Woman's Place: Discourse and Design in *La pícara Justina*," in *La Chispa '85 Selected Proceedings*, The Sixth Louisiana Conference on Hispanic Languages and Literatures, ed. Gilbert Paolini (New Orleans, La.: Tulane University, 1985), 115–23. See also his recent book, *The Antiheroine's Voice: Narrative Discourse and Transformations of the Picaresque* (Columbia: Univ. of Missouri Press, 1987).

19. Perry, "Deviant Insiders," 141.

20. Mary Douglas, *Purity and Danger: An Analysis of Concepts of Pollution and Taboo* (New York: Praeger, 1966), 162.

21. Perry, "Deviant Insiders," 141.

22. Ibid.

23. See Ann M. Pescatello, *Power and Pawn: The Female in Iberian Families, Societies, and Cultures* (Westport, Conn.: Greenwood, 1976), 21.

24. José Antonio Maravall, *El mundo social de "La Celestina"* (Madrid: Editorial Gredos, 1964), 71.

25. Alan Deyermond, "Divisiones socio-económicas, nexos sexuales: La sociedad de *Celestina*," *Celestinesca* 8 (1984): 8.

26. Delicado translates the island's name as "the couples," stating that he sends Lozana and Rampín there because it had previously served as a prison for dangerous criminals, who were sent there without mates (250). However, he may also have had in mind Boccaccio's *Decameron*, whose second story of the fifth day ends with its lovers reunited on the island.

27. See Umberto Gnoli, *Cortigiane Romane: Note e Bibliografia* (Arezzo: Edizioni della Rivista "Il Vasari," 1941), 11–14. Paul Larivaille confirms that Gnoli's estimated ratio is accurate, at least in the decades preceding the Counter-Reformation. *La vie quotidienne des courtisanes en Italie au temps de la Renaissance: Rome et Venise, XVe et XVIe siècles* (Paris: Librairie Hachette, 1975), 32.

28. For a different view which maintains the relevance of Lozana's Jewish heritage and the novel's realistic portrayal of prostitution, see Angus MacKay, "Averroístas y marginadas," *Actas del IIIer. Coloquio de Historia Medieval Andaluza: La Sociedad Medieval Andaluza, Grupos No Privilegiados* (Jaén, 1984), 247–61; and his unpublished article, "A Lost Generation: Francisco Delicado, Fernando del Pulgar, and the *Conversas* of Andalusia."

29. Hanrahan, *La mujer en la novela picaresca*, vol. 1, 85ff.

30. Bruno Damiani, *Francisco López de Ubeda* (Boston: Twayne, 1977), 135–49. Ubeda might also have read Aretino's *Ragionamenti*, acknowledged to have been influenced by the *Lozana andaluza*.

31. Marcel Bataillón, *Pícaros y picaresca: La pícara Justina* (Madrid: Taurus, 1969), 44ff.

32. Ibid., 125ff.

33. "Porque, así como la naturaleza . . . hizo a las mujeres para que encerradas guardasen la casa, así las obligó a que cerrasen la boca" [Because, as nature . . . determined that women should remain enclosed, guarding the home, so it required them to keep their mouth closed]. *La perfecta casada y poesías selectas*, ed. Florencia Grau (Barcelona: Obras Maestras, n.d.), 110.

34. See Bataillón, Ch. 10, "Los cristianos nuevos en el auge de la 'novela picaresca,' " 215–43.

The Empire's New Clothes: Refashioning the Renaissance

Marguerite Waller

I. An Observation

Recently, at the University of California, San Diego, where I had been visiting, two "new historicist" Renaissance scholars spoke on two successive days. The first day Stephen Orgel presented a masterfully detailed historical account of the instability of the Shakespearean text. The next day, Jonathan Goldberg gave an equally impressive, imaginatively structured and researched presentation concerning *Hamlet* and Renaissance handwriting. A third new historicist, Louis Montrose, was in the audience of both lectures. His elegant synthesis of theoretical and archival historicizing, "The Elizabethan Subject and the Spenserian Text," had just been published in the collection *Literary Theory/Renaissance Texts*.[1]

This confluence of scholars put me in a taxonomic mood. Each has been identified, and has identified himself, as a participant in a new group or school whose common theme, Montrose explains, is "its refusal of traditional distinctions between literature and history."[2] He goes on to say that this orientation is "new in resisting a traditional opposition of the privileged individual—whether an author or a work—to a world outside."[3] For a long time I had been puzzling over Stephen Greenblatt's *Renaissance Self-Fashioning: From More to Shakespeare*, the book often thought of as inaugurating this movement in Renaissance Studies.[4] I had found the book captivating and maddening. I would find myself assenting to the explicit politics of the "voice" of the book while disagreeing vehemently with the readings it presented of texts I knew well—Book 2 of Spenser's *Faerie Queene*, Shakespeare's *Othello*, and the sonnets of Sir Thomas Wyatt, to name the main ones. As it happened, I had already worked out my own close readings of two of the Wyatt sonnets Greenblatt discusses, and I could see in minute detail how my readings and his did not agree. I was already wondering, when I found myself in the same room with Orgel, Goldberg, and Montrose, why it was that although Greenblatt said he was interested in the same problems I was interested in—roughly, power, selfhood, and cultural imperialism—our results were so different. Finding myself in this distinguished company, each member of which, I might stress, has his own distinctive interests and modes of argumentation, I became aware that Greenblatt's and my particular missing of the minds might usefully be located within the larger frame of a comment on the new historicist project in general.

"History" is, of course, a tricky term, as Montrose fully acknowledges. It tends to answer only those questions that are asked of it, and it tends to assume the shape of the asker's desire.[5] It was gradually coming clear to me on that memorable afternoon in La Jolla that my desire is different from what I deduce to be the desire of the new historicists. To be blunt, their own discursive practices bespeak a desire for, an investment or belief in, the epistemology of authority. Their modes of historicizing may be loose, the historical materials they unearth may be off-beat, unsystematically selected, and playfully arranged, but the effect they are after is one of grounding. Orgel's point was the instability of the Shakespearean text, but his proof consisted largely of historical documents, read as if they escaped the textual problematics whose inescapability they were supposed to demonstrate. In this way, Orgel could argue, and even seem to agree with, a theoretical point without allowing his own discourse to fall prey to the consequences of that point. To indulge in a pop cultural comparison, this stance is a little like that of Star Trek's Captain Kirk, mapping the universe from the relative safety of his Federation star ship, making occasional forays into the unknown, but always secure in the knowledge that Scotty can beam him up if he encounters any truly intransigent *aporias*. Shakespeare's texts are left to suffer their instability alone. Literature is not opposed to or distinguished from history, it is true. But it tends to *become* history—not a new history in which the historian's position as knower is represented as being just as historical and textual as the material under scrutiny, but the old kind which delivers "knowledge"—be it pro- or anti-Establishment.

I have a harder time spatializing the stances of Goldberg and Montrose. Goldberg's talk about some of the material characteristics of Renaissance handwriting was a welcome extension of theoretical discussions of "écriture." His examples suggested that readability, in the sense of legibility, was not necessarily the first priority, or even a desired effect, in the play of calligraphic styles and genres to be found in the archives. Goldberg's performance implicitly denaturalized or "demythologized," to use Roland Barthes' term, all technologies of writing, doing for the materiality of writing something akin to what Derrida has done for the philosophical idea of writing. Montrose, meanwhile, has published a cogent critique of Greenblatt's treatment of Spenser, and has himself suggested that the "new historicism" has something of the academic fashion about it, conceding that "the theoretical and methodological assumptions, principles, and procedures of such a project have yet to be systematically articulated." [6]

There is a certain pathos, however, accompanying Montrose's theoretical statements about his own work and that of others. At one point he explains that to give themselves the sense that their own writing is "a mode of action" in "a system of higher education increasingly geared to the provision of highly specialized, technological, and preprofessional training," new historicist critics may justifiably indulge in a little "anti-reflectionism." Too much formal analysis may have led to a "nagging sense of professional, institutional, and political impotence." [7] You see what I mean about the desire for some kind of ground, the kind of ground that would legitimate the critic's authority in the context of a positivist setting? The trace of this desire for ground can also be seen in Goldberg's ingenious strategy of taking as his topic the material *base* of writing. Some threat is, momentarily at least, postponed. What is that threat? Montrose's candidate, as I have indicated, is what he calls "structuralist and poststructuralist formalisms." In "The Elizabethan Subject and the Spenserian Text," he writes: "Current invocations of History . . . seem to me at least in part a response to (or, in some cases, merely a reaction against) various structuralist and poststructuralist formalisms that have seemed, to some, to put into question the very possibility of historical understanding and historical experience." [8] But *whose* historical understanding and historical experience has theory put into question? I would ask. And how did those "understandings" and "experiences," or their written representations, come to be equated with "knowledge" in the educational establishment? What *kind* of history presents itself as a ground of or for stable meaning, and in doing so implicitly denies the possibility that the shape of *your* desire might not be the shape of *my* desire?

There are ways of living and writing historically in which the *aporias* of knowing do not present themselves as the occasion for pathos, or result in feelings of powerlessness, or, in any sense, suggest that history is inaccessible. As this volume and others testify, there is a second new development in Renaissance studies—a less magisterial, less "liberal" rewriting of early modern social, political, and literary practices.[9] This work not only starts from explicitly ideological positions, usually foregrounding class, or gender, or both, but also assumes that to be historical is to be in motion. The motive for going to the archives, a vexed question in both Montrose's and Jean Howard's discussions of the new historicism, is not to thicken the description or to broaden, in a simple Euclidian sense, the field of inquiry.[10] The motive, the desire, of this historical research is to demonstrate how our representations of the past *move,* how different they are depending upon what kinds of conceptual categories are or are not brought to bear on, what social categories are or are not included in, the analysis. Did women have a Renaissance?[11] How does a text by Rabelais exclude the feminine from the possibility of identity or presence?[12] The historian/critic shifts her own position (from excluded reader to dialogical writer) and enters a relationship, not *to,* but *in* a situation (so that the relationship becomes nonhierarchical— neither the past nor the present speaks for the other). In so doing she changes the situation itself (which becomes open, subject to still further change). Unlike the new historicists, she does *not* want the position from which she begins to be validated, and it would defeat the purpose of her performance if it were.

In short, the new historicism looks from here a lot like a flight, not only from theory, but also from the implications for historical thought of Marxism and feminism. Class- and gender-centered historiographies no less than deconstruction (and often with its help) are showing that the kind of knowledge for which new historicism seems to be nostalgic depends upon exclusivity, the privileged position of one class, race, or gender. The sense of powerlessness Montrose speaks of could be read as an accurate sign, not necessarily negative or unfortunate, that a political challenge to the discourses of intellectual authority is beginning to be felt. If the new historicists are indeed as concerned with the terrors of power as they say they are, they could use this occasion to see how they themselves have been shaped by the power/knowledge game which has for so long underwritten white, male privilege. Although no one wants to see him/her self as the class enemy, when reflection and analysis make us feel disenfranchised, we need to look at the conditions that allow us to feel entitled.

Let me emphasize that I do not mean to impugn the characters or the motives of any of the new historicists. But if, as it sometimes promises, this movement is to inaugurate a phase of politically oriented Renaissance scholarship, then the sooner its own ideological operations come under discussion, the better. The rest of this essay will focus on Stephen Greenblatt's book, *Renaissance Self-Fashioning*, the text which has catalyzed these reflections. In a counterreading of one of Greenblatt's selected texts, Sir Thomas Wyatt's sonnet "Whoso list to hunt," and its Petrarchan "model," "Una candida cerva" ("A white deer"), I will demonstrate how the selfhood Greenblatt has demarcated as his object of study—and, finally, as a kind of irreducible entity—leads to a symptomatic denigration and exclusion of woman. Greenblatt's text claims to be engaged in an analysis of upper-class English Renaissance male selfhood, critical of the ravages committed in the name of that selfhood, both privately—in the family—and publicly—in the New World, in Africa, and within British society itself. But in the heat of his readings, the critic more often simply identifies with that model of selfhood, romanticizing and reinscribing it within his own critical discourse. That is, his text repeatedly reinscribes as absolute the very concepts it also presents as rhetorical and political. The cognitive imperialism that it deplores, as I will illustrate, it also exercises. In doing so, I will also argue, Greenblatt's text becomes unselfconsciously sexist. It addresses a male audience whose empirical experience is called upon to ratify readings which are, in effect, heavily freighted ideologically. Essentially mimetic, these readings neglect the rhetorical operations of their texts— the rhetorical operations which underwrite both male and female selves.

As one consequence among several, the positions of certain key female figures are not attended to. He thereby misses what could be a central—perhaps the central—source of insight into the fashioning of the elitist male self.

II. A Homily

The appeal of the book for me, and I am sure for many Renaissance scholars, lies in its contextual information and emblematic anecdotes. The six chapters, discussing respectively Thomas More, William Tyndale, Thomas Wyatt, Book II of Spenser's *Faerie Queene*, Marlowe's *Tamburlaine*, and Shakespeare's *Othello*, are generally introduced by an historical vignette or some other extraliterary, usually historical, speculation which eloquently signals the literary critic's overt politics. The chapter on Marlowe, for example, opens with the chilling tale of a merchant fleet which sets in at Sierra Leone, where the English seamen, after admiring a finely built and well-organized native village, set fire to it. (The U.S. in the Third World?) The chapter on Wyatt brings alive the pathologies of Henry VIII's absolutist court. (Modern American corporate life?) The chapter on Shakespeare's *Othello* is set up in terms of a story about how the Spaniards tricked some Bahamian natives into going to work in the mines of Hispaniola by promising to take them to the paradise that the natives' indigenous religion promised them after death. Here Greenblatt's point is that the Spanish see Bahamian religion, though not their own, as a manipulable construct, and, further, that the compulsion of their own creed is only strengthened by their contemptuous exploitation of an analogous symbolic structure.

But over and over again the politically engaged historian fails to be similarly vigilant toward his own treatment of self and other. Consider the following passage from Greenblatt's commentary on Sir Thomas Wyatt's sonnet, "Whoso list to hunt":

> The drama of the lyric is the passage from Petrarch's vision of the world to Wyatt's or rather to the vision we ourselves constitute on the basis of the poet's deliberately allusive self-representation. Of course, the effect is diminished if we are unfamiliar with the source, but it is by no means entirely lost, for the reader is in any case implicated in the sonnet's essential activity, the

transformation of values. The poet twice addresses the reader as a potential hunter—"Whoso list to hunt," "Who list her hunt"—both inviting and dissuading *him,* making *him* reenact the poet's own drama of involvement and disillusionment. *We* share the passage from fascination to bitterness, longing to weariness, and we do more than share: we are forced to take responsibility as translators in our own right. It is *we,* after all, who refuse to take *noli me tangere* in a religious sense, *we* who understand Caesar not as God but as an all-too-human protector, we who hear—as Wyatt's contemporaries may have done—Anne Boleyn and Henry VIII where there is only talk of a hind and her hunters. It is as if a whole mystical visionary ethos gives way before our eyes and *under our pressure* [*sic*] to a corrupt and dangerous game of power (149, emphasis mine, except where otherwise indicated).

Greenblatt's text here treats the historically remote personae of Petrarch's and Wyatt's poems similarly to the way the Spanish are said to have treated the Bahamians. The sonnet enacts a transformation of values, he says; Wyatt's world is different from Petrarch's. But somehow here in our contemporary world of twentieth-century academic criticism, we are not so uncomfortably subject to relativism. We know who we are, and where we stand. "We" *know* when to refuse to read *noli me tangere* in a religious sense, "we" *know* Caesar for what he is, and "we" hear the *real* historical reference behind what appears to be only a remark about the nature of the relationship between aristocratic males and their ladies. This is the language of imperial history, not of cultural criticism. The essentializing rhetoric suggests that twentieth-century readers have achieved what previous ages lacked, a perspective beyond contingency from which texts and events can be known absolutely. This apotheosis of the present as a position of privileged knowledge coincides with a remarkable disregard for the differences and divisions between positions in our own society. Coinciding with the essentializing rhetoric of the passage, there seems to be an assumption that the owner of this absolutist twentieth-century perspective is both male and heterosexual. The pronoun "he," referring to the male reader implied by Wyatt's poem, is unselfconsciously elided with a "we," referring to Greenblatt and his readers, who are decidedly not generically human, but stereotypically male: "The poet twice addresses the reader as a potential hunter— 'Whoso list to hunt,' 'Who list her hunt'—both inviting and dissuading *him,* making *him* reenact the poet's own drama of involvement and disillusionment. *We* share the passage from fascination to bitterness" (emphasis mine). In other words, Greenblatt's text not only exploits the Wyatt poem to enhance its own authority, but, in the bargain, obliterates the position of the female (or nonheterosexual male) reader. The two gestures, in fact, go together. The liberal guilt which Greenblatt so graciously wishes to share with his reader ("*we* are forced to take responsibility as translators in our own right") does not undo the act of usurpation and colonization being perpetrated either on Wyatt's text or on the reader who does not identify with the thrills and disillusionments of the male traffic in women. On the contrary, the expression of guilt is one more indication that the critic wants his own position to be regarded as "natural," as politically and epistemologically beyond question. (One feels guilty about that which one assumes one knows and controls.) To put the case conversely, Greenblatt's own rhetoric of critical mastery effectively delegitimates both the past in relation to the present and the female in relation to the male.

The strange mixture of insight and blindness Greenblatt so usefully identifies in the Spaniards' behavior toward the Bahamians shows up in modern dress throughout this book. It was difficult for me, on a first reading, to know whether to credit the one or the other. The passage I have quoted is more obviously objectionable than most of the text. The description of the Spaniards, on the other hand, is so astute and impassioned that one can hardly believe that the critic fails to grasp its application to himself—except, of course, there is Greenblatt's own illuminating example of the Spaniards to help us. I have finally decided that the issue lies in Greenblatt's disinclination to contextualize and relativize—to consider as an ideological construct—the critical ground from which he is operating. No matter how much he "knows" discursively about the ungroundedness of the "self-fashioner," this knowledge remains compartmentalized, powerless to change the way he reads and writes—powerless, that is, to open up alternative conceptual fields in which the burdens and compulsions of one notion of selfhood could present themselves differently. To demonstrate what I mean, I will offer an alternative reading to one of the texts dealt with by Greenblatt—Wyatt's sonnet "Whoso list to hunt." The differences between our readings, and the difference this makes in how these texts respond to the questions I share with Greenblatt about a model of male selfhood which is still with us, should show, not how much more disinterested my interpretive position is, but, on the contrary, what different literary histories can be generated from different sociological and ideological positions.

III. H(e)arts and Hinds:
Two Portraits of Male Desire

> My sympathy deserts my own sex: I feel how very disagreeable it must be for a woman to have a lover like Wyatt. But I *know* this reaction to be unjust; it comes from using the songs as they were not meant to be used.—C. S. Lewis (*English Literature in the Sixteenth Century Excluding Drama*, 229, emphasis mine)

> Whoso list to hount, I knowe where is an hynde,
>   But as for me, helas, I may no more:
>   The vayne travaill hath weried me so sore.
>   I ame of theim that farthest commeth behinde;
> Yet may I by no meanes my weried mynde
>   Drawe from the Diere: but as she fleeth afore,
> Faynting I folowe. I leve of therefore,
>   Sins in a nett I seke to hold the wynde.
> Who list her hount, I put him owte of dowbte,
>   As well as I may spend his tyme in vain:
>   And, graven with Diamonds, in letters plain
> There is written her faier neck rounde abowte:
>   *Noli me tangere,* for Cesars I ame;
>   And wylde for to hold, though I seme tame.[13]

From the arguably nonexemplary position of a female reader and teacher of Renaissance literature, Sir Thomas Wyatt's sonnet "Whoso list to hount, I knowe where is an hind" inscribes a very obvious absence. This absence is *so* obvious that when it is missed, or unselfconsciously repeated, I suspect that a nontrivial ideological operation is taking place. This textual effect, which is often repeated but rarely "seen" in the criticism of the poem over the last forty years, is none other than the denial of the position of any reader who is not male, heterosexual, and politically privileged.[14] Or rather, if a position cannot be denied which was never implied, then a great many readers of this poem, be they sixteenth-century aristocratic or twentieth-century American women, contemplate an image of their own nonidentity or noncoincidence with themselves when they try to read themselves as readers of this poem.[15] In the very act of trying to come into "being" as a reading self, a woman comes face to face with a kind of "nonbeing" when she tries to read herself in the story of the hunter/readers identified definitely and exclusively as male in lines 9 and 10 (emphasis mine):

> Who list her hount, I put *him* owte of dowbte,
>   As well as I may spend *his* tyme in vain.

The quotation with which the poem closes goes even further. This text, which at least thematically provides the ground or occasion for the lines that precede it, not only masculinizes the place of the reader, but also actively usurps the place of woman as speaker or writer, as producer of language, especially in its odd appropriation of the first person singular pronoun "I":

> And, graven with Diamonds, in letters plain
> There is written her faier neck rounde abowte:
>   *Noli me tangere*, for Cesars I ame;
> And wylde for to hold, though I seme tame.

Though the lines in quotation marks are presented as inscribed by a male hand, and addressed to readers who are male, this unseen authorial hand—that of a Caesar who evidently wields considerable political and linguistic as well as sexual power—exploits the inevitability with which the shifter "I" refers to or suggests a speaking subject. The quotation thus implies the presence of a female self different and distinct from the male writer. The illusion generated by the poem, of a female speaker or writer describing herself, is, however, patently an effect of this male writing—a writing which, furthermore, would not even be visible to, let alone readable by, the figure it would appear, or attempt, to identify.

The question of how a female reader, or a feminist reader of any sex, might read a text that denies woman any place—whether that of reader, speaker, or writer—in its discourse draws me next to the relationship between the lines within quotation marks and the rest of the sonnet. The scandalously usurptive, proprietary "Caesar" named in these lines might make the male poet, to be inferred from earlier uses of the pronoun "I," look good by comparison, despite the poet's displacement of woman as reader. But the illusion that there are two male figures here, and two texts, is itself a function of the same kind of gesture—really the same gesture—whereby a female subject was somewhat clumsily and ineffectually implied. More subtly, and conspicuously so, the poet's portrayal of himself as a reader of another man's text performs the same power play we see within the quotation. The subjectivity of an other is suggested by the image of a text authored by that other, while, in fact, that textual image is constituted in and by the text of the sonnet. What "Caesar" is made to do clumsily, the sonneteer appears to do exceedingly well, beating this ventriloquist's dummy of a Caesar at his own game.

The difference between this reading of Wyatt's Caesar and Greenblatt's reading provides a good illustration of the difference between reading rhetorically and reading mimetically or thematically. Greenblatt's Caesar is far more substantial than mine. He is treated, in fact, as if he, not the poet, were the poem's originary figure. "The poet's inner life," Greenblatt comments, ". . . is shaped by the relation of Caesar and the object of desire" (150). Up to a point the thematic relationship between poet and Caesar seems, in fact, to be the inverse of what it is rhetorically. The sonneteer portrays Caesar as a powerful owner and protector of property, and the producer and inscriber of an ineradicable writing, while he presents himself as nearly impotent, his only capabilities (not unlike those of a literary critic) being to read and to quote. From the poet's thematically-stated position it is, of course, possible to ironize the figure of Caesar, and this he does with a vengeance, as I shall show in a moment. But in so directing the forces of irony against "Caesar," the poet also reinscribes the hierarchy in which Caesar appears powerfully central while he, the poet, seems at first marginal and weak.

The means by which the (apparent) centrality of the figure of Caesar, though not the structure of centrism itself, is subverted by the lines in quotation marks may be described in any number of ways. One of the most economical would be to comment on the act or concept of quotation itself. Within the lines set off by quotation marks there is a citation from the Vulgate Bible which graphically (or typographically) as well as rhetorically suggests the impossibility of owning the medium—writing—in which Caesar's proprietary claim is made. The phrase that reads "Do not touch me" is neither untouchable nor sacred, although it has been used before in a sacred context. It occurs in John 20:17, where the risen Christ says to Mary Magdalene, "Noli me tangere, nondum enim ascendi ad Patrem meum" [Do not touch me, for I have not yet ascended to my Father].[16] The phrase has also been used by Wyatt's Caesar, whose use of the phrase to characterize the hind is an aspect of his own characterization by the poet. The poem, through its presentation of Caesar's appropriation of the words of the biblical Christ, arguably suggests that language belongs at once to no one and to everyone (provided that the everyone is male), implying that any sense of mastery coming from, mediated by, or directed toward language must be illusory. One may possess the power to place the *Noli me tangere* sign on a woman, but this will not prevent potential rivals from reading this sign as an allegory of its own highly contingent status, its dependence upon context, its lack of transcendental meaning. Similarly, the very fact that the poet (he claims) has succeeded in coming close enough to the deer to read the words on her collar might suggest that Caesar's power is not nearly as far-reaching and complete as the tone and deployment of his discourse might otherwise imply.

As for the thematic ironies which interpreters may discern in the poem's evocations of biblical and also Petrarchan contexts, no one critic could foresee and describe all of them. I will, nevertheless, play with a few. In John's Gospel, Christ says *"Noli me tangere"* not to signify that he is the private property of God and therefore not available or accessible to Mary Magdalene, but to warn her that his situation is one of ambiguity and transience. He is neither of this world nor of the next, at this point, but appears as a kind of afterimage of his historical incarnation—beyond history, but not yet beyond the problematics of signification. He is still subject to misappropriation and misunderstanding, as Mary's mistaking him at first for the gardener testifies. If the situation of Caesar's deer in Wyatt's poem shares any of these characteristics, Caesar betrays his own cause by calling the world's attention to them. Though he may think that he is claiming only that the status of his lady is not what it appears to be to her would-be hunters, his terms unleash questions about the transient and ambiguous status of any figure of the self—even, or especially, a theologically grounded one. The very possibility of ownership and private property in terms of which Caesar describes his relationship to his lady might seem, with reference to the Biblical text, illusory. The echo in "for Caesar's I am" of Matthew 22: 21—"Render therefore to Caesar the things that are Caesar's, and to God the things that are

God's"—intensifies the irony of Caesar's proprietary claims.[17] In this second biblical passage, the Pharisees, hoping to entrap Jesus into either defying Roman law or selling out Hebrew society, ask him whether it is lawful to pay taxes to Caesar. Christ takes a coin and asks, "Whose likeness and inscription is this?" In other words, he asks his interlocutors to see the coin as an icon of Caesar's political and economic (but not spiritual) centrality rather than as an index of private wealth. Disrupting his antagonists' logic, he calls attention to the public, political structure underwriting what was being presented as private property so that the latter virtually disappears as an operable category. By so problematizing the system of reference and meaning upon which the circulation of money depends, he displaces money as measure or mediator of what the self has or is.[18] If, then, the lady in Wyatt's poem resembles this coin, as her inscribed collar suggests she does, she may be read as connoting the contingency of Caesar's wealth and power, not to mention the coercive, but less than absolute, imperialistic, perhaps illegitimate political structure which underwrites that position. The image of the coin may also bring with it the suggestion that the lady has been in circulation—thus, in a different way, undermining Caesar's claim.

Two more points. As most commentators including Greenblatt mention, the poem is probably making reference to the relationship of Henry VIII to Anne Boleyn, Anne having probably been a lover of Wyatt's. If so, then the conflation of Christ's and Caesar's words in lines 11 and 12 may also allude to Henry's making himself the head of the English Church when the Pope refused him the divorce he needed to marry Anne. One more implication set in motion by Wyatt's Caesar's garbling of Scripture would then be that Henry's conflation of church and state amounts to a cynical and unconvincing usurpation. Yet another echo for the Renaissance reader might have been Plutarch's account of Julius Caesar's divorce from his wife Pompeia. She was rumored to have committed adultery, and though she was proved innocent, Caesar divorced her anyway, saying that Caesar's wife must be above suspicion. This echo registers the political irrelevance of the ambiguity between wildness or tameness in the Wyatt sonnet. Whether the female figure appears wild or tame, "free" or domesticated, her status depends upon the will of Caesar.

But before we become lost in admiration for the number and variety of

ways in which this sonnet gets the better of the big, bad authority figure
through what Greenblatt terms its "immense power of implication," let
us recall, as I noted earlier, that this is fake combat. Wyatt's Caesar is
as much Wyatt's creation as Wyatt's Caesar's lady. We could also note
that the central conceit of the poem—the hunt—still casts the poet in
the role of aristocratic hunter and the beloved in the role of an animal to
be hunted. As Helmut Bonheim has observed, the sonnet conveys the
impression that certain members of the society in question "have a license to approach such game as the hind, whereas others lower down on
the social ladder have none," and, further, "that women are there to be
hunted or possessed." Both points, the poet's superior social status and
the inferior status of the woman, are "matters which the poet seems to
accept rather than grumble about." [19] Thirdly, and for me the most subtle
and disturbing symptom of the ideological operation being performed in
this sonnet, is the matter of the displaced woman reader.

Before showing that the poet's pursuit of the woman is no less fake
than the apparent competition with "Caesar," let me make a detour to
Wyatt's Italian model, the sonnet from Petrarch's *Canzoniere* which begins "Una candida cerva." Greenblatt, too, refers his reading of Wyatt
to Petrarch's poem, but he treats Petrarch's project (very cursorily) as
mimetically as he does Wyatt's. "Petrarch depicts an experience of illu-
mination and loss" (146). I have argued at length elsewhere, however,
that Petrarch's highly formal poetics resists any kind of narrative reading
other than that of the story of its own writing.[20] Petrarch's persona, as
I read "him," is a self-proclaimed descendent of Ovid's Narcissus. He
alternately displays and acknowledges the illusoriness of the kind of self
that would be needed to ground the signifying processes which make
the self "knowable"—the illusoriness, that is, of the operative model
of selfhood that Greenblatt most often takes for granted. The figure of
the self as an autonomous, self-identical, ontologically grounded being
who knows what he sees and knows how he feels about it disintegrates
again and again in the Petrarchan text, shown repeatedly to be as much
an effect as a cause of its own reading and writing. Sonnet 190, "Una
candida cerva," provides a good example.

> Una candida cerva sopra l'erba
> verde m'apparve, con duo corna d'oro,

fra due riviere, all'ombra d'un alloro,
levando 'l sole a la stagione acerba.

Era sua vista sìdolce superba,
ch'i' lasciai per seguirla ogni lavoro:
come l'avaro che 'n cercar tesoro
con diletto l'affanno disacerba.

"Nessun mi tocchi—al bel collo d'intorno
scritto avea di diamanti et di topazi—:
libera farmi al mio Cesare parve."

Et era 'l sol già vòlto al mezzo giorno,
gli occhi miei stanchi di mirar, non sazi,
quand'io caddi ne l'acqua, et ella sparve.[21]

From the outset the poem suggests that the figure of the deer is just that—a *figure* (not a "mystical vision," as Greenblatt describes it) that *appears* as a function of the configuration of two bodies of water, the shade of a laurel, and the lover's position in that particular landscape. By the end of the poem this figure has become so clearly a Narcissistic projection that when the sun reaches its zenith and the lover must lean out over the water to keep the image in view, he falls in, and the image disappears. Building up to this implosion of self and other are a number of rigorously conceived details which further elaborate the connection between the figurative status of the image of the beloved and the status of the self. The lover's desire, the given of the poem, defines him as a self that is wanting or lacking in some way. A self who desires, any self who acknowledges himself as a sexual being, cannot, strictly speaking, escape a fundamental instability. Such a self cannot "know" itself and the world in the totalizing way that Greenblatt so often assumes in his commentary because its own partiality implies, by definition, that there are other positions different from its own. As the French feminists have put it, all positions, all "selves," are equally "castrated."[22] Only an imbalance in political power between the two sexes has arbitrarily designated the "phallus," or the male position as the locus of truth, the site of a self-identical presence existing outside the relational play of difference. Woman in this schema, then, becomes not an "other" signifying the mutual otherness of male and female alike, but *the* "other," the castrated one, existing in a hierarchical relationship vis-à-vis the male. This denial of relational difference, as feminists have further noted, requires that woman be treated not as herself a desiring being, but as an object. If she is fetishized as a possessable thing, her difference from the male can be, at least momentarily, neutralized as a source of "castration anxiety."[23] The male's confrontation with the originary "otherness" that constitutes his position is thereby forestalled.

So is his confrontation with the figural, diacritically related status of both positions. This is the strategy that comes under scrutiny in the second quatrain of the sonnet, where the lover compares himself to a miser. The puzzling reference to a pleasure which "disembitters" ("disacerba") the travail of the pursuit of the object signals the paradox of this mode of channeling desire, namely, that the object must never be fully obtained or the ruse will be revealed. It is the pleasure of the pursuit, the pleasure of feeling oneself always about to be completed, that matters. For the miser, as for the Narcissistic lover, actually possessing or coinciding with the image of desire, be that image money or woman, would block the self-transcendence which is being sought. The self that projects its own ontological lack as an objective, external object will not be any less lacking if or when that particular objectification of desire is obtained.

The writing encircling the neck of Petrarch's doe in the third quatrain acknowledges this paradox as concisely as Narcissus's lament, "Plenty makes me poor."[24] Although the words, "Let no one touch me. It has pleased my Caesar to make me free," are neither written nor read by the beloved, they are also not appropriative. They say that no one does or shall own her. Here are no rivals and no competing hunters, collaborating in the illusion that there is some external obstacle to the lover's desire. Instead, this writing within the writing of the poem suggests the incommensurability of the lover's desire and its object. What he wants he cannot have, not because of some circumstantial prohibition, but because it does not exist in the form in which he conceives it. Specifically, it is his writing which is problematic. The "shade of the laurel" within which, in the first stanza, this internal drama is said to take place (the phrase "all'ombra d'un alloro" ambiguously modifying either the position of the deer or the position of the lover, or both the one and the other) is the shadow cast by the poet's language, as Petrarch's multiple puns throughout the *Canzoniere* on the laurel as poetry and the laurel as the beloved make clear. Like the pool within which Narcissus sees the reflection which allows him at first to see what he takes to be the object of his desire, then to see "himself" (but a self which is constituted by that reflection), the lover's writing is the only ground of the images of both self and other at play in this poem. They are both equally figural, and there is no way, as the use of quotation marks around the words which are around the neck of the figural deer emblematizes, to get from the figural stratum within which such a desire could be conceived to a literal stratum within which it could be satisfied. There can only be figures within figures, writing upon writing that, beautiful and informative as they may be, ultimately resist the efforts of the self (itself a figural creature) to fix or break through to a stable, literal reality. The "I" referred to in the last line of the poem—"quand'io caddi ne l'acqua et ella sparve"—can only "fall" into the water (water having been established in the *Canzoniere* cycle as another of Petrarch's metaphors for writing). He does not attain sovereign selfhood (which requires the illusion of the literal), but allows the unraveling process inaugurated by the investigation of the status of one image, a male image of woman, to engulf the image of the male self as well.

Not coincidentally, the poem does not exclude the female reader. Or rather it excludes all readers—all readers who would try to read themselves as stable beings in relation to a stable, unproblematically referential text. Here the male lover/reader joins woman in that unread and unreadable limbo I claimed she was consigned to by the critic's disinclination to put his own signifying practices into question. However uncomfortable within the context of Western thought this limbo may be (and some readers have been made very uncomfortable by what they take to be Petrarch's "lack of assurance" or "volatility"[25]), this (non)position has the advantage of making other, more "ordinary" discourses appear less than self-evident. Their ideological workings, in other words, become more accessible to analysis. And, to paraphrase a contemporary theoretician of ideology, when we are summoned by the persistence of sexual, class, and racial oppression, we need all the analytical help we can get.[26]

The relatively simple point I want to make about Wyatt's sonnet is that, though it deploys a very similar unraveling process against "Caesar" (as we have seen), it stops short of implicating the poetic subject, the "lover," in the indeterminacy of language. And the figure that operates rhetorically to insure the integrity of the male self is woman, defined as a nonhuman, nonself. Let me recapitulate. Greenblatt, as I have indicated, reads the poem mimetically, that is, as if it were descriptive rather than constitutive of a rhetorical situation. Although he claims to be concerned with the interrelationship of rhetoric and power, he does not look to the poem as an instance of rhetorical power playing, but as a record of the results of a preexisting power play—that of Caesar. The poet's position, he assumes, is what it is from the start of the poem and works itself out as a frustrated, but rich and interesting, suspension between a realistic rendering of individuality and the necessities of diplomacy, between "transcendentalism and cynicism" (146). The poet's political and sexual alternatives then appear to be either domination and possession or disengagement. Or when these two possibilities lead to an impasse, the goal becomes to attempt at least "a clear statement of its (the hunt's) hopelessness, its 'vanity' " (147).

But these are not at all the goals and achievements of this poem's rhetorical strategizing. If it is read, not as a "*witness* to his (the poet's) continued obsession even as it *records* the attempt to disengage himself from it," (147, emphasis mine), but as a performative gesture in its own right, then the plot and its outcome are very different. Both the shadowboxing with "Caesar" and the pursuit of the female figure work instead to create a male persona whose status over the course of the poem becomes more, rather than less, secure. The fetishized figure of woman is the linchpin of this rhetorical operation. Because the beloved is defined as a nonhuman, nonself who, at least potentially, can belong to someone, and because this fetishized figure of woman does not disappear by the end of the poem, the male self, which logically should have succumbed to the same ironization to which Caesar is subjected, remains intact. Or, to put the case more fully, the poem sets up a three-way situation involving the lover's relationship to a figure of absolute power, his relationship to male rivals of his own station, and his relationship to a female figure defined as an object. This situation, far from being problematic for the sovereign male self, includes precisely the elements necessary to the emergence of such a self.[27] Here is how the poem, as a "self"-producing artifact, works.

The king, Caesar, is set up as the chief obstacle to the poet's appropriation of the image of his desire. The would-be lover "knows" where to find the "hind," but cannot capture her because another man, whose power is greater than his own, has prohibited it. The poet and the hunters, meanwhile, through their competition with the king for the power to "own" the image of sexual desire, serve as obstacles to the king's full possession of the authority which seems to block their way. In this curious round-robin of power and sex, the status, ontological as well as political, of all the male figures is heightened and reinforced. The hunters will hunt happily in vain, neither giving up nor succeeding in the hunt, deriving their status as contenders for sovereign selfhood from the status of the man who seems to stand in their way. Meanwhile, the king's claim to sovereignty will remain happily at risk as long as he has sexual and political rivals. In short, all the male figures are put in the best of all possible positions for maintaining the illusion of the stable, sovereign subject—that of having the image of desire within sight, but just out of reach or made slightly insecure, due to some external obstacle.

Note that the Wyatt persona is, therefore, dependent for its very existence upon what Greenblatt terms the poem's "impasse." This kind of self can emerge at all only by neither succeeding nor leaving off the pursuit. Furthermore, this self depends upon *maintaining* the power structure of absolutism. Relative positions within the structure may be at stake, but never the structure itself. "Caesar" may be superficially ironized, but never done away with. In fact, the very brilliance of Wyatt's lover's challenge serves to enhance the prestige of the figure who evokes it.

The political economy of sovereign male selfhood is equally dependent upon reducing woman to the status of an object. Without the fetishized female, the political economy of sovereign male selfhood would fall apart. Without this reduction of woman, politics and ideology threaten to invade the self. Not just positions within a structure, but the structure which underwrites those positions would come into question. This means, of course, that the woman who makes the competitive male relationship, and hence the sovereign self, possible, is herself placed in a highly unstable, highly unflattering, perilous and powerless double bind. She is structurally required, only to be denied and despised, abused for her role in a dynamic not of her own choosing and out of which she stands to gain nothing. As Wyatt's address to an all-male readership implies, she is effectively banished from the company of selves. As his metaphor of the hunt underscores, she comes to be articulated as rightful prey for the fierce, insatiable appetites built into self-fashioning.

This reading of the poem hardly compels me to "share" or to "take responsibility for" the pathos of the Wyatt persona. What seems to me important about the poem is the brilliance with which it either masks or reveals (depending upon whether one reads it narratively or rhetorically) the interdependence of sovereign selfhood, a highly centralized, hierarchical, nondemocratic political structure, and misogyny. It is not just the conscious politics carried out by Greenblatt's "self-fashioners" but the political conditions necessary for the emergence and perpetuation of such a model of selfhood that readers need to attend to if the sins of the fathers are not to be visited upon their daughters and sons. When, instead, "the lady vanishes" as a subject from the text of the critic as well as from the text of the Renaissance writer, the critical text becomes complicit with the forces of absolutism and sexism whose sixteenth-century effects it deplores.

NOTES

My thanks to Robert Doran, Jim Rothenberg, and especially Andrew Szegedy-Maszak for their timely editorial, scholarly, and electronic contributions to this project.

1. Louis Adrian Montrose, "The Elizabethan Subject and the Spenserian Text," *Literary Theory/Renaissance Texts*, ed. Patricia Parker and David Quint (Baltimore and London: Johns Hopkins Univ. Press, 1986), 303–40.

2. Though other critics and I include Jonathan Goldberg among the "new historicists," I am also aware of the gravitation of his work toward a certain theoretical vocabulary, or I should say, vocabularies. One problem with his 1986 book, *Voice Terminal Echo: Postmodernism and English Renaissance Texts* (New York: Methuen), is its lack of differentiation among such disparate and incompatible academic figures as Jacques Derrida, Stephen Greenblatt, Thomas Greene, Geoffrey Hartman, and Emile Benveniste. In addition, theoretical points are taken to be quite portable, as if they did not have everything to do with the specificity of their staging. One of the readers' reports from the University of Tennessee Press suggests that in a forthcoming essay on *Macbeth* Goldberg "seems much more an (apolitical) orthodox Derridean deconstructionist than a 'new historicist.' " I cannot speak to the *Macbeth* article, not having read it, but in my lexicon "orthodox deconstruction" is an oxymoron, and the apolitical

Derrida an Anglo-American invention. Based on the work I do know, my sense is that Goldberg's theoretical interests are subordinate to a desire to generate and participate in a discourse of "knowledge," not compatible with Derrida's project.

Edward Pechter also refers to Goldberg as a new historicist in his article "The New Historicism and Its Discontents: Politicizing Renaissance Drama," *PMLA* 102, no. 3 (May 1987): 292. Pechter and I otherwise disagree. He criticizes new historicism as a version of Marxism; I am interested by instances in which some form of history writing works conservatively, against the grain of Marxist and/ or feminist analysis.

Jean E. Howard also refers to Goldberg as a new historicist. See her review, "Old Wine, New Bottles," *Shakespeare Quarterly* 35, no. 2 (1984): 236, and her article "The New Historicism in Renaissance Studies," *English Literary Renaissance* 16, no. 1 (Winter 1986): 13, where she also includes the work of Stephen Orgel under the new historicist rubric. Goldberg has, of course, written his own account of new historicism: "The Politics of Renaissance Literature: A Review Essay," *ELH* 49 (1982): 514–42.

As I hope the anecdotal informality of my opening signals, however, taxonomy is not fundamental to my argument about discourse and desire.

3. Montrose, 304. For an elaboration of the theoretical argument in this article see his "Renaissance Literary Studies and the Subject of History," *English Literary Renaissance* 16, no. 1 (Winter 1986): 5–12.

4. Stephen Greenblatt, *Renaissance Self-Fashioning: From More to Shakespeare* (Chicago and London: Univ. of Chicago Press, 1980). Quotations from this volume will be cited by page number.

5. Montrose, in "The Elizabethan Subject and the Spenserian Text," warns that "History," like "Power," is a term "now in constant danger of hypostatization" (304). Jean E. Howard, whose excellent discussion of the new historicism is less explicitly feminist than mine, writes that "when a new historian looks at the past he or she is as likely as an old historian to see an image of the seeing self, not an image of the other" (16). I have substituted "desire" for "the seeing self," but I think we both have Narcissus on our minds. See Howard, "The New Historicism in Renaissance Studies," *English Literary Renaissance* 16, no. 1 (Winter 1986): 13–43.

6. Montrose, "The Elizabethan Subject and the Spenserian Text," 304.

7. Ibid., 332.

8. Ibid., 304.

9. See especially *Rewriting the Renaissance: The Discourses of Sexual Difference in Early Modern Europe*, ed. Margaret Ferguson, Maureen Quilligan, and Nancy Vickers (Chicago and London: Univ. of Chicago Press, 1986) which, incidentally, includes essays by Goldberg, Orgel, and Montrose. Also the recent work of British and American Marxists, including Jonathan Dollimore, *Radical Tragedy: Religion, Ideology and Power in the Drama of Shakespeare and his Contemporaries* (Chicago and London: Univ. of Chicago Press, 1984) and *Political*

Shakespeare: New Essays in Cultural Materialism, ed. Jonathan Dollimore and Alan Sinfield (Ithaca, N. Y., Cornell Univ. Press, 1985).

10. Howard, 26 and 31.

11. I am referring of course to Joan Kelly-Gadol's article by that name in *Becoming Visible: Women in European History*, ed. Renate Bridenthal and Claudia Koonz (Boston: Houghton Mifflin, 1977).

12. See Carla Freccero's "The Other and the Same: The Image of the Hermaphrodite in Rabelais," in *Rewriting the Renaissance*.

13. This version of Wyatt's sonnet is taken from *Collected Poems of Sir Thomas Wyatt*, ed. K. Muir (Cambridge, Mass.: Harvard Univ. Press, 1950). The modernized version Greenblatt quotes is not identified.

14. See, for example, Raymond Southall, *The Courtly Maker: An Essay on the Poetry of Wyatt and his Contemporaries* (Oxford: Basil Blackwell, 1964), who not only leaves out of account the poem's exclusion of the female reader, but has harsh words for Patricia Thomson's article, "Wyatt and the Petrarchan Commentators," *Review of English Studies* 10, no. 39 (Aug. 1959), which, though equally impressionistic, characterizes the poem's sentiment as "arrogant and cynical" (225). For Southall, the poem represents an advance over Petrarch's poetics toward "a firm grip on reality" (90). In other words, like Greenblatt's reading, his naturalizes Wyatt's rhetoric. Thomson's does the same, universalizing her reactions without taking into consideration her own position as a female critic, but the sharp differences in their reactions to Wyatt's persona are suggestive of the importance of gender and other aspects of social position in reading regardless of the reader's own theoretical and political orientation. For Southall's discussion of "Whoso list to hunt," see 86–91. See also his discussion of the sonnet in *Literature and the Rise of Capitalism: Critical Essays mainly on the Sixteenth and Seventeenth Centuries* (London: Lawrence and Wishart, 1973), 22–36. C. S. Lewis, with his customary acuity, feels that there is something "oppressive" and "suffocating" about Wyatt's address to women, but explains away his feeling with an argument about the use of the poems as songs to be "sung in a room with many ladies present." He apparently considers the court women fully capable of defending themselves against the aggression of Wyatt's sonnets in the dramatic situation of a live performance, a presumption not borne out by recent social histories of the period. See *English Literature in the Sixteenth Century Excluding Drama* (Oxford: Clarendon Press, 1954), 229–30. Thomas Greene in *The Light in Troy: Imitation and Discovery in Renaissance Poetry* (New Haven and London: Yale Univ. Press, 1982) speaks of the poem only briefly but includes a comment about its "refusal of illusions about the woman" (262), again naturalizing the poem's sexual politics. Only the non–Anglo-American critic Helmut Bonheim, who mentions having been made more politically aware by his students in the sixties, notes what he calls the "sociological relevance" of the poem. See my discussion of his conclusions below, p. 173. "Notes on a Sonnet by Sir Thomas Wyatt," *Literatur im Wissenschaft* 5 (1972).

15. Other Renaissance scholars have begun noting other canonical texts (and

their canonical readings) that speak the exclusion of the feminine subject. Carla Freccero's work (see note 12 above) parallels in many ways my work with Wyatt.

16. All citations from Scripture are quoted from the Vulgate Bible. The edition used here is the Biblia Sacra, Vulgatam Clementinam, ed. Alberto Colunga and Laurentio Turrado (Salmantica: Biblioteca de Autores Cristianos, 1959). Passages are identified by book, chapter, and verse. The Latin text of John 20: 15–17 reads, "Dicit ei Iesus: Mulier, quid ploras? quem quaeris? Illa existimans quia hortulanus esset, dicit ei: Domine, si tu sustulisti eum, dicito mihi ubi posuisti eum; et ego eum tollam. Dicit ei Iesus: Maria. Conversa illa, dicit ei: Rabboni (quod dicitur Magister). Dicit ei Iesus: Noli me tangere, nondum enim ascendi ad Patrem meum."

17. Ibid. The Latin text reads, "Reddite ergo quae sunt Caesaris, Caesari: et quae sunt Dei, Deo."

18. Modern scholars have, in fact, stressed that the phrase from John is the present imperative ("Do not cling to me"). See R. Brown, *The Gospel of John* (Garden City, N. Y. : Doubleday, 1970), 1011–15, which argues that the reply of Jesus is to show that He has not come back the same; His presence from now on will be in a different mode, via the Spirit.

There is a range of opinion on the Matthew passage. Some hold that it means one should obey Caesar and obey God. Others maintain that the saying is a witty evasion, which satisfies for the moment but on reflection can mean whatever one wants it to. A full discussion is found in F. F. Bruce, "Render to Caesar" in *Jesus and the Politics of His Day*, ed. E. Bammel and C. F. D. Moule (Cambridge: Cambridge Univ. Press, 1984), 249–63. The coin *is* generally seen as representative of the socioeconomic power of Rome, but possibly of its religious power as well.

My readings of both passages are my own. The poem seems to me to provoke, rather than to limit or try to regulate, such strong, not necessarily orthodox, readings. This provocation, I am arguing, is part of the poem's seduction. Irreverence can be, ultimately, if properly staged, fuel for sovereign selfhood.

19. Bonheim, 2.

20. See my *Petrarch's Poetics and Literary History* (Amherst, Mass.: Univ. of Massachusetts Press, 1980), especially the chapter on the *Canzoniere*, 27–104.

21. Quoted from *Canzoniere*, critical text and introduction by Gianfranco Contini and annotations by Daniele Ponchiroli (Turin: Einaudi, 1968). The following English translation is that of Robert M. Durling in *Petrarch's Lyric Poems* (Cambridge, Mass.: Harvard Univ. Press, 1976), 336.

A white doe on the green grass appeared to me, with two golden horns, between two rivers, in the shade of a laurel, when the sun was rising in the unripe season.

Her look was so sweet and proud that to follow her I left every task, like the miser who as he seeks treasure sweetens his trouble with delight.

"Let no one touch me," she bore written with diamonds and topazes around her lovely neck. "It has pleased my Caesar to make me free."

And the sun had already turned at midday; my eyes were tired by looking but not sated, when I fell into the water, and she disappeared.

22. I am thinking of the feminist students of Jacques Lacan and their use of his theory of castration; they include Hélène Cixous and Luce Irigaray especially. See also Shoshana Felman's commentary on Luce Irigaray in "Women and Madness: The Critical Phallacy," *Diacritics* 5, no. 4 (Winter 1975): 2–10.

23. This is an expansion of the French feminist discussion of castration as it has been applied to classic American cinema by Laura Mulvey in "Visual Pleasure and Narrative Cinema," *Screen* 16, no. 3 (Autumn 1975): 13–14.

24. Publius Ovidius Naso, *Metamorphoses*, vol. 1 (Cambridge: Harvard Univ. Press, 1971), bk. 3, l. 466. The Latin reads, "inopem me copia fecit."

25. Greene, 101 and 100, respectively.

26. Andrew Parker, "Futures for Marxism: An Appreciation of Althusser," *Diacritics* 15, no. 4 (Winter 1985), 71.

27. For a much fuller discussion of how individuals negotiate with their societies for empowerment through the play of desire and identification, see Eve Kosofsky Sedgwick's brilliant argument and extensive literary analyses in *Between Men: English Literature and Male Homosocial Desire* (New York: Columbia Univ. Press, 1985), passim. See also Montrose, "The Elizabethan Subject and the Spenserian Text," for a rhetorical reading of the poetic subject in passages from Spenser's *The Faerie Queene* in many ways parallel with my reading of Wyatt's poetic subject. Montrose's critique of Greenblatt's reading of Spenser usefully extends and elaborates several points of my argument. See especially his discussion of the difference it makes to the structures under discussion when the sovereign is a woman.

Textual Intercourse:
Anne Donne, John Donne, and the
Sexual Poetics of Textual Exchange

Janet E. Halley

Some things we know quite irrefutably about the life of Anne More Donne, the wife of the famous poet. We know that she was the daughter of Sir George More and was taken into the household of the powerful Sir Thomas Egerton, Lord Keeper of the Great Seal—a sign that allows us to infer that her relatives intended her to make an aristocratic match. We know that she met an aspiring but impecunious John Donne, Egerton's secretary, when she was about fourteen.[1] We know that they fell in love, married surreptitiously in 1601, and incurred the immediate wrath of her powerful father.[2] We know that her husband lost his position with Egerton and began fourteen years' desperate search for preferment at Court and in its aristocratic surrounds—a search that ended only with his ordination in 1615. We know that she gave birth in 1603, 1604, 1605, 1607, 1608, 1609, 1611, 1612, 1613, 1615, 1616, and 1617.[3] She died, probably of puerperal fever, shortly after the birth of her last infant.[4] She was 33.

Beyond bare facts such as these, we know very little of this woman. We don't know what these events meant to her—we know nothing of her attraction to her clandestine suitor, her understanding of his motives, her experience of her father's anger and of her exile from the class to which she was born, her feelings about her incessant pregnancies and the embraces that caused them. We don't even know whether she was literate. Statistical studies suggest it is highly unlikely that she was: David Cressy has shown that female literacy remained low throughout the period during which Anne Moore would have received her education and well beyond it.[5] But statistics cannot speak to individual cases: perhaps she could read but not write; perhaps she was taught to read and write as a girl but lost both skills through disuse in the óbstacle race of her twelve pregnancies; perhaps she wrote, but no documentary evidence remains; perhaps her writings remain, but no one has found them or can identify them as hers. Amid the great torrent of words that her husband let loose, Anne Donne is silent.

With perhaps unusual clarity, the confluence of Anne Donne's historical silence with her husband's prodigious noise forces on us the temptation to read *his* writing for indications of *her* presence. Such a temptation frequently besets—and overcomes—feminists seeking signals of women's history in the overwhelmingly masculine literary product of the early modern period. It is my purpose here to suggest, however, that a search for Anne Donne's historical presence in the writing of her husband not only displaces the historical woman with masculine desire but also occludes the actual traces of her history inscribed in his texts. Anne More Donne offers, then, a case study in the feminist project of recovering lost and silent women—a case study that warns us to examine carefully the forms, and the limits, of our knowledge.

Selections from the lengthy shelf of John Donne biographies demonstrate that a full respect for Anne Donne's historical actuality is imperiled by efforts to discover her presence in her husband's literary product. In the authoritative life of Donne, R. C. Bald is nonplussed—but not enough—by the problem of Anne Donne's silence: "The personality of his wife inevitably remains elusive, although to Sir John Oglander, her brother-in-law, she was 'the best of women', and all Donne's references reveal his devotion to her."[6] Though acknowledging that Anne Donne herself cannot be directly known, Bald is pleased to accept, as an adequate substitute, evaluations of her character by men who enjoyed, as she did not, the power to leave documentary records. The character that emerges is, not surprisingly, that of the woman-whose-virtue-evoked-men's-praise. Admittedly unable to compose an historical account of the woman, Bald displaces her with expressions of masculine perception and desire.[7] The next step, of course, is to find in her death the occasion for her husband's final fulfillment: "The death of his wife marked a turning-point in Donne's life; it deepened his sense of religious vocation, and produced something much closer to a conversion than the feelings which had prompted him to enter the Church."[8]

A more recent literary biography of John Donne, on the other hand, demonstrates that even more precipitous displacement can result from scholarly efforts to treat Anne Donne as available to historical recovery. Arthur F. Marotti demonstrates (conclusively, I think) that John Donne can be read as a "coterie poet," carefully restricting the circulation of his poetry to a select number of friends and associates. For certain love poems, "Anne was the intended primary audience"[9]—although even here Marotti finds within these poems repeated indications that they were also intended for circulation to male friends. To have knowledge of Anne Donne as a reader would be something indeed, but Marotti's discovery[10] is too positive in several respects.

First, he repeatedly infers Anne Donne's status as primary audience from various poems' lack of formal or rhetorical sophistication: difficult passages could not be intended for her.[11] These conclusions depend on a silent assumption that she was ignorant of the poetic vocabularies of her age—precisely the sort of knowledge about her subjective life which we most acutely lack.

Second, Marotti never acknowledges that a peculiar historiographical problem arises when the status of the historical female reader is to be inferred from poems in which she is only ostensibly the sole audience, and which are ultimately available to us because of their circulation among men. Explicating a poem which he argues was composed during the courtship of Anne More and John Donne, Marotti finds that certain blunt, "antisentimental" lines were intended "for a primarily male audience fond of such aggressive wit," yet concludes that "the whole piece is a dramatic performance for the benefit of a mistress."[12] While recognizing that the poem contemplates a "double audience," Marotti fails to account for the duplicity itself.

The pattern repeats itself when Marotti turns to a series of poems which he argues were written after the poet's marriage and probably during his travels in 1605.[13] These poems are read in the supposed "context" of Anne Donne as their exclusive audience: so placed, they are interpreted as orchestrating the poet's gradual disengagement from his wife and as recording his emotional reparations to her for his simultaneous turn towards the world of masculine striving. Marotti's own introduction would suggest, however, that the very fact of our inheriting these poems through the manuscript culture of coterie exchange demonstrates irrefutably that they circulated, initially at least by Donne's consent, among a narrow and select group of male friends.[14]

In both instances, Marotti has constituted Anne Donne as a historical presence from poems which, by their circulation among male friends, render that presence extremely problematic. We might as well admit that our inclusion as readers of these poems brings us into kinship not with Anne Donne but with the male coterie readers from whom we obtain them. Along with them, we are invited by the poet to peer into the privacy of her relationship with him and to see her as he can construct her, the reader of his texts.

That is to say, when Donne placed his poems into circulation among his male confidants, he created for his friends the image of his wife's reading them. This specular effect does not depend on her *actually* reading and would occur even without it. Instead, it is the product of the poem's placement into textual exchange among men. Under such circumstances, the sight-line along which an image of Anne Donne becomes visible, and not the woman herself, is the proper object of historical recovery.

For all readers except the historical Anne Donne, then, her appearance as a reader of these poems is a product of the duplicitous theatrics of their circulation. Not only is she displaced once by the coterie readers who take up her position as reader; she is displaced again by the mirage of her presence they enjoy by their inclusion in the private exchange of lovers' talk. To mistake this double displacement[15] as an historical woman's presence is to fool ourselves, and to forswear awareness of Anne Donne's actuality, however lost to us.

If Bald's work suggests a willingness to abandon the problem of Anne Donne's historical presence for the satisfactions of representing an entirely masculine history, Marotti purports to recover Anne Donne without acknowledging that the object of his rescue is her representation in masculine exchange. Anne Donne herself is either lost completely or rendered falsely present. These unacceptable alternatives, then, pose a slightly different challenge than the one articulated above. Rather than demand that an overwhelmingly masculine historical record make Anne Donne *present* to us, we might ask whether, in the man's writing, we can read the woman's *absence*. Can we respect the subjective, historical existence of Anne Donne not only by recognizing her presence in history, but also by acknowledging her absence to us? Is it possible to hear her silence?

ADVOCATING A RETURN FROM "GYNOCRITICS" [16] to the predominantly male-authored canon, Adrienne Munich urges us to seek in the latter "signs of real female power": "Feminist critics of the literary canon can expose women's presence in writing by men as well as in writing by women." [17] The case of Anne Donne poses a caveat to Munich and others engaged in the project of discovering "woman" within male-authored texts, by reminding us that *woman* and *women* are not necessarily coterminous categories. If we admit that women in their historical actuality remain the political constituency of feminist criticism, [18] we oblige ourselves to keep in mind that the subjective experience and authority of women are, perforce, absent from representations of them. From this vantage point, an unbridgeable chasm appears between two projects Munich proposes without distinguishing between them. She exhorts us not only to "refus[e] to accept texts as unaffected by women," but also to "expose women's presence in writing by men." [19] While the first of these recommendations must be crucial to the feminist critical undertaking, the second reflects an exaggerated estimation of the powers of feminist criticism. Nevertheless, if we can steel ourselves to abandon this second, possibly nostalgic, project, the path to Munich's first goal becomes clearer. Precisely by maintaining our awareness of actual women's absence from texts written by men, we can pursue the challenge Munich proposes when she declares that "Suppression, distancing, alteration or any other defences against woman's role in a text's creation are compelling examples of women's history, and are therefore a vital subject for feminist criticism." [20]

John Donne and his silent wife offer an unusually concise case on which to test this hypothesis. Donne wrote a large body of letters, in prose and verse, and many of them directly refer to Anne Donne's presence outside the circuits of epistolary exchange. These letters, when read with a feminist commitment to the silent actuality of Anne Donne, do indeed constitute such a "compelling example of women's history." Several letters, indeed, were written in Anne Donne's presence or about her and provide fundamental information about her relation to the gendered exercise of literacy in her era and class.

Many of these letters, not surprisingly, were written to Donne's close friend Sir Henry Goodyer. Goodyer and Donne exchanged letters weekly, and a great number of Donne's letters survive. In one of these weekly letters, Donne states that he writes from neither of his usual *scriptoria,* the library and the open road, but

> from the fire side in my Parler, and in the noise of three gamesome children; and by the side of her, whom because I have transplanted into a wretched fortune, I must labour to disguise that from her by all such honest devices, as giving her my company, and discourse, therefore I steal from her, all the time which I give this Letter, and it is therefore that I take so short a list, and gallop so fast over it.[21]

Donne's sense that he is obliged to disguise Anne's situation from her, even as it provides us with evidence of his domestic solicitude, reminds him of his own entrapment: he complains of not being away from home since he received Goodyer's last packet of letters and calls that duration an experiment "in how I can suffer a prison." And the melancholy thoughts that this reflection promotes must, too, be hidden from Anne: "I sit by one too tender towards these impressions, and it is so much our duty, to avoid all occasions of giving them sad apprehensions, as S. *Hierome* accuses *Adam* of no other fault in eating the Apple, but that he did it *Ne contristaretur delicias suas*" [lest he sour her pleasures]. The letter then closes in a catalogue of letters, news, and promises in which Donne and Goodyer jointly exercise their frustrated ambitions. This letter distinguishes sharply between the feminine domestic world in which it is inappropriately (and, Donne laments, badly) written, and the masculine terrain of the library and the highway, bound together by a network conveying packets of letters. As an interloper into the female world by the hearth, the letter writer "steal[s]" discourse from Anne to share it with Goodyer, attempting to hide from her not only her misery, but also his sense of entrapment, his yearning for the open world of masculine discourse and courtly preferment. He is trying to hide from her the fact that they do not share the same "wretched fortune," and to do this he attempts to hide, by writing hastily, the fact that he is writing at all.

This letter tells us something important about Anne Donne's relationship to literary production. Her husband uncomfortably discovers himself in a scene at once private and feminine; his mere act of writing to Goodyer constructs a distinction between his domestic situation and the circumstances invoked by the letter, a public world managed by literate men. For all his tenderness towards her, he excludes her from that second world. As I observed above, however, her exclusion is not complete: the letter, once actually conveyed to Goodyer, makes her husband's solicitude for her—and so, at two removes, the woman herself—an object of public, literary, male intercourse. In a gesture that articulates his friendship with Goodyer by distinguishing it from his relationship with his wife, Donne places his image of his wife into circulation.

Anne Donne is thus revealed to us as functionally illiterate in two senses: not only has she been unable to convey to us any writing over her own signature, but she also appears in her husband's letter as the excluded object of literary exchange. In another letter, Donne suggests that both aspects of her exclusion from literacy were, precisely, feminine: "When I began to apprehend, that even to myselfe, who can releive myself upon books, solitairines was a little burdenous, I beleeved yt would be much more so to my wyfe, if she were left alone." [22] Donne describes his reading as phallic, a kind of intercourse with a text implicitly figured as female. His language here suggests that he regarded his wife's inability to read as sexually appropriate: if he regards the written text as a feminine figure, if his relation to it is erotically heterosexual, then his wife is the living analogue of the text. If reading is heterosexually masculine, Anne Donne quite properly does not do it. And conversely, if Anne Donne is excluded, as a woman, from the world of literacy, she can reappear there metaphorically, as the text itself.

Donne's practice of textual intercourse begins to emerge in this letter, as he engenders the text as feminine and the acts of writing and reading as masculine. In such a textual practice, female desire is not only excluded from the power to express itself, but is displaced by the male author's representation of it. Donne's domestic letters effect this displacement not only when they refer to Anne Donne, but also when Donne describes his efforts to provide his eldest (and favorite) daughter, Constance, with a husband (#61). Donne informs his friend that a proposed match for Constance has just fallen through: though the prospective father-in-law was willing to accept the small dowry Donne could offer, his son resisted the profession (the cloth) proposed for him, and pleaded, successfully, to be allowed to travel. The question of Constance's participation in the plans for her marriage was a nice one in 1622, the date of this letter,[23] for, as Lawrence Stone has shown, cultural habits were then in transition. Parents in the propertied classes had largely relinquished the powers they routinely exercised in the sixteenth century, to force their eldest sons and their daughters to accept arranged marriages, but they had not yet retreated to their eighteenth-century position, in which they exercised a veto over the initial choices of their children. Stone suggests that uncertainty as to practice was at its highest during the first four decades of the seventeenth century, as parents continued to arrange marriages but began to accept their children's right to veto their plans. Young women's powers to refuse arranged marriages were particularly slow to materialize, "the most severe parental pressure . . . inevitably [being] exercised on daughters."[24] Stone concludes:

> Conditions varied from family to family according to the temperament of the father, and daughters continued to be under heavy parental pressure for several centuries, but on the whole contemporary [early seventeenth-century] comment suggests that this significant advance in the history of the emancipation of women took place between 1560 and 1640.[25]

Constance's marriage plans were being worked out just when the conditions and significance of women's subjective assent to their conditions of existence were being articulated. Clearly, Donne's temperament in these matters would make him a more rather than a less indulgent father: we would look for him in the vanguard of the formation of the "affectional marriage" (to borrow Stone's term). His narration to Goodyer is therefore highly suggestive. It opens with Donne's advice, "Tell both your daughters a peece of a storie of my *Con*. which may accustome them to endure disappointments in this world," and closes, "The girle knows not her losse, for I never told her of it: but truly, it is a great disappointment to me." The first sentence implies that it is daughters who endure disappointment when arranged marriages fail, but the second assimilates their desires to those of their fathers: Constance is understood to have undergone an ordeal of which, thanks to her father's solicitude, she is unaware.

This letter forcefully reminds us that we need all our scepticism when confronted by male-authored texts that represent the subjectivity of women. Constance's wishes are created in exchanges between men, first in the negotiations between her father and her proposed father-in-law and husband, and second in the exchange of letters between Donne and his closest male friend. In the exchange of letters just as in negotiations over the marriage contract, men enjoy the power to define women's desires. Constance's relationship to the transaction planning her marriage is echoed in her relationship to the letter about it: both mirror her mother's position vis-à-vis John Donne's writing. Mother and daughter alike are specifically excluded from the representation of their wishes and desires.

Taken together, these domestic letters warn feminist readers that, if we undertake Adrienne Munich's full project and attempt to find Anne Donne's presence in the texts left by her husband, we will lose precisely whom we seek. The warning is particularly difficult to hear because all three letters evince Donne's tender solicitude for the emotional life of his wife and daughter. His recognition of the subjective presence of these women suits well the poet who is widely admired for creating a poetry of "mutual love."[26] Here, if anywhere, the erotic life of a seventeenth-century woman would be refracted through the writings of the man who loved her.

But note that, when Donne worries that his wife's illiteracy renders her incapable of enduring solitude or sadness without his company, he inserts his own presence as the medium of hers. Her illiteracy is complemented by his literacy, her text by his reading, so that she is whole only when she is joined by him. The pattern is repeated in an acutely ugly form in Donne's letter to his bride's father, communicating the fact of their marriage. The letter concludes by reminding Sir George More "that yt is irremediably donne; that if yo[w] incense my L[ord] [Egerton] yo[w] destroy her and me; that yt is easye to give us happines, and that my endevors and industrie, if it please yo[w] to prosper them, may soone make me somewhat worthyer of her."[27] Donne's biographers, though willing to admit that this disastrous letter voices an inappropriate jauntiness,[28] have refused to concede its plain sense—that Donne, having gained Anne More's love and hand, deploys them as bribes for her father's patronage.[29] Even as he seeks to avert his wife's destruction and to secure her happiness, Donne transforms her capacity to suffer and enjoy into his hostages. Written at a time when Anne Donne had just exercised what her culture understood to be female choice, the letter co-opts the lovers' union, making its representation a token in the jealous negotiations between Donne and More.

This construct suggests that we limit very carefully our speculations about Anne Donne's subjective engagement in the complementary whole made up of these two lovers. But, as historians of women seeking knowledge of women's actual lives, we do not go away empty-handed. Anne Donne is absent from these texts, but their strategies depend on her passionate presence outside of them. These letters insist, again and again, that the material and literary traffic in women in which Donne engages requires not only women's absence from the exchange itself, but their presence somewhere else.

IT WILL NOT DO TO EXAGGERATE our positive knowledge of Anne Donne, that almost paradigmatically silent woman. Rather, to read with Anne Donne persistently present beyond the margin of the text is continually to rediscover our failure to know her. That does not mean that we learn nothing of her history. Instead, by abjuring to seek in the texts written by her husband reliable references to her actuality, we are freed to observe the uses of her exclusion and of his literacy in a cultural practice of literary exchange that belongs as insistently to her history as it does to his. As the "domestic" letters just analyzed suggest, Donne described that exchange as a textual intercourse whose product was his friendship with other men: in it, Anne Donne's history is inscribed as a sequence of displacements.

Crucial to that textual intercourse as a social practice is the activity of exchanging letters and poems. Donne frequently adverted to that activity even as he participated in it, and his reflections both describe and enact a complex sexual dynamic in which he repeatedly likens the exchange of letters between friends to the consummation of sexual love. In a letter to Goodyer which Donne wrote during his 1611 sojourn on the Continent (#41),[30] Donne opines that "when Letters have a convenient handsome body of news, they are Letters," and goes on to declare:

You (I think) and I am much of one sect in the Philosophy of love; which though it be directed upon the minde, doth inhere in the body, and find piety [*sic*] entertainment there: so have Letters for their principall office, to be seals and testimonies of mutuall affection, but the materialls and fuell of them should be a confident and mutuall communicating of those things which we know. How shall I then who know nothing write Letters?

Donne expatiates here on an analogy between the philosophy of love and that of letters: just as sexual love is "directed upon the minde," unifying partners in their highest faculty, so does friendship consist most essentially in "mutuall affection"; and just as sexual love cannot perform its lofty function unless it "inhere in the body," so must friendship find consummation in the exchange of "a convenient handsome body of news," the "confident and mutuall communicating of those things which we know."

Wherever he invokes this analogy, Donne carefully prohibits it from collapsing into an identity. In the letter to Goodyer he confesses finally, "How shall I then who know nothing write Letters?", describing himself as bereft of the means of physically consummating this act of friendship: the reason, he informs Goodyer, is "that I dyed ten years ago, . . . when my courses were diverted." The reference, of course, is to 1601, when he married Anne More. The existence of Anne Donne not only explains Donne's supposed lack of news (in fact, the letter proceeds to retail four pages of this substance which Donne claims to lack) but also draws a crucial distinction between sexual and textual intercourse: the latter not only requires the woman's absence but inserts in her place the body of the letter. As Donne suggested to Sir Henry Wotton, the result of this displacement was not merely a different but a superior form of communion: "Sir, *more* then kisses, letters mingle Soules." [31]

Not a little anxiously, this careful distinction argues that, if Donne practices the philosophy of love with his wife, he must be doing something else with Goodyer. This implied denial of homosexual longing is no simple repression of a "truer" subtext. Instead, as Donne reveals in an epigram, a representation of heterosexual desire functions as a token which, when exchanged between men, gives positive meaning to their relationship. Donne wrote:

Thou call'st me effeminat, for I love womens joyes;
I call not thee manly, though thou follow boyes. [32]

Rejecting as "pointless" this epigram's MS title "The Jughler," Donne's modern editor has given it the appropriate title "Manliness." [33] But the original title, surely, is not the nonsense "Jughler," but "Ingler": the *OED* defines the noun "ingle" as "a boy favourite (in a bad sense) [*sic*]; a catamite." The immediately apparent purpose of the epigram is to express the speaker's contempt for, and disavowal of, homosexual desire. But Milgate correctly concludes that the overarching issue here is the poet's masculinity, his sexual solidarity with men. The speaker founds his argument for his manliness not only on his denial of homosexual desire but on his affirmation of the supposed contrary, on his commitment to heterosexual love. The form of manliness proposed here depends on the speaker's avid appreciation of "women's joyes"—and that point depends on the existence of women who (we are told) fully relish Donne's sexual attention. In order to affirm his inclusion within the masculine kinship that was threatened by the jibes of his unknown interlocutor, Donne sets into circulation an image of women's presence outside the network of textual exchange.

These transactions, though they require that real women should exist, give no readily interpretable signs of their actual desires. Instead, the pattern that emerges from Donne's letters of male friendship repeats, at the level of literary practice, the "traffic in women" which Gayle Rubin deduced from Lévi-Strauss's theory of cultural production: "If it is women who are being transacted, then it is the men who give and take them who are linked, the woman being a conduit of a relationship rather than a partner to it." [34] And indeed, as Eve Sedgwick has suggested in her elaboration of this triangle, patriarchal power will often be found articulating the relations between men by constructing dynamics that are apparently purely heterosexual. Sedgwick's studies of the eighteenth- and nineteenth-century novel demonstrate that, where patriarchy joins forces with homophobia (and assuredly it did in late sixteenth- and early seventeenth-century England), representations of heterosexuality will often describe and enforce both of these forms of oppression. In such representations, women appear as the mutual focus of male desire in order to produce a sharp and, for homophobic purposes, reassuring distinction between homosexual and homosocial desire—and thus to generate the meanings and the terms of male ascendency.[35]

It is only by drawing his careful distinction between sexual and textual intercourse that Donne is able to secure the benefits of this symbolic traffic in women. By inserting representations of women's sexual subjectivity into texts that function to realign his relationships with men, Donne assures that those images function not to describe real women, but to pass as currency in masculine exchange, and so to articulate the alliances and rankings between men. When Donne confides in Goodyer that "You (I think) and I am much of one sect in the Philosophy of love," he merely *refers* to heterosexual love; far more immediately he *performs* a gesture uniting the two friends. To rephrase this point: the belief that heterosexual intercourse unites the minds of heterosexual lovers, unites the male friends. Though the very structure of male friendship as Donne practices it here depends on the men's shared acknowledgment of Anne Donne's presence somewhere else, that shared acknowledgment constitutes the totality of our information about her. Moreover, she is not the point; the point is the two friends' intimate exchange of thoughts about her.

The representations of Anne Donne that we have inherited from her husband function no differently in the context of male textual exchange than do Donne's representations of that quintessentially fictional female, the Muse. Consider a verse letter Donne wrote "To Mr. I. L." [36] after the latter had retired to his country estate with a new wife:

> Your Trent is Lethe; that past, us you forget.
> You doe not duties of Societies,
> If from the'embrace of a lov'd wife you rise,
> View your fat Beasts, stretch'd Barnes, and labour'd fields,
> Eate, play, ryde, take all joyes which all day yeelds,
> And then againe to your embracements goe:
> Some houres on us your frends, and some bestow
> Upon your Muse . . . .
>
> (ll. 6–13)

Donne complains that his friend has fallen into the same epistolary neglect of which, as we have seen in two of Donne's letters to Goodyer, he repeatedly accused himself—and he ascribes much the same reason to I. L.'s failure. Masculine friendship, it seems, does not comport well with a man's absorption with feminine company. To remedy this problem, Donne invites his friend to divert some hours of sensual delight from his wife to his Muse—twice excluding that real woman from the society the two men would constitute. First, of course, her sexual presence must be driven to the margin; second, her role is to be fulfilled by a literary figure, the Muse. Though "Societies" here are male domains, dichotomized from the world of domestic heterosexuality, the former, homosocial world is mediated by the Muse—that is, by woman absent as a person but present as a figure.

Men who can be divided by one man's exclusive enjoyment of a real woman may be, Donne's verse letters suggest, reunited by their shared attention to—indeed their circulation of—the female figure and the texts they beget on her. Two poems from Donne's literary friendships— one from and one to Donne—provide evidence of the sexual combinations Donne rejected in designing this interaction. In a sonnet "To Mr. B. B.,"[37] Donne specifically disavows the homoerotic implications of male friendship mediated by the Muse:

> If thou unto thy Muse be marryed,
> Embrace her ever, ever multiply,
> Be far from me that strange Adulterie
> To tempt thee and procure her widowhed.
>
>   (ll. 1–4)

Donne not only refuses to tempt B. B. from his Muse's embraces, he also rejects any proposal that he should annex B. B.'s Muse in his own *ménage à trois* ("I can take no new [Muse] in Bigamye," l. 7). Neither do we find in any verse letter by Donne the remarkable relations proposed by his friend T. W.:[38]

> Haue mercy on me & my sinfull Muse
> W^c rub'd & tickled wth thyne could not chuse
> But spend some of her pithe and yeild to bee
> One in y^t chaste & mystique tribadree.
> . . . .
> Thy Muse, O strange & holy Lecheree
> Beeing a Mayd still, gott this Song on mee.
>
>   (ll. 11–14, 19–20)

T. W. imagines his and Donne's Muses uniting in a lesbian consummation, or "tribadree," but cannot resist assimilating that image to one of erection and ejaculation ("spend some of her pithe"). This disturbing and ambiguous image is promptly replaced with another only slightly less so: Donne's Muse who, though a maid, begets a poem on T. W.

These two poems give us some idea of the dispositions Donne rejects in his figuration of male friendship: no erotic contact between Donne and the friend or between Donne's Muse and the friend; no erotic autonomy of Donne's and the friend's Muses. The sexual dynamics Donne invokes in his verse letters to male friends follow a simpler design, in which neither the Muses nor the poets enjoy each other; rather, the Muses *are enjoyed by* the poets, who need sacrifice neither their masculinity nor their detachment. Requesting a letter from the uncommunicative R. W. (Roland Woodward?), Donne argues,

> Our Minds part not, joyne then thy Muse with myne,
> For myne is barren thus devorc'd from thyne.[39]
>
> (ll. 11–12)

The poet's potency relies not on any erotic relationship between himself and his friend, and not on any agency of his Muse, but on the friends' shared possession of a composite female figure.

As these verse letters developing Donne's use of the Muse figure suggest, his sexual poetics of textual exchange depends on the displacement of real women by texts endowed with a feminine gender; but it would be a mistake to characterize the resulting textual intercourse as "mere" imagery. By exchanging these images Donne constituted a social practice of literary exchange that articulated the meanings of male power and the power of male meaning, *within* the social world inhabited by the historical women it strove to exclude. For example, a verse letter to Roland Woodward reveals Donne involved in his painstaking management of the circulation of his erotic verse. The poem attempts to excuse Donne's refusal to send Woodward an unspecified manuscript of Donne's work:

> Like one who'in her third widdowhood doth professe
> Her selfe a Nunne, ty'd to retirednesse,
> So'affects my muse now, a chast fallownesse;
>
> Since shee to few, yet to too many'hath showne
> How love-song weeds, and Satyrique thornes are growne
> Where seeds of better Arts, were early sown.[40]
>
> (ll. 1–6)

It is safe to infer that the poems at issue are Donne's love lyrics. Woodward was the collector and scribe of the Westmoreland Manuscript, one of the most authoritative manuscript collections of Donne's verse.[41] The most glaring gap in this rich collection is the *Songs and Sonnets* (it contains only one love lyric, "A Jeat Ring Sent"); also missing are three epithalamia, all Donne's verse letters to women, all Donne's funeral elegies, the *Anniversaries*, and, except for *La Corona* and the *Holy Sonnets*, all his sacred verse. To one asking which deficiency Woodward sought to remedy and Donne refused to supply in this verse letter, the date of the exchange appears as the decisive fact. Whether one accepts Milgate's date for it of 1597 or Grierson's and Empson's of 1603–4,[42] the verse letter is too early to refer to anything but love lyrics. Virtually none of the other missing texts could have been written by either date.[43] One scarcely need point, then, to more subtle arguments, such as the unlikelihood that Woodward would ask for poems Donne had allowed to be printed (the *Anniversaries*), or the improbability of Donne's describing epithalamia, funeral elegies, letters to patronesses, or sacred verse in the terms discovered in this interesting verse letter.

For Donne figures the circulation of his love songs and his satires as the public exposure of a sexually profligate Muse. Donne teases his reader's expectations: "[T]o few, yet to too many'hath [she] showne"— what? Even as he retreats to a "how" clause and towards the more chaste register of agricultural imagery, Donne imagines his texts as the displayed clothing (the "weeds") of a lascivious Muse and figures his friends' reading, like his own in the letter about Anne's illiteracy, as sexual penetration. Donne withholds circulation of his poetry in an effort to prevent mis-conceptions resulting from other men's erotic interactions with his texts: he hopes, instead, to foster the "seeds" of his own "Arts." Donne here gathers to himself a power he shared whenever he circulated the figure of the Muse, the feminine text, or the figure of his own wife: the masculine power to control the meaning of the feminine.

Donne's cultural ceremonies of textual circulation thus enact the symbolics of textual intercourse: the historical woman, excluded by her functional illiteracy, reappears as (fictionalized) text, the exchange of which generates male social control over signification. This control, the letter to Woodward suggests, takes the form of constraining circulation of the feminized text, thus rarefying it and amassing in Donne's hands the power to determine its value. A neat emblem of this power appears in a letter I have already discussed, the letter to Goodyer about Donne's frustrated plans for his daughter Constance's marriage. With the letter

Donne sent a "schedule," a cypher or secret code encrypting the name of the erstwhile groom; Donne eagerly asked Goodyer to burn this enclosure once he had deciphered it. Textual and sexual exchange dovetail here, as Donne exercises two closely interpolated powers. By circumscribing textual signification he negotiates the terms and the value of female desire; and conversely, in defining female desire he exercises his power to circumscribe textual signification.

We know, from the prodigious scholarly and critical efforts of some of Donne's best readers, that he devoted painstaking care throughout his life to curtail the circulation of his poetry, to maintain its private character, and thus not only to fend off the "stigma of print" but also to accumulate the benefits of coterie alliances.[44] What has too rarely been recognized is the extent to which these practices exploited and perpetuated a gendered culture of literacy and literature.[45] Perhaps this historiographical hesitance arises from the fact that it is the absence of historical women that is present to study in Donne's textual practice. Reading that absence is not easy, but it has its acrid rewards. Among those, I would suggest, is a sense of a new syntax and a new conception of loss in the famous line, "John Donne, Anne Donne, Un-done."[46]

NOTES

I am grateful to the Kirkland Endowment for its support.

1. R. C. Bald, *John Donne: A Life* (New York: Oxford Univ. Press, 1970), 96.

2. Ibid., 128–40.

3. Ibid., Appendix B, "Donne's Children," 547–56.

4. Ibid., 324–25. The speculation about the cause of Anne Donne's death is Edward Le Comte's, *Grace to a Witty Sinner* (N.Y.: Walker, 1965), 170; it is substantiated by the epitaph John Donne wrote for her: "vii post xii[m] partum (quorum vii superstant) dies / Inmani febre correptae" (Bald, 325). To translate these lines rather liberally: "seven days after the birth of the twelfth child (of whom seven survive her) she was destroyed by a fierce fever."

5. David Cressy, *Literacy and the Social Order: Reading and Writing in Tudor and Stuart England* (New York: Cambridge Univ. Press, 1980), 128–29, 144–49. Cressy's figures show that, during Anne Donne's lifetime, female illiteracy rose from 84 percent to 91 percent in London, and fell from 100 percent to 93 percent in East Anglia (Table 7.2, p. 144).

6. Bald, 326.

7. One biographer of Donne goes even further, inferring from Anne Donne's relentless childbearing the persistent mutuality of the couple's love: "I do not doubt it [the love of Anne Donne and John Donne] was mutual and true and lasting unto the grave and beyond. . . . [Her] repeated pregnancies . . . signif[y] that he continued to find her, or they each other, irresistible." Edward LeComte, "Jack Donne: From Rake to Husband," in *Just So Much Honor: Essays Commemorating the Four-hundredth Anniversary of the Birth of John Donne*, ed. Peter Amadeus Fiore (University Park: Pennsylvania State Univ. Press, 1972), 22–23.

8. Bald, 328.

9. Arthur F. Marotti, *John Donne, Coterie Poet* (Madison: Univ. of Wisconsin Press, 1986), 139.

10. As Marotti recognizes (see p. 137 and notes), the notion that certain poems were addressed to Anne Donne can be traced back to Walton's Life of Donne, and features in the work of J. B. Leishman, *The Monarch of Wit: An Analytical and Comparative Study of the Poetry of John Donne*, 4th ed. (London: Hutchinson, 1959), and of Helen Gardner, ed., *John Donne: Elegies and Songs and Sonnets* (New York: Oxford Univ. Press, 1965). His reading strikes one as a "discovery" because of its focus on the social history of the poems.

11. Marotti, 143–44, 149.

12. Ibid., 141. The poem is "The Broken Heart," and the lines purportedly directed to the male friends are these: "He is starke mad, who ever sayes / That he hath been in love an hour" (lines 1–2).

13. Ibid., 168–78. The poems examined are "A Valediction: of the booke," "A Valediction: of Weeping," and "A Valediction: Forbidding Mourning."

14. Ibid., 17; 297–98 n. 62. Marotti occasionally verges on an acknowledgment of this second audience (171–72, 178).

15. Gayatri Chakravorty Spivak, "Displacement and the Discourse of Woman," in *Displacement, Derrida and After*, ed. Mark Krupnick (Bloomington: Indiana Univ. Press, 1983), 169–95; see "Introduction: The Lady Vanishes," p. 12, above.

16. The term is Elaine Showalter's, "Feminist Criticism in the Wilderness," *Critical Inquiry* 8, no. 2 (Winter 1981): 179–205.

17. Adrienne Munich, "Notorious Signs, Feminist Criticism and Literary Tradition," in *Making a Difference: Feminist Literary Criticism*, ed. Gayle Greene and Coppélia Kahn (New York: Methuen, 1985), 252.

18. See Toril Moi, *Textual/Sexual Politics: Feminist Literary Theory* (New York: Methuen, 1985), 13.

19. Munich, 252.

20. Ibid., 244.

21. Letter #44, in John Donne, *Letters to Severall Persons of Honour*, ed.

Charles Edmund Merrill, Jr. (New York: Sturgis & Walton, 1910), 118–19. This volume reproduces the 1651 edition of Donne's letters produced by his eldest son, John Donne, Jr. Unless otherwise indicated by an endnote, all quotations from Donne's prose letters are from this edition, to which reference will be made by the inclusion of each letter's number in the text.

22. Letter #41, in *The Loseley Manuscripts*, ed. A. J. Kempe (London, 1935), 345.

23. Bald, 439; Appendix B, "Donne's Children," 547.

24. Lawrence Stone, *The Crisis of the Aristocracy, 1558–1641* (Oxford: Oxford Univ. Press, 1965), 594.

25. Ibid., 597. See also Stone, *The Family, Sex and Marriage in England, 1500–1800* (New York: Harper & Row, 1977), 179–189, 390.

26. The term is Helen Gardner's; she argues that the subject appealed to Donne primarily for philosophical reasons but concedes that his "own experience" may have played some role. *John Donne: The Elegies and The Songs and Sonnets*, ed. Helen Gardner (Oxford: Oxford Univ. Press, 1965), liii, lxii. For a vehement argument that shared sexual passion, not philosophical speculation, underlies Donne's great love lyrics, see William Empson, "Rescuing Donne," in *Just So Much Honor*, ed. Fiore (University Park: Pennsylvania State Univ. Press, 1972), 95–148. See also Marotti, 135.

27. Letter #132, *The Loseley Manuscripts*, 329.

28. Ibid.

29. See LeComte, *Grace to a Witty Sinner*, 79; Marotti, 135.

30. Though the 1651 edition of Donne's letters indicates that this letter was addressed to Sir Henry Wotton, I. A. Shapiro has demonstrated that the actual addressee was Goodyer. Shapiro also provides the date, 14/24 January 1611/12. Shapiro, "The Text of Donne's *Letters to Severall Persons*," *Review of English Studies* 7 (1931): 294–96. For further confirmation of Shapiro's thesis that John Donne, Jr., altered the addresses of his father's letters while compiling the 1651 edition, see Roger E. Bennett, "Donne's *Letters to Severall Persons of Honour*," *PMLA* 56 (1941): 120–40. Bennett discusses this and other letters written by Donne during his Continental travels in another article, "Donne's Letters from the Continent in 1611–12," *Philological Quarterly* 19 (1940): 66–78.

31. "To Sir Henry Wotton," l. 1, in *John Donne: The Satires, Epigrams and Verse Letters*, ed. W. Milgate (Oxford: Clarendon Press, 1967), 71 (emphasis added). In subsequent notes, this edition will be cited as "Milgate, *Verse Letters*."

32. Milgate, *Verse Letters*, 52.

33. Milgate, *Verse Letters*, 200.

34. Gayle Rubin, "The Traffic in Women: Notes on the 'Political Economy' of Sex," in *Toward an Anthropology of Women*, ed. Rayna R. Reiter (New York: Monthly Review Press, 1975), 174.

35. Eve Kosofsky Sedgwick, *Between Men: English Literature and Male Homosocial Desire* (New York: Columbia Univ. Press, 1985), 1–5, 29, and passim.

36. Milgate, *Verse Letters*, 67. Milgate is unable to determine the identity of the addressee.

37. Ibid., 68; again, the addressee is not identified.

38. Ibid., 212. Milgate notes that the Westmoreland manuscript associates this poem with Donne's verse letters, and concludes that T. W. probably wrote it in response to a verse letter from Donne; T. W., Milgate suggests, may be Roland Woodward's brother Thomas Woodward, but the identification cannot be certain (*Verse Letters*, 211).

39. Ibid., 62.

40. Ibid., 69.

41. Gardner, *The Elegies and the Songs and Sonnets*, lxxii; Milgate, *Verse Letters*, xlvi; Marotti, x.

42. Milgate, *Verse Letters*, 223; Empson, 129–32.

43. For dates of the epithalamia and funeral elegies, see Bald, 177–79, 269, 274, 466. For dates of the verse letters to women, see Milgate, *Verse Letters*, 242–78. For dates of almost all Donne's sacred poems, see *John Donne: The Divine Poems*, 2nd ed., ed. Helen Gardner (Oxford: Oxford Univ. Press, 1978), 92–109, 132–35, 138–41. The *Anniversaries*, of course, were written after the death of Elizabeth Drury in 1610 (Bald, 238).

44. See J. W. Saunders, "The Stigma of Print: A Note on the Social Bases of Tudor Poetry," *Essays in Criticism* 1 (1951), 139–64; Margaret Maurer, "The Poetical Familiarity of John Donne's Letters," *The Forms of Power and the Power of Forms in the Renaissance*, ed. Stephen Greenblatt, spec. issue of *Genre* 15, nos. 1–2 (Spring/Summer 1982): 183–202; Annabel Patterson, "Misinterpretable Donne: The Testimony of the Letters," *John Donne Journal* 1, nos. 1–2 (1982): 39–53; Marotti, passim.

45. For a rare exception, see Maurer's essay, "The Real Presence of Lucy Russell, Countess of Bedford, and the Terms of John Donne's 'Honour is So Sublime Perfection,' " *ELH* 47 (1980): 205–34.

46. The only evidence of Donne's having written this line comes to us from Izaak Walton's *The Life of Dr John Donne, Late Dean of St Paul's Church, London*. I have relied on the text in *Izaak Walton's Lives* (London: Thomas Nelson and Sons, n.d.), 22.

The Identity of the Reader in Marie de Gournay's *Le Proumenoir de Monsieur de Montaigne* [1594]

Patricia Francis Cholakian

> "Qui écrit? A qui? Et pour envoyer, destiner, expédier quoi?
> A quelle adresse?"
> [Who is writing? To whom? And to send, to forward, to
> expedite what? To which address?]
>
> Jacques Derrida, *La Carte Postale*[1]

Educated almost entirely by reading the works of male classical authors and imbued with the unexamined presupposition that these works were "universal," early women writers were caught between their ambition to write like men and their need to write as women. When they tried to emulate their fathers, they wrote as daughters, but often their message was really addressed to other women, to whom they offered maternal advice and comfort. The relationship between author and audience in their texts was thus linked to and made problematic by their gender. The resulting confusion as to the identity of both reader and writer provides a special context in which to ask Derrida's question "Who is writing? To whom?" Concomitantly, the search for an answer makes it possible to read these heretofore neglected works in a new way—as attempts to deliver a message which has been misaddressed.

Marie de Gournay's *Le Proumenoir de M. de Montaigne* offers a dramatic case in point. This little-known novel, which has generally been dismissed as pedantic, dull, and unoriginal,[2] was dedicated to the great French essayist Michel de Montaigne. It carried his name in its title, was preceded by a letter addressed to him, and contained numerous asides which invoked his presence as the reader. Yet its author stated in her prefatory letter that books such as hers are useful because they warn women to stay on their guard (3 v°)[3]—a message certainly not intended for Montaigne. To whom, then, was Gournay really writing? And in what capacity?

MARIE DE GOURNAY WAS THE ONLY professional woman writer of her age. Deprived of a formal education because of her sex, she had taught herself Latin by comparing French translations with the originals and had become sufficiently knowledgeable to translate the second book of the *Aeneid* into French verse.[4] She discovered Montaigne's *Essais* in her teens and immediately recognized in them the greatest literary work of her era. In the spring of 1588, she sent their author a note expressing her admiration, to which he responded by adopting her as his "fille d'alliance." [5] After Montaigne's death, she devoted herself to a literary career. A member of the impoverished nobility, she refused to live under the protection of friends or relatives. Instead, she installed herself in an attic apartment in Paris, where she eked out a frugal income, writing, translating, and reediting the *Essais*.[6] Often mocked by the literary establishment, unable for many years to find the patronage which would have given her some measure of security, she nevertheless participated actively in the linguistic and critical debates which gave birth to French classicism.[7]

The months following her meeting with Montaigne had been the turning point in her existence. The great man seems to have found in her a substitute for his long dead friend La Boétie. He paid several visits to her family in Picardy, and there "father" and "daughter" read, talked, and went for long walks together. When Montaigne departed for Bordeaux, Gournay wrote down a story she had told him during one of their conversations. She framed it with a letter in which she begged him to correct her style:

Vous entendez bien, mon père, que je nomme cecy vostre Proumenoir, parce qu'en nous proumenant ensemble, il n'y a que trois jours, je vous contay l'histoire qui suit; comme la lecture que nous venions de faire d'un subject de mesme air (c'est des accidens de l'amour en Plutarque) m'en mit

à propos. L'occasion qui m'esmeut à la coucher maintenant par escrit, et
l'envoyer depuis vostre partement, courir apres vous, c'est afin que vous
ayez plus de moyen d'y recognoistre les fautes de mon stile, que vous
n'eustes en mon recit qui passa soudain. Goustez le donc et me corrigez
(2 r° and v°).

[You understand, my father, that I am naming this your Proumenoir (Prome-
nade), because as we were walking together only three days ago, I told you
the story which follows; as a similar subject (the accidents of love in Plutarch) had reminded me of it. The present occasion moves me to set it down
in writing now and to send it running after you, since you have departed, so
that you will have a greater opportunity to recognize the faults of my style
than you had in my retelling, which passed quickly by. See how you like it,
then, and correct me.]

She goes on to say that she had read the story somewhere, but cannot
remember either the author's name or the title:

Je rapporte l'argument de ce comte d'un petit livre que je leuz d'avanture,
il y a quelque an et d'autant que je ne l'ay sçeu revoir onques puis, j'ay
mesme oublié son nom et celuy de l'aucteur encore (3 r° and v°).

[I found the plot of this story in a little book which I read by chance some
years ago, and since I have never been able to see it since, I have even
forgotten its name and, what is more, that of its author.]

There is no doubt, however, that *Le Proumenoir* departs only mini-
mally from the "Second Discours" of Claude de Taillemont's *Discours
des Champs Faëz*. Both versions tell of a princess (Laurine in Taillemont's story, Alinda in Gournay's) whose father attempts to force her to
marry an enemy ruler in order to ransom her uncle the king. En route
to meet her bridegroom, Alinda is persuaded by a handsome admirer
named Leontin to elope with him. They are shipwrecked near Thrace,
where a nobleman Orthalcus and his sister Ortalde immediately fall in
love with Alinda and Leontin, respectively. The princess remains faithful to her lover, but Leontin is easily captivated by Ortalde. Overhearing
him promising marriage to his new love, the heartbroken Alinda pre-
tends to agree to marry Orthalcus but in fact arranges to have herself
killed in the place of a servant. When Leontin learns of her death, he
stabs himself and they are buried in a common grave.

Taillemont's story is framed by a series of refined discussions in the
style of Bembo's *Asolani*. His narrator, Philaste, a practitioner of amor-

ous servitude, respectfully addresses both his narrative and his asides to "mes dames," a group of noblewomen with whom he discourses in a meadow not far from Lyon. He exhorts them to follow his heroine Laurine's example and to remain faithful to their lovers even when they are betrayed—"En quoy aurez d'autant plus d'honneur et louange, comme y surpasserez les hommes" [In which you will earn so much more honor and praise that you will be superior to men].[8] The narrative voice is that of a man telling a "piteous tale" to women, who are advised to profit from his heroine's example. There is never any question as to the relationship between speaker and audience. The male speaks and the female listens. It is not within her power to re-act, let alone to act. Her role is purely passive.

Gournay discards completely this fictional frame and addresses her story to Montaigne, not only in her covering letter, but throughout the novel itself. The audience is no longer a group of female listeners who are supposed to learn a lesson, but a male *author*ity, who is supposed to pass judgment on the form (although not necessarily the content) of that lesson. Since the story's subject (female reaction to male infidelity) remains the same, the presence of a female audience cannot be eliminated, however, if the message is to reach its *destinataires*.

The situation is further complicated by the fact that the passive female who listens without comment in Taillemont's text now speaks through Gournay, the woman author who represents the female audience. She has read his story and reacted to it. It is no longer clear, therefore, who is writing to whom or what the relationship between author and audience is supposed to be.

As the reader of Taillemont's story, Gournay draws a very different lesson. Taillemont holds up his heroine as an example to be imitated by other women, urging them to remain faithful to their suitors, even when they are betrayed. Gournay interprets Alinda's tragedy as a warning, a case which women should guard against. Thus although both are giving advice to women, their goals are very different. Taillemont's message would ultimately benefit not women but men, who would be assured of having constant wives and mistresses even when they themselves were unfaithful. On the other hand, by rejecting his advice and advocating that women guard themselves against false promises, Gournay is trying to protect women from suffering at the hands of men. Speaking as a member of the sex to whom Taillemont would assign the role of listener and victim, Gournay thus erases in the *Proumenoir* not only his name and his title but his message as well. But by directing her message to Montaigne, she diverts it from the female audience who would benefit from it and places it under the sign of paternal patronage.

Le Proumenoir differs from its source in another important respect. Unlike Taillemont's story, which is broken only by brief asides to "les dames," Gournay's is frequently interrupted by classical quotations and lengthy digressions.

At first glance these extracts, principally from Virgil's *Aeneid* (Book 4), Catullus 64, and Ovid's *Metamorphoses* (Philomela), appear to be nothing more than proofs of Gournay's erudition. After all, it was crucial for her as Montaigne's heir apparent to display the credentials which the Renaissance mind regarded as essential to the educated MAN.[9] These insertions may also be explained away as her attempt to imitate Montaigne's practice of strewing his *Essais* with Latin quotations (which Gournay as his posthumous editor helped to identify and translate).

Her purpose in inserting these passages was not, however, merely to imitate her "father," or as her critics later alleged, to prove that she could read Latin and Greek.[10] She was trying to establish a kinship between her heroine and the betrayed women of classical antiquity—Dido, Ariadne, and Philomela.

As she writes at the end of a long passage from Catullus (Ariadne's lament, 64, vv. 136–48),

> Ces vers de la chétive Ariadné devroient estre escrits par tout dans les heures des dames, et quiconque soit celuy qui premier leur defendit la science comme allumette de lasciveté, je croy . . . qu'il craignoit qu'elles l'en missent au rouet le second jour de leur estude, mon père. Le vulgaire dit qu'une femme pour estre chaste ne doit pas estre si fine: . . . Au contraire il la faut subtiliser tant qu'on peut, afin que si chacun est assez meschant pour la vouloir tromper, personne ne soit assez fin pour le pouvoir (41 r° and v°).

> [These verses of poor Ariadne should be written everywhere in ladies' books of hours, and whoever was the first [man] to deny them learning on the grounds that it kindles lasciviousness, I think that he must have feared . . . that they would make him sit in front of the spinning wheel on the second day of their studies, my father. The common man says that in order to be chaste a woman should not be clever. . . . But on the contrary, she should become

as cunning as possible so that if each man is wicked enough to try to deceive her, no man will be clever enough to do so.]

Thus, the female author reacts as female reader through the expansion of *discourse,* that is, of inserted commentary on the story line.[11]

Gournay's handling of classical quotations pinpoints the problem we are discussing here, the confusion between reader and writer. She inserts her quotations *to prove that she has read them.* But she also inserts them *to prove that women should be able to read them.* The works which she quotes constitute her proposal for a program of obligatory reading for women. But since women have been denied access to the Latin texts to which she refers, they must first be educated before they can profit from the lessons they contain:

> Les dames au demeurant trouveront dans les livres que qui mieux congnoist les hommes plus s'en deffie, et que le plus fiable des prometteurs de constance est celuy qui ne sçauroit tenir promesse, par instabilité de la nature humaine. Elles en rapporteront le mespris de mille et mille amans que les femmes ignorantes admireroient, et tel qui feroit delices pour celles-là leur feroit penitence à elles (43 r°).

> [Consequently ladies will find in books that those who know men best are the most sceptical and that the most trustworthy man who promises constancy is the one who would be most incapable of keeping his promise because of the instability of human nature. They [the ladies] will come away scorning the thousands of lovers whom ignorant women would admire, and a man who would be the delight of the latter would be a penance for the former.]

The use of the third person and the future and conditional tenses makes it clear that female readers are not yet capable of reading these texts; whereas Montaigne, who learned Latin before he learned French, will recognize and read them without difficulty. The message for women which is encoded in the citations from antiquity has therefore been channeled through the man who penned the following with regard to education for women:

> Si toutes-fois il leur fache de nous ceder en quoy que ce soit, et veulent par curiosité avoir part aux livres, la poësie est un amusement propre à leur besoin: c'est un art follastre et subtil, desguisé, parlier, tout en plaisir, tout en montre, comme elles. Elles tireront aussi diverses commoditez de l'histoire. En la philosophie, de la part qui sert à la vie, elles prendront les discours qui les dressent à juger de nos humeurs et conditions, à se

deffendre de nos trahisons, à regler la temerité de leurs propres desirs, à ménager leur liberté, alonger les plaisirs de la vie, et à porter humainement l'inconstance d'un serviteur, la rudesse d'un mary et l'importunité des ans et des rides; et choses semblables. Voilà, pour le plus, la part que je leur assignerois aux sciences.[12]

[If, however, it vexes them to cede to us in anything, and if they want to have their part of books, poetry is an amusement proper to their needs: it is a frivolous and crafty art, deceptive, talkative, all for pleasure, all for show, like them. They will also draw diverse lessons from history. In philosophy, the part which is useful for living, they will take the discourses which teach them to judge our humors and conditions, to defend themselves from our betrayals, to manage their liberty, increase life's pleasures and endure humanly the faithlessness of a lover or the brutishness of a husband and the importunities of age and wrinkles; and such things. This, at most, is what I would assign to them for learning.]

Gournay's campaign for female education is thus a reply to Montaigne's condescending program. He would allow women to amuse themselves and teach them to submit to their unhappy fate; she would instruct them to take charge of their own lives.

But in order to accomplish this, women will have to learn from the works of male authors. Thus the introduction of classical quotations further confuses the identities of reader and writer. Who in fact is writing about Dido and Ariadne? Virgil and Catullus? Or the female author, who has appropriated their words in order to incite women to profit from their lessons?

GOURNAY'S SECOND RADICAL DEPARTURE from her source is her insertion of lengthy asides which, like the citations, interrupt Taillemont's linear narrative. During these digressions, the "daughter's" voice seems particularly aware of the "father's" critical attention, addressing him directly as "mon père" and alluding to the intertextual bonds between her *Proumenoir* and his *Essais*. For example, at the very beginning of the book, when Alinda's father the Satrap delivers a long sermon on the duties of princes in order to convince her that she must marry the Parthian king and ransom her uncle, the author reminds Montaigne that in the *Essais* he has outlined a work which he wishes that "their" Justus Lipsius would undertake:[13]

Vous desirez en voz Essais mon père . . . que nostre Justus Lypsius voulut
entreprendre un certain, utile et bel oeuvre, je luy ay plusieurs fois souhaitté
l'entreprise d'un autre, encore auquel il nous instruisit du devoir mutuel des
Princes et des peuples, et jusques où s'estendent les privileges des uns vers
les autres. Le discours precedent du Satrappe m'en a faict ressouvenir
(10 v° and 11 r°).

[You desire in your Essays, my father, . . . that our Justus Lipsius should
undertake a certain useful and fine work. I have several times wished that
he should undertake another, in which he would teach the mutual duties of
Princes and peoples and how far the privileges of one extend toward the
other. The preceding discourse of the Satrap has put me in mind of it.]

By equating Montaigne's idea for a treatise to be written by Lipsius with
her own, Gournay is claiming the right to enter into the dialogue between
the two men.

The chronology involved here is intriguing. Montaigne's remark was
published in the revised edition of the *Essais* which appeared in June
1588, a few months after he met Gournay. Lipsius' *Politicorum sive
Civilis doctrinae libri sex qui ad Principatum maxime spectant* appeared
in 1589. It is in fact a collection and classification of citations on the
subject of political power, and upholds the idea that to be legitimate,
power must be conferred by law or custom and exercised for the good of
the people. He amplified his ideas on the responsibilities of the prince
in *Monita et exempla politica. Libri dui, qui virtutes et vitia principum
spectant,* which appeared in 1605, but which he began working on in
1596.

In or around 1590 Gournay wrote to Lipsius in Latin, thanking him
for his praise of the *Essais*. His reply, published in his *Centuria Secunda*
(1590), reads in part, "Who can you be who write me thus? A maiden?
Scarcely can I believe it from what you write. Is it possible that so keen
an understanding and so solid a judgment, not to speak of such wisdom
and knowledge can be found in one of your sex and in such times as
these?" [14] He also praises the pages from a book which she included and
wishes that she had sent the entire manuscript. [15]

In the margin of the *Proumenoir* (1594) this annotation has been
added: "Il semble qu'elle donnast en cecy quelque presage des Politiques
qu'il a depuis escrites" [It seems that she was anticipating here the

Politics, which he has since written] (10 v°). This marginal notation is retained through the 1599 edition. Gournay evidently wished to give the impression that she had not read Lipsius' *Politics* when she composed the Satrap's discourse.

Her suggestion for a literary project to be undertaken by the great Dutch humanist is, however, the one which the Persian satrap has just delivered to his daughter. Thus Gournay addressing her "father" [Montaigne] replaces a learned man [Lipsius] through the fiction of a father [the Satrap] preaching to *his* daughter [Alinda] and interjects her own opinions into the exchange between the two male authors. Writing to Montaigne what should have been written by Lipsius, Gournay has composed the work on the duties of princes and delivered it in the guise of a fatherly sermon.

The point of departure for this discourse, however, is Alinda's resentment at being "confisquee par droict de victoire" [confiscated by right of victory] (7 v°), and the Satrap's words are immediately followed by a description of the heroine's tears "chasque fois qu'elle venoit à se representer le contentement et les avantages qu'on luy arrachoit, en la banissant de son pays" [each time that she began to think of the contentment and advantages which were being taken from her by banishing her from her country] (11 v°).

The story line, which tells of the daughter Alinda, who is exchanged for a prince, constitutes an ironical commentary on the political theories which her father the Satrap sets forth. In the first place, the sermon on the duties of princes does not apply to Alinda, who is not a prince but a prin*cess* and (as her father knows perfectly well) cannot reign. The text states clearly that if the Satrap hesitated to agree to the marriage, it was not for Alinda's sake, but because he would be deprived thereby of seeing her *children* on the throne. His daughter must fulfill the *duties* of princes, but their *privileges* will fall to her *sons*.

It is at this precise point in the text (the moment when the Satrap hesitates to agree to the exchange because it will deprive Alinda's sons of the succession) that Gournay accomplishes one of the most amazing deconstructive feats in the entire book. The passage begins, "Le père de la dame" [the lady's father], but between the subject and its qualifiers, "sage vieillard et seconde personne de la Perse" [a wise old man and second of rank in Persia], she inserts a long quotation from Catullus 64 which describes how tenderly Ariadne was raised by her *mother*. The passage in its entirety reads,

> Le père de la dame
>   virgo
> Regia, quam suavis expirans lectus odores
> Lectulus, in molli complexu matris alebat
> Quales Eurote progignunt flumina myrtos,
> Aurave distinctos educit verna colore
> sage vieillard et seconde personne de la Perse, se trouvoit importuné d'un mariage estranger, d'aultant qu'il se voioit privé par là, du regne future des enfans de sa fille, à qui le Royaume tomboit, le Roy n'espérant point avoir de race.

In English, the sentence, minus the passage from Catullus, would therefore read, "The lady's father . . . [passage from Catullus] . . . a wise old man and second in rank in Persia was not happy at the idea of a foreign marriage, inasmuch as he saw himself deprived thereby of the future reign of his daughter's children, to whom the Kingdom would fall, since the King had no hope of offspring" (7 r°). The two feminine nouns of the citation, "virgo" (referring to Ariadne) and "regia" (referring to her mother), divide two masculine subjects; and "regia" seems to be in apposition with "le père de la dame" [the lady's father]. The quotation from Catullus thus makes a tacit commentary on the father's patriarchal bias. It contrasts his disappointment at not being the grandfather of kings with the nurture which *mothers* lavish on their daughters. The essential opposition between paternal and maternal attitudes towards offspring is thus encoded in this jarring passage in which the two feminine nouns literally tear apart the syntactical unit "Le père de la dame, [. . .] sage vieillard et seconde personne de la Perse."

Excluded because of her sex from the privileges of which her father speaks, Alinda is a sacrifice to the *res publica*. The treatises which men like Lipsius compose are totally irrelevant to women's estate. When male authors theorize about legitimizing power, they are writing for and about men: "Nous sommes donnéz aux hommes, afin que nous leur soyons comme la nourrice à l'enfant," says the Satrap [We are given to men so that we may be like the nurse to the child] (8v°). It does not occur to political theorists to enfranchise women, let alone to place them in positions of responsibility. By framing the Satrap's discourse with Alinda's impotent laments, Gournay's text demonstrates how the power which men define, and which princes wield, is procured through the exchange of women.[16] But by daring to write such a discourse in Lipsius' place, the female author does what prin*cesses* cannot do: she simultaneously enters and rejects the male arena of politics.

The longest digressive "essay," inserted just before Alinda's death, once again intersects with Gournay's reading of the *Essais*. This aside, already referred to above, follows Ariadne's lament. It argues in favor of education for women and points out how disadvantaged they are by the customs and prejudices of society (42–58). About a third of the way through, the authorial voice speaks directly to Montaigne:

> Or vous defendez, mon père, en vos Essais . . . Plutarque et Seneque, de quelques reproches qu'on leur faisoit: je veux aussi defendre et consoler en votre Proumenoir Paule et Menalia [*sic*] (49 r° and v°).[17]

> [You defend in your *Essais*, my father, Plutarch and Seneca . . . from some reproaches that were inveighed against them. I also want to defend and console in your Proumenoir Paula and Melania.]

Since her "father" has defended Seneca and Plutarch from calumny in his *Essais*, she too will write a defense of those who have been unjustly accused. The objects of her defense will not be the two Latin authors, however, but two obscure women mentioned by St. Jerome. Jerome wrote in order to defend himself from the false accusation that he had been having illicit relations with Paula and Melania. He argued that the extreme asceticism (and physical undesirability) of the two women rendered the charge ridiculous.[18] In the same way that Gournay assumed Lipsius' place when she composed the Satrap's discourse on the duties of princes, here she substitutes herself for both Montaigne and St. Jerome, rewriting their texts in such a way as to replace men by women. St. Jerome defended the two women only incidentally. His main concern was his own reputation. Gournay, however, not only makes them the center of her defense but also argues that they were calumniated because of their gender:

> [M]ais les femmes en particulier y ont double malheur, car on ne pince que les actions sages aux hommes, à elles on pince le nom mesme de la sagesse, et quand il n'y auroit que ce tiltre seul d'une habille femme on en dira du

mal. Y a il personne si meschant d'oser penser . . ᵧ qu'il y eust jamais nul subject que cestuylà qui fit medire des sainctes Paulle et Menalia ces grandes Dames Romaines (47 v°–48 r°).

[But women in particular are doubly unfortunate, for men are robbed only of their wise actions, but women are robbed of the very name of wisdom, and the title of clever woman alone causes people to speak ill of them. Is there anyone so wicked as to dare to think . . . that there was ever any other reason behind the evil talk about Saints Paula and Melania?]

The fault lies, she says, in society's unjust treatment of women. Carried away by the force of her argument, Gournay momentarily forgets that she is writing to Montaigne and speaks directly to the two Roman matrons. What if Socrates had been a woman? she asks: "*Vous* suffise donc, *pauvres dames Romaines,* que si Socrates eust esté femme on n'en eust pas bien parlé non plus que de *vous*" [*You* may be assured, *poor Roman ladies,* that if Socrates had been a woman, he would have been no better spoken of than *you*] (49 v°, emphasis mine). Even Saint Paul himself would have been a failure as a woman:

Davantage *consolez vous* que si S. Paul eust esté de *vostre sexe* il n'eust jamais peu se maintenir dame de réputation en establissant l'Eglise Chrestienne, et en ouvrant au genre humain les portes de Paradis. Car il luy fallut procéder en son dessein par pérégrinations, conversations, et assistences, qui de vray sont bien dignes de sainct Paul et d'un instrument du salut des hommes, mais non pas d'une femme de bien (50 v°–51 r°, emphasis mine).

[Furthermore *console yourselves* that if St. Paul had been of *your sex* he would never have been able to maintain his reputation as a lady while establishing the Christian Church and opening to humanity the gates of Paradise. For he had to carry out his design by journeys, conversations, and gatherings, which in truth were quite fitting for St. Paul and an instrument of men's salvation, but not for an honest woman.]

The social codes have imposed silence on women and have prevented them from participating in the world of ideas and words:

Car estre femme pudique selon le monde, ce n'est pas garder la pudicité, c'est despouiller l'ingénuité, renoncer à la franchise des parolles, des moeurs, et encores du jugement. (50 r°).

[For to be a modest woman in the world's eyes is not to preserve one's modesty, it is to divest oneself of all that is natural, to renounce freedom in words, customs, and even judgment.]

By the act of writing, and what is even more daring, by *rewriting the words of men*, Gournay is herself defying the very codes which she denounces. In fact her entire argument shifts the ground of the discourse in such a way as to undermine the homosocial assumptions of these male authors who read and write about other men. In Montaigne's text, women are totally absent as subjects;[19] in Jerome's they exist only marginally, as literary weapons which are used either to disestablish or to reestablish the good name of the man of God. Gournay's defense of Paula and Melania fills the gap in male texts which is due to the absence of women.

In her fervor, Gournay turns away from Montaigne. She addresses the Roman women directly, reassigning to them the "you" hitherto reserved for "mon père." Only at the end of the passage does she assume once again the humble attitude of dutiful daughter, excusing herself on the grounds that she has been following Montaigne's advice in daring to speak out so forcefully:

> Mais, mon père, qui me pourroit pardonner la longueur de mon caquet en ceste digression, sinon vous qui me reprenez que je suis d'ordinaire trop taciturne en récompense (58 r°).

> [But my father, who could forgive me this long gabby digression if not you who are always telling me that I am too taciturn.]

Throughout *Le Proumenoir* the authorial voice alternates abruptly between the deference of the daughter, and the outspokenness of the woman writer who intrudes herself into male discourse. Sometimes she speaks in the tones of a simpleminded girl:

> Encore moins la simplesse qui est en moy pourroit elle deviner avec quelles persuasions Leontin peut mener à chef le monstrueux dessein qu'il accomplit en Alinda (20 r°).

> [Still less can a simple person like me guess with what persuasions Leontin could succeed in his monstrous design.]

But at other times she abandons her air of modest diffidence. Then she speaks out strongly on women's behalf, telling them to demand that their lovers prove their constancy by more than empty vows:

> [I]l leur falloit dire: Mes amis pour nous faire croire que vous serez constans, il ne sert non plus de nous monstrer que vous estes passionnez à outrance, que si vous nous faisiez veoir que vous avez les bras forts pour

> acquerir reputation de bien courre. . . . Mais faictes-nous paroistre que vous
> ayez la suffisance d'Epaminondas et de Xenophon, et puis nous croirons que
> vous serez capable de la fermeté (30 v°–31 r°).

> [They should be told: My friends, to make us believe that you will be con-
> stant, it is of no more use to show us that you are passionate in the extreme
> than it would be to make us see that you have strong arms in order to be
> reputed as good runners . . . . But make it appear to us that you have the
> steadfastness of Epaminondas and Xenophon, and then we will believe that
> you are capable of firmness.]

The assertive tone is accompanied by a shift away from Montaigne.
When she addresses him directly, she habitually does so in self-depreca-
tory tones, but when the "vous" designates some one other than the
paternal critic, then she expresses her opinions forthrightly, abandoning
the modest demeanor of filial piety. Yet no matter how forcefully she
speaks out, behind her brave display lies the painful recognition that she
is in alien territory where she will be tolerated only so long as she stays
close to the great man who has invited her in as an honorary guest.

The strategy is peculiarly "feminine." By casting herself in the role of
helpless female, she hopes to enlist Montaigne's aid and benefit from his
prestige, but more importantly, she also draws attention away from her
daring invasion of the male world of letters. The asides to "mon père"
serve not only to flatter him but to dissimulate the revolutionary nature
of her project: taking up her pen, she has rewritten Taillemont's story,
contradicting his moral lesson and inscribing subversive digressions into
his plot. Substituting herself for Lipsius, she has written in his place a
political treatise which she has then proceeded to deconstruct by setting
it within the context of the exchange of women. She has even had the
temerity to *re*-write both Montaigne and St. Jerome, inserting a woman's
perspective into texts preoccupied with male concerns.

In her anxiety to placate her "father," however, Gournay is never able
to address her female reader directly, except for occasional outbursts like
those mentioned above. For the most part, her concern for the members
of her own sex is manifested indirectly. As a result the mother's advice
to the daughter is encoded within the daughter's message to the father.
Thus wavering between the roles of daughter and mother, the authorial
voice of *Le Proumenoir* remains undecidable. Since it is not clear *who* is

writing, it also becomes impossible to answer the question "To whom"? The indeterminate identity of the reader is thus causally linked to the writer's inability to accept the full implications of her maternal authority.

THE AUTHOR'S "MATERNAL" STANCE is concealed within her sympathetic retelling of Alinda's story, for like Gournay, Alinda also fails to measure up to *her* father's rigorous standards, as he sets them forth in his discourse on the duties of princes. Gournay portrays the young woman as torn between her respect for the paternal precepts and her desire to determine her own destiny.

She assigns to Alinda a series of soliloquies in which her sense of guilt, connected with the sign of the father, alternates with her need for comfort and solace, personified by her lost mother. Her greatest regret at being forced to marry the Parthian king comes from being forced to renounce the "sein de sa mère" [her mother's breast] (7v°). She sets off on her journey "confite en douleurs et en pleurs sur l'adieu de sa mère" [dissolved in sorrow and tears at bidding her mother adieu] (11 v° and 12 r°). The wily Leontin's success is due in large part to the way in which he skillfully exploits her bitterness at being separated from her mother, thus undermining the Satrap's insistence on her duty to her country:

> Heureuses les filles basses et populaires, [he says to her] qui sans jamais bouger du giron de leur pays, escoutent un jour celle qu'ils [*sic*] ont appelé mère, instruire leurs petites creatures (qui commencent à desnoüer la langue) à les saluer à leur tour de la douceur de ce nom (16 r°).

> [Happy are the lowly daughters of the people who, without leaving the lap of their country, may listen someday to the person they call mother, teaching their little creatures (who are beginning to use their tongues) to call them in their turn by that sweet name.]

In the beginning, Alinda attributes to the maternal figure the attitudes and beliefs of the father. Struggling to resist the temptation to elope with Leontin, she imagines that her fault will be held up by mothers everywhere as an example.

> Est-il dit que ce soit à jamais sur l'horreur de mon exemple, que les mères instruiront leurs filles à fuir le mal? (20 v°–21 r°).

[Shall it be said that forevermore mothers will use my horrible example to instruct their daughters to avoid evil?]

In Alinda's mind, the signs of father, king, and god are linked to betrayal of duty:

Neantmoins, Dieux, donnez moy pardon, ou si ma faute ne mérite grace, vueillez la conceder à ma penitence. Pardonne moy, mon père: tu n'es pas encore parfaitement père miserable, s'il peut advenir que jamais on ne t'aille racompter de quelle punition les Dieux auront aujourd'huy jugé ton enfant digne pour l'offence qu'elle t'a faite (59 v°–60 r°).

[Nevertheless, gods, grant me pardon, or if my fault does not deserve grace, allow it as my penance. Forgive me, my father. You are not yet the most miserable of fathers, if it comes to pass that you never learn of the punishment to which the gods have condemned your child today because of the wrong she has done you.]

As the narrative progresses, Alinda's image of a judgmental mother, who upholds and perpetuates the patriarchal structure, gives way to that of a compassionate mother, grieving for her lost daughter:

Au moins auray-je dequoy consoler ma dolente mère, quand le regret de mon desastre l'aura chassée entre les morts avec moy (40 r°–v°).

[At least I will have something with which to console my grieving mother when the pain of my disaster has driven her to join me among the dead.]

The figure of the mother in *Le Proumenoir* comes more and more to represent nonjudgmental consolation and compassion for the daughter's suffering. When Alinda is silenced by death, it is the authorial voice which laments the mother's absence at her deathbed:

Il ny eust poinct là de tendre mère qui par la chaleur de ses baisers semble luy vouloir inspirer une nouvelle âme. . . . Point de maternelle main pour clorre ses doulx yeux, et pour oindre ce beau corps de baulme et de larmes . . . (61 v°).

[No tender mother was there, trying it would seem to breathe into her a new soul with the warmth of her kisses. . . . No maternal hand to close her sweet eyes, and to anoint that lovely body with balm and tears . . .]

A deep yearning for the absent mother pervades the story which so conspicuously advertises the father's name.

The mother's absence is filled by the authorial voice that discourses on education for women and denounces the repressive social structures in which they are trapped. The understanding, forgiving mother, whom Alinda imagines grieving for the daughter's tragedy, is Gournay herself. It is she who is instructing her daughters to flee from evil, not out of respect for patriarchal duty, as Alinda had at first supposed, but in order to avoid future suffering.

Who then is writing? The answer would seem to be—both the dutiful daughter and the absent mother. And in the same way, the answer to the question, "To whom?" would seem to be that two readers are projected for the text, the paternal critic, to whom it is ostensibly addressed, and the vulnerable woman, to whom it is meant to offer solace and salvation.

AS FAR AS IS KNOWN, MONTAIGNE never replied to Gournay's letter or corrected the manuscript she had sent to him. After his death in 1592, his relatives found *Le Proumenoir* among his papers and sent it back to her along with a request to publish a posthumous edition of the *Essais*.[20] The appeals to the paternal reader remained therefore without response; and Montaigne's silence called into question not only the identity of the reader, but the validity of her entire enterprise. Undaunted, Gournay decided to publish her novel anyway, presumably in the same form in which she had sent it to Montaigne. She even retained the cover letter which called attention to the absence of the father, now rendered forever present in the capacity of silent judge.

But since Montaigne's *imprimatur* had never been received, a note from *l'imprimeur,* the printer, was added to justify its publication.

Il y a quelques anneés que ce livret fut envoyé à feu monseigneur de Montaigne par sa fille d'alliance: dont ayant esté depuis son decés trouvé parmy ses papiers, messieurs ses parens me l'ont faict apporter, pource qu'ils l'ont jugé digne d'estre mis en lumière, et capable de faire honneur du deffunct: s'il se peut adiouster quelque chose à la gloire d'un si grand et si divin personnage. Voy donc que c'est, Lecteur (1 v°).

[Some years ago this little book was sent to the late Monseigneur de Montaigne by his adopted daughter; and having been found among his papers after his death, my lords his relatives had it brought to me, because they judged it worthy of being brought to light and doing honor to the deceased, if it is possible to add anything to the glory of so great and divine a personage. See then what it is, reader.]

This note substitutes the father's surrogates—"messieurs ses parens"—for the original *destinataire*. In the absence of the great man himself, it is they who have judged her book and found it worthy. Significantly "the printer" cites Montaigne's *male* relatives, although his immediate family consisted only of his wife and daughter, thus making it clear that authentication proceeds through the male line.[21]

The style of this note indicates beyond much doubt that the "printer" is none other than Gournay herself, who feels called upon to explain why her book deserves to appear under the father's name. Since, however, her framing letter continues to address a paternal critic, the identity of the final reader remains undetermined. Was the "reader" to whom the "printer" wrote a man of letters who was expected to take the place of the dead father and correct the author's mistakes? Or was she an unwary female who might profit from Gournay's maternal advice and learn to guard herself from falling victim to an inconstant lover?

THE UNCERTAIN IDENTITY OF *Le Proumenoir*'s reader continued to plague its insecure female author. She was never able to decide whether she was addressing herself to a female audience or to a male critic. As a result, Gournay was driven to revise *Le Proumenoir* with each successive reprinting, trying anxiously to meet the impossible demands of male readers for whom her story had never really been intended.

Since the *Proumenoir* had not undergone the paternal corrections, the "daughter" was forced to become her own corrector. Of course, Montaigne himself had been engaged in revising the *Essais* up to the time of his death, and by imitating his practice, Gournay was proving once again the lasting effects of the "father's" influence, marking her text as forever his. But by revising her own text, she was also displacing a male correcting *his* text by a female correcting *hers*.

The gender of the reader and the writer remained both crucial and undecidable through each successive edition of the book. The original version of *Le Proumenoir* was reprinted four times in as many years. Then in 1599 the frontispiece announced a new edition purporting to be "plus *correcte* et plus ample que les précédentes" [emphasis mine]. In it Gournay eliminated altogether the eighteen-page digression in which she had advocated education for women and pleaded the cause of Paula and Melania. Stanton has pointed out that this radical amputation of the pages which plead for women's rights alters significantly the message of *Le Proumenoir*, definitively reducing its female author to the dutiful daughter who stands corrected.[22] It is true that Gournay subsequently incorporated many of its ideas into her two treatises, *Egalité des hommes et des femmes* (1622) and *Grief des dames* (1626),[23] but by removing her feminist digression from the body of her novel, she robbed the book of its power to suggest a new plot in which women would not have to die for love.[24]

The evidence suggests that the members of the literary establishment had not hesitated to proffer the criticisms from which Montaigne had abstained. Their comments have survived indirectly in the preface which precedes *Le Proumenoir* in Gournay's collected works (*L'Ombre de la damoiselle de Gournay*, 1626).[25] In this "Advis sur la nouvelle édition du Proumenoir de Monsieur de Montaigne" [Remarks on the new edition of the Proumenoir . . .], she defends her novel against those who had disapproved of it. They had objected first of all, it would appear, to the classical citations, "quelque ornement en langue estrangere" [some embellishment in a foreign language]. Some "joyeux" [ridiculous people], she writes, "disent, que nous les servons de ceste viande, pour monstrer que nous sçavons du Latin . . . . Ils alleguent, que ceux qui citent, ou nomment les Autheurs en leur texte, le font par vanité de pedanterie, pour monstrer qu'ils les ont leuz" [say that we serve up this food in order to show that we know Latin . . . They allege that those who cite or name these authors in their text do so out of vain pedantry, to prove that they have read them] (*Ombre*, 647). Another serious criticism had been directed at her discursive digressions. The critics had accused her of breaking the rules governing the narrative genre.

The very innovations which make *Le Proumenoir* an original work— the insertion of classical citations and the digressions, the passages in which the woman writer speaks most insistently as *mother* rather than *daughter*—were those which had been singled out for attack. Defending what was, in her mind, the heart of her book, Gournay wrote tartly,

> Mais nous voicy derechef aux mains avec ces correcteurs: ils ne souffrent point un Roman discourant, car sa tablature d'esprit le défend, à leur advis, et luy commande sans respit et sans intermède la suitte de son adventure. . . . je diray seulement sur une si plaisante vision; qu'ils me

font faveur de m'accuser du trop, veu que j'estois en peine de m'excuser du peu (*Ombre*, 651–54).

[But here we are once more confronted by these correctors. They do not admit the possibility of a discursive novel, for in their opinion, the rules of the genre forbid it and demand the continuation of the story without respite or interval. . . . I shall simply say of such an amusing fantasy that they are doing me a favor to accuse me of too much, when I was feeling guilty for adding too little.]

Undoubtedly it was such reproofs which had caused Gournay to *correct* the 1599 edition by deleting from it the eighteen-page "feminist" digression. Her remark about feeling guilty for adding too little indicates, however, that she had not done so without an inner struggle. Nevertheless, the version of the novel which Gournay published in 1626 had again been drastically revised. The large number of changes (even the letter addressed to Montaigne has been rewritten!) betrays the awe in which she still held the figure of the paternal corrector. But the sharp tone of "L'Advis" makes it clear that in her heart of hearts she still believes in the validity of her original text.

In the 1626 edition, she completely revised her use of classical citations, eliminating many and translating the others into French. In so doing she renounced what had been for her a point of honor—her proof of competency in Latin and Greek.[26] Moreover, she reassigned the "virgo regia" passage from Catullus (which had deconstructed the Satrap's desire to become the grandfather of kings) to a sentence with a female subject, Alinda, thus nullifying the shocking apposition of masculine and feminine nouns.

As if to defy those readers who had found fault with her discursiveness, however, she inserted a new digression, this time on the nature of love. This insertion occurs at the moment when the seductive Leontin makes his first appearance (*Ombre* 667–74) and has male charm as its point of departure. The arguments it sets forth are so complex, if not embroiled, that they are almost impossible to summarize. Beginning with the idea that charm is ultimately more powerful than physical beauty, Gournay seems to be arguing in favor of some kind of amorous relationship which would not be based on the senses. But she is not able to reach any coherent conclusion, perhaps because of her half-conscious perception that all her male sources including Plato ultimately reduce women to passivity. Like the "feminist" digression on the education of women, this digression on the nature of love suggests, by its intrusion into the plot, the possibility of another dénouement. What is more, it challenges the authority of the "correctors" who had obliged her to amputate her text and asserts the female author's right to determine the form of her discourse.

The "Advis" also acknowledges overtly the existence of her women readers:

> [J]e croirois avoir autant de tort de refuser quelques Dames du premier rang, qui me commandent de luy faire revoir la lumière à present, que j'en aurois de le composer en l'aage où je suis aujourdhuy (*Ombre*, 644).

> [I would feel myself as wrong in refusing some ladies of the first rank, who order me to have it reappear now, as I would in composing it at my present age.]

She has republished *Le Proumenoir* at the express request of *women*, whose opinions she values and respects. In "L'Advis" she no longer finds it necessary to seek Montaigne's approbation. Furthermore, the printer's note has disappeared and the asides to "mon père" have become less frequent in the body of the text. The Satrap's discourse on the duties of princes makes no reference to either Montaigne or Lipsius. It is also worthy of note that some verses by Sappho have been added to the classical citations.

The appearance of *L'Ombre* did not cause her critics to fall silent with admiration. They immediately attacked her choice of a title. Gournay had based it on the words, "L'homme est l'ombre d'un songe, et son oeuvre est son ombre" [Man is the shadow of a dream and his work is his shadow]. Her detractors objected so sharply to this conceit that when she published a revised edition of her works in 1634, she bowed to pressure and changed her title to *Les Advis ou les presens de la Demoiselle de Gournay*.[27]

This surrender evoked, however, a foreword in which she addressed her female supporters directly. She prefaced the collection with a "Discours sur ce livre" addressed to "Sophrosine," perhaps an idealized woman reader or even an actual patron.[28] In this foreword she speaks of "Vostre tendresse aux interests du sexe et aux miens" [Your sympathy for the interests of the [female] sex and for mine] (n. p.)—and of their close friendship, "Vous qui m'avez fait l'honneur, Illustre Sophrosine, de prendre plaisir à me cognaistre intimement. . ." [You who have done me the honor, Illustrious Sophrosine, of taking pleasure in knowing me intimately]. It seems that Sophrosine has asked her to clarify her reasons for changing the title of her collection:

> Les riottes opiniastres . . . que vous avez sceues, Dame tres-illustre et tres vertueuse, vous ont conviée à me commander de vous esclaircir de mes raisons pour ce regard.

> [The stubborn mockeries . . . which you have heard about, most illustrious and virtuous Lady, have inspired you to command me to enlighten you as to my reasons for this change.]

The female reader now seems to play the role of confidante and advisor which Gournay had tried to assign to Montaigne forty years earlier. Sophrosine knows of the attacks on *L'Ombre* and it is she who has persuaded Gournay to defend herself in writing. Writing to her female supporter, Gournay expresses frankly the bitterness of the woman writer:

> Il sera bon de voir après quel Livre de femme vainqueur de la malice des temps et des hommes sera capable d'effacer le mien: je dis vainqueur de la malice des temps et des hommes: car quels ravages n'ont-ils point fait de cette part sur les Corinnes, les Saphons, les Hypathies, les Aretes et autres?

> [It will be interesting to see what woman's book, overcoming the malice of the times and of men, will be capable of causing mine to be forgotten; I say overcoming the malice of the times and of men, for what ravages have they not made in this way on the Corinnes, the Sapphos, the Hypatias, the Aretaeas and the others?]

This list shows that over the years Gournay had come to know the women writers of antiquity and to identify herself with them. She had also come to understand that the attacks against her writings were related to her gender.

"A Sophrosine" refers to *Le Proumenoir* only in passing, speaking of it as a "gentillesse," but unfortunately in this brief aside the author disavows what had been one of its central theses, Alinda's innocence. Gournay explains that she has included the novel because it shows "la peine qui suit la coulpe" [the punishment which follows guilt]. Instead of exonerating her heroine, as she had in 1594, she seems to be condemning her for misconduct.

At the very moment, then, when Gournay cancels out the paternal reader and redirects her novel to its true *destinataïre,* she disavows the maternal viewpoint and realigns the authorial voice with the paternal doctrine of the guilty female. The final text emerges as more problematic than the original. Before, a woman's message was addressed to a man. Now, a man's message is directed to a woman. It is less certain than ever who is writing to whom.

DERRIDA'S POSTCARD REPRESENTS Socrates seated at a desk writing, while Plato stands behind him (dictating?), an amazing reversal of roles which transforms the speaker into the writer and the son into the father. Likewise in *Le Proumenoir* the identities of reader and writer seem to be reversed. Having first metamorphosed herself from anonymous reader (of Taillemont and Montaigne) into privileged interlocutor, at the moment of composition Gournay assumes the place of the writer, while casting Montaigne in the role of reader.

In the same way that Derrida's postcard stimulated him to speculate in ever more daring hypotheses on the relationship between the celebrated father and son, *Le Proumenoir,* which encloses the couple Montaigne / Gournay, also gives rise to new and complex questions on the relationship between reader and writer. The questions "Who is writing?" and "To whom?" must be posed again and again, as must the questions "Who is correcting whom?" and "Who is refusing to correct whom?"

Perhaps the ultimate addressee of early women's texts is the reader who realizes that the questions they raise are more important than the answers.

NOTES

1. *La Carte Postale: de Socrate à Freud et au-delà* (Paris: Flammarion, 1980), 9 [translation mine].
2. See, for instance, G. L. Michaud's remarks in "Le 'Proumenoir de Montaigne' " *Revue d'histoire littéraire de la France* 41 (1934): 397–99. He asserts that the work contains nothing original aside from the digressive "dissertations de genre moral, plus ou moins fatigantes et pédantesques qui n'ajoutent rien à la valeur de l'oeuvre" [dissertations of a moral nature, all more or less tiresome

and pedantic, which add nothing to the value of the work]. According to Paul Stapfer, "Le roman conté à Montaigne par Mlle de Gournay, puis rédigé par elle en beau style, est mortellement ennuyeux" [The novel told to Montaigne by Mlle de Gournay, then written by her in fine style, is mortally boring]. *La famille et les amis de Montaigne* (Paris: Hachette, 1896), 165. Mario Schiff has this to say: "A nos yeux, le seul mérite de cette nouvelle . . . est d'avoir distrait l'auteur des *Essais*" [In our eyes, the only merit of this novel . . . is that it amused the author of the *Essais*]. *La Fille d'Alliance de Montaigne. Marie de Gournay* (Paris: Champion, 1910), 7. Alan M. Boase comments that "it shows her exaggerated intellectualism applied to love. Nevertheless, the digressions of the *Proumenoir* contain much good sense, and just the conception of love which a predestined old maid of considerable ability would inevitably develop as a shield to her self-respect." *The Fortunes of Montaigne—A History of the Essays in France, 1580–1669* (New York: Octagon, 1970), 55–56. Writing of his painstaking study of all the versions of the *Proumenoir*, in "Note bibliographique sur les diverses éditions du *Proumenoir de M. de Montaigne*," *Bulletin du Bibliophile*, XIVe série (1860), 1285–87, Jean-François Payen said, "[J]'ai dû les lire à peu près complètement pour rédiger cette note, mais, en terminant, je suis tenté de dire . . . COMBIEN QUE JE NE CONSEILLE A HOMME D'AINSI FAIRE! [*sic*]" [I had to read them almost completely in order to compose this note, but in conclusion I am tempted to say . . . HOW MUCH I DO NOT ADVISE ANY MAN TO DO LIKEWISE!].

3. Unless otherwise indicated, all references and quotations are taken from *Le Proumenoir de M. de Montaigne par sa Fille d'Alliance*, introd. Patricia Francis Cholakian (Paris: Abel l'Angelier, 1594; Delmar, N.Y.: Scholars Facsimiles and Reprints, 1985). I have modernized spellings slightly, especially with regard to accents. All translations are mine.

4. This translation was printed after the *Proumenoir* in the 1594 edition.

5. It was a custom during the French Renaissance for two people who discovered a spiritual kinship to declare themselves related "par alliance."

6. See Cathleen M. Bauschatz, "Marie de Gournay's 'Preface de 1595': A Critical Evaluation," *Bulletin de la Société des Amis de Montaigne*, nos. 3–4 (Jan.–June 1986): 73–82; and Maryanne Cline Horowitz, "Marie de Gournay, Editor of the Essais of Michel de Montaigne: A Case-Study in Mentor-Protégée Friendship," *The Sixteenth-Century Journal* 17, no. 3 (Fall 1986): 217–84.

7. For Gournay's biography see Marjorie H. Ilsley, *A Daughter of the Renaissance: Marie le Jars de Gournay: Her Life and Works* (The Hague: Mouton, 1963).

8. Claude de Taillemont, *Discours des champs faëz à l'exaltation de l'Amour et des Dames* (Lyon: Michel Du Bois, 1553), 278.

9. Walter Ong believes that, during the Renaissance, learning Latin was imposed on boys as a rigorous initiation rite. It was supposed to develop in them tough-mindedness and disciplined powers of concentration, which would fit them

for success in the economic and political arenas. Since women were expected to marry and bear children as soon as they reached maturity, they were excluded from this process. See Walter Ong, "Latin Language Study as a Renaissance Puberty Rite," in *Rhetoric, Romance, and Technology: Studies in the Interaction of Expression and Culture* (Ithaca: Cornell Univ. Press, 1971), 113–41.

10. In her preface to the 1626 edition, she mentions these criticisms. See below.

11. I use the word "discourse" here in the sense defined by Benveniste, who distinguishes between the story line or *récit,* which narrates past events, and the *discours,* which presupposes a speaker who attempts to influence a listener. Emile Benveniste, *Problèmes de Linguistique Générale* (Paris: Gallimard, 1966).

12. *Essais,* bk. 3, ch. 3, Pléiade edition, ed. Albert Thibaudet (Paris: Gallimard, 1950), 920.

13. See *Essais,* bk. 2, ch. 12: "Combien je desire que, pendant que je vis, ou quelque autre, ou Justus Lipsius, le plus sçavant homme qui nous reste, . . . eust et la volonté, et la santé, et assez de repos pour ramasser en un registre, selon leurs divisions et leurs classes, sincerement et curieusement, autant que nous pouvons voir, les opinions de l'ancienne philosophie sur le subject de nostre estre et de noz meurs" (651–52). [How I wish that while I live, either someone else, or Justus Lipsius, the most learned man who is left to us, . . . had the will, the health, and enough leisure to collect into a register, according to their divisions and classes, sincerely and curiously, as much as possible of the opinions of ancient philosophy on the subject of our being and our customs.] This passage was inserted by Montaigne into the 1588 edition (Paris: Abel l'Angelier), in the same year that he met Marie de Gournay and she wrote the *Proumenoir.*

14. Translation from the Latin in Ilsley, 37.

15. Ibid., 37.

16. For a study of *Le Proumenoir* within the context of Lévi-Strauss's theory of the exchange of women, see Domna C. Stanton, "Woman as Object and Subject of Exchange: Marie de Gournay's *Le Proumenoir* (1594)," *L'Esprit créateur* 23, no. 2 (Summer 1983): 9–24.

17. The essay in question is the "Defence de Seneque et de Plutarque,"bk. 2, ch. 32, pp. 807–14. Paula and Melania (Melanium) were two Roman matrons eulogized by St. Jerome in Letter 45, "To Asella," in *The Principal Works of St. Jerome,* trans. W. H. Fremantle (New York: The Christian Literature Co., 1893), 58–60. Gournay seems to have reversed unconsciously the *n* and the *l* of Melania's name.

18. "Of all the ladies in Rome but one had power to subdue me, and that one was Paula. She mourned and fasted, she was squalid with dirt, her eyes were dim from weeping. . . . Of all the ladies in Rome, the only ones that caused scandal were Paula and Melanium, who, despising their wealth and deserting their children, uplifted the cross of the Lord as a standard of religion. Had they frequented the baths, or chosen to use perfumes, or taken advantage of their

wealth and position as widows to enjoy life and to be independent, they would have been saluted as ladies of high rank and saintliness." *The Principal Works of St. Jerome*, 59.

19. The chapter in question refers to women only to prove how stubborn they can be: he retells the old story about the drowning woman who made the sign of killing lice above her head to prove that her husband was covered with vermin (811). Later, in book 2, ch. 35 ("De Trois Bonnes Femmes") he tells of three exceptional women who were *not* overjoyed by their husbands' deaths.

20. Gournay learned of Montaigne's death only indirectly in 1593 through a letter from Lipsius. Evidently the family's announcement was lost, an occurrence not hard to understand considering the fact that France was in the throes of a civil war. She probably received the manuscript of *Le Proumenoir*, along with the revised edition of the *Essais*, in the spring of 1594. *Le Proumenoir*, written in 1588, appeared in 1594 and her posthumous edition of the *Essais*, accompanied by a controversial preface, in 1595. That Gournay remained on good terms with Montaigne's family is proved by the fact that she paid them a long visit in 1595–1596.

21. At the end of her letter, Gournay had sent her greetings to Montaigne's brothers, "messieurs de la Brousse et de Mattecoulon vos freres" (5 r°).

22. Stanton, 23.

23. A primitive version of the *Grief des dames* had appeared in her 1595 preface to the *Essais*.

24. Very significantly, this edition also contains the original version of her 1595 preface to Montaigne's *Essais*, which critical opinion had caused her to retract in 1598. This first preface was a highly emotional response to Montaigne's critics and detractors. Thus it looks very much as if she sacrificed the feminist digression in *Le Proumenoir* to filial piety.

25. *L'Ombre de la Damoiselle de Gournay* (Paris: Jean Libert, 1626). The title of this collection may be translated into English as "Miss Gournay's Shadow."

26. In this regard it is interesting to take note of Jean-Regnault de Segrais' comment more than half a century later that Madame de LaFayette knew Latin, but took care not to show it in order to prevent the other ladies from becoming jealous. *Segraisiana* (Paris: La Compagnie des libraires associés, 1721), vol. 1, p. 102.

27. Paris: Toussainct Du-Bray, 1634; Paris: Jean Du-Bray, 1641. The title means "Miss Gournay's Opinions or Offerings."

28. Sophrosine means *prudent* or *wise* in Greek.

Reading Ben Jonson's *Queens*

Margaret Maurer

> If to a Womans head a Painter would
> Set a Horse-neck, and divers feathers fold
> On every limbe, ta'en from a severall creature,
> Presenting upwards, a faire female feature,
> Which in some swarthie fish uncomely ends:
> Admitted to the sight, although his friends,
> Could you containe your laughter?
>
>   (*Horace, His Art of Poetrie*, made English
>   by Ben. Iohnson, ll. 1–7; vol. 8: 305)[1]

William Drummond says Ben Jonson told him "that he wrott all his [verses] first jn prose, for so his master Cambden had Learned him" (*Conversations with Drummond*, xv, ll. 377–78; vol. 1: 143). A poem to Jonson is first of all a concept, an idea, or (to use Sir Philip Sidney's well-known word for it) a foreconceit that can be formulated without the language in which it is ultimately expressed. Neither Sidney nor Jonson can maintain the dualistic sense of poetry on which this theory depends. In his *Defence*, Sidney admits to "finding [himself] sick among the rest" of those who pursue verbal ingenuity as an end in itself;[2] and while Jonson, Drummond records, said "That Verses stood by sense without either Colour's or accent . . . yett other tymes he denied [it]" (*Conversations*, xv, ll. 379–80; vol. 1: 143). Finally uncompromised by such qualifications, however, this understanding of a poem as primarily its informing idea is the ground of poetry's defense because it is that idea that is the vehicle of didactic intent. In these terms, poetry can be rescued from the charge that it is a diversion and promoted instead as meaningful activity. Only dealing in beauty, not serving it, the poet pursues truth and attempts thereby to induce virtuous conduct in those who read his work. Not surprisingly, the formal restraint characteristic of neo-classicism is attractive to the poet with this sense of his vocation. Conventions of genre and the more generalized distrust of verbal and formal ingenuity for its own sake control the extraneous flourishes of invention that might interfere with the poem's virtue-breeding idea.

Any consideration of the place that women can have in the tradition of canonical literature must begin by recognizing the paradigm shaping this defense of poesy: Sidney's poet writes in just the terms that Count Baldasarre Castiglione's Bembo teaches the courtier to love. He must keep in mind that the pursuit of particular beauty is justified only as it can be sublimated to larger concerns, and that act of sublimation requires him to assert control over the object of his affection.[3] The analogy between the Renaissance courtier's *ars poetica* and *ars amatoria* helps discover why poetry that is written or read as canonical, that is, as effectively meaningful, will be explicitly or implicitly misogynous. Basically, women's historically incidental status undermines the significance towards which poetry strives. Women in their particular actuality, therefore, are not a poet's direct concern; and if they are somehow involved in his poem, their influence must be rigidly controlled.[4] The threat they pose to poetry also emerges indirectly in the terms that prescribe the education of the poet to mastery in his craft. Insofar as he sets about to prove himself a man by writing significantly, all inhibitions to that significance— weak elements of invention, extraneous "Colour's" and rhetorical embellishments—are effeminate tendencies to be subdued and overcome in himself. Jonson accuses the poetaster outright of sexual dysfunction:

> Others there are, that have no composition at all; but a kind of tuneing, and riming fall, in what they write. It runs and slides, and onely makes a sound. Womens-*Poets* they are call'd: as you have womens-*Taylors*.
> *They write a verse, as smooth, as soft, as creame;*
> *In which there is no torrent, nor scarce streame.*
> You may sound these wits, and find the depth of them, with your middle finger. They are *Creame-bowle*, or but puddle deepe (*Discoveries*, ll. 710–18; vol. 8: 585).

Jonson's anxiety to assert his poetry's power to an audience of men hardly conceals his fear of appearing impotent in their eyes. No less vulnerable to this fear, though perhaps less literally so, are we professors of literature today, who need to find in poems enough transcendent meaning to make them items of the discourse men speak with men.

Jonson's *Masque of Queens* is the occasion of a particularly belabored struggle, begun by Jonson himself and continued on his behalf by his readers, to represent women (historically inconsequential women; some might even say, silly women) meaningfully. The masque's action, enshrining Bel-Anna, presented by Queen Anne, in Chaucer's House of Vergil's Fama, is Jonson's self-conscious proof of his poetical powers as he derives them from his two great masters. Although in some ideal formulation, that is, with respect to something we might conceivably articulate as its foreconceit, the masque can be seen to accomplish a didactic end by imagining the Queen as a projection of the heroic virtue of the King's pacifistic policy, its presentation at court and subsequently in print became a far cry from that elegant notion. Indeed, the fully annotated text of the masque as Jonson prepared it for readers soon after its performance at Whitehall, February 2, 1609, and then published it, first in a quarto edition of that year and then in the 1616 folio edition of his "workes," seems to confess its difficulties in handling its female elements.

To be sure, a reader of modern texts of and commentary on the masque is not encouraged to acknowledge these difficulties.[5] Glosses ignore the identity of the women who participated in *Queens* and for whom, at least in some sense, Jonson wrote it; and editors slight or even excise Jonson's detailed commentary and obsessive annotations, particularly those focused on the incantatory verses of the hags in the antimasque. Alongside such subdued renditions, *Queens* as Jonson printed it has a monstrous look, its text swelling with apparently incidental invention. When we examine these excrescences, we find warrant for the sex-based categories of neo-classical literary criticism. With more actuality than we might expect the ladies of *Queens* to have as far as we stand from them, they are lurking in the shadows of Jonson's text, daring us to imagine them and the threat they pose to the masque's meaning.

One point in the text of *Queens* is especially exemplary of this effect. To mark the entrance of the court ladies into the performance, Jonson lists the names of the queens from antiquity that the ladies impersonate, providing at some length an account of their historical exploits. This is one of those conspicuously pedantic embellishments of the written text about which Jonson's commentators have relatively little to say. Its enormity becomes interesting, however, once we realize that it has been written to fill the vacancy created because Jonson does not describe the spectacle as the audience of Whitehall might have appreciated it—seeing actual ladies in the costumes of fictional queens. Jonson will do nothing but describe the fictional dimensions, for reasons he acknowledges in a single sentence with a surprising lapse at the crucial point:

> And here, wee cannot but take the opportunity, to make some more particular description of the *Scene,* as also of the *Persons* they presented: w^ch, though they were dispos'd rather by *chance,* then *Election,* Yet is it my part to iustefie them all vertuous; and, then, The Lady, that will owne her presentation, May (*The Masqve of Qveenes*, ll. 475–80; vol. 7: 306).

That is, instead of displaying his poetical power to rename the ladies, associating each in a delightfully instructive way with an ancient queen, Jonson credits "*chance*" rather than "*Election*" with controlling this element of the masque's meaning; and he passes on to a long description of the historical queens that is, by his own admission, inconsequential in its particularity.

And suddenly some dim traces of the actual masquing ladies are before us, too disembodied to be described with certainty, but nonetheless disrupting the masque's progress toward meaning and so complicating our efforts to read and interpret it coherently. Each lady attendant on the Queen is implicated in this challenge to Jonson's authorial control, first in her act of choosing her "presentation" and then in her reservation to herself of the circumstances under which she will "owne" it. Jonson's uncharacteristic willingness to let the matter go at that suggests, if not necessarily helplessness, an attitude of exasperation with the ladies. Too frivolously concerned with costume, perhaps, to care for the significance of the roles they played; too caught up in the trick of disguise as an end in itself, maybe, to permit the moment of meaningful disclosure; too liable, one might suppose, to change places in the chariots to assert precedence or sit near a new friend—these ladies give no reason for not cooperating; indeed, they can have no other than a woman's reason.

It is not usual to be concerned with this passage in a reading of *The Masque of Queens,* and it is still less ordinary to read a remark in the text of a masque as an allusion to something off the page which one proceeds then to imagine. In pursuing the sometimes barely perceptible intimations a reader may experience of the actual women participating in this masque, I, like the lady masquers, only in another context, am challenging any purely idealized meaning that *Queens* may be said to have. My techniques are defensible because, in many of its present academic manifestations, literary discussion has taken Jonson's theory of poetry to a level of abstraction beyond what he assumes in his texts, confining the actual persons associated with them to only so much particularity as is consistent with an utterly transcendent idea. Jonson's full texts, however, are more dynamic than they appear in our editions, and they provoke extraliterary imaginations.

Queens, in particular, seems to beg the observation that, whatever we make of Bel-Anna, Jonson did not succeed in presenting Queen Anne as the type of feminine virtue nor did he do anything to improve her standing in the House of Fame. Her name requires a footnote; and once that footnote goes beyond the merest factual comments, it will describe, in an idiom hardly more reliable than gossip, a lady scarcely worth celebrating.[6] To acknowledge the essential irony of the masque's conceit whereby this lady becomes the focus of Fame's exertions and to admit, as an aspect of that irony, the insubstantial nature of the evidence on which a perception of the irony depends is to be suddenly expelled from the world imagined in the masque proper, where Fame is the dutiful daughter of Heroic Virtue, and thrust into the world of the antimasque of hags, where something called Mischief is the presiding influence, her various aspects embodied in Ignorance, Suspicion, Credulity, Falsehood, Murmur, Malice, Impudence, Slander, Execration, Bitterness, and Rage. In his antimasque, in other words, Jonson seems momentarily to justify all that a reader might hear, know, or suspect about the frivolity of the Jacobean court. It is by succumbing to the impulses of the antimasque that a reader imagines the actual ladies of *Queens*.

This reading of *Queens*, preoccupied with those ladies, makes then what I would call mischief in the text. It does so by focusing at first mainly on the commentary in the text proper, then on Jonson's manipulation elsewhere in his writing of the identity of the masquing ladies, and finally, generally, on the implications of the antimasque and Jonson's heavy annotations of it. In other words, though I acknowledge the origin of my reading the masque this way in such unworthy motives as impudence, ignorance, and even some bitterness, this undertaking has some of the virtues of literary analysis, if not precisely the heroic ones. In this reading, Jonson is not a Vergil, a poet resting assured of the power his work will always have to promote virtue; but he is a Horace, a courtier-satirist locked in heroic struggle with what he would call the effeminate impulses of triviality and vulgar pleasure.[7] This reading does not really discount *Queens* as a poem nor Jonson as a poet; rather, it credits Jonson with anticipating the resistance of his masque's subjects and creating a complex structure to accommodate that resistance. I am not denying that Jonson has represented women meaningfully; I am saying that to do so he must represent them as monsters.

The important question that attends women's study of canonical works is whether investigating the sense in which women have an actual place in them can have any satisfactions. In Horace's hypothetical anecdote, the painter's friends laugh at him because they abhor his picture; and it is odd to be a woman and to be among them. My reading of *The Masque of Queens* has therefore an epilogue, describing one heartening incident I have found of ladylike resistance to the constraints Jonson has imposed on us by the foreconceit of *Queens*.

SOME IDEA OF *The Masque of Queens* had to exist and be approved before its author began to negotiate over the points of its production; if Jonson composed as Drummond says he says he did, it existed before any speeches were even written. A document from British Museum MS. Harley 6947 is clearly an account of the masque that, in projecting its elements, has assigned a meaning to those elements in just the form we would expect a foreconceit to be articulated. There are points in this document that suggest that some slight changes in the details of the production were introduced into the court performance, and these are of some interest;[8] but I want to quote the document in full primarily to set the interpretation it specifies for the masque's crucial elements against Jonson's description of those elements in the more poetical text he published.

The dominant attitude in the document is explanatory: it describes the elements of the masque by giving them names, and their names explain their various functions in the masque's conceit:

When the kinge is set and the full expectation of the spectacle raised there shalbe hearde a strange murmur with a kind of hollowe and infernall musike when sodainely an orcus or poeticall Hil [hell?] is discouered and from the sides of it comminge forth a maske of hags or Sorceresses se⟨ue⟩rally attired, with thire spindles reeles and other magicall instruments makinge a confused noise with strange gestures. Thire names are *Ignorance, Falshoode, suspicion, Credulity, Murmur, Impudencie, Malice, slaunder, Execration, Bitternes,* and *Fury* the opposites of glory To these comes Ate the goddes of mischiefe and makinge vp the 12. bids them and encourageth them to goe forwarde to disturbe the peace of the night and place, as they doe to all goodnes, wherevpon fallinge a fresh to thire daunces and incantation:

Thus in this document the antimasque is clearly a foil to the main masque, delineating the glory of the queens by force of contrast. The argument is likewise obvious that the antimasque is dispelled by the force of Heroic Virtue, who articulates the fiction behind the next event, the spectacle of queens in the House of Fame:

on the instant a loude triumphant musicke sounds at which as at a blast they all vanish, and the place is changed into a bewetifull and magnificent buildinge to shewe that the sounde of a virtuous fame is able to scatter and affright all that threaten yt. out of this place comes forth a person signifiinge *Heroicke Virtue,* the father of goode fame. He tels that this was the pallace of his daughter, where there were a selecte number of Queenes who for thire virtues while they were on earth haue had the honour since to liue celebrated in the ⟨pallace⟩ of Fame foreuer. These hearinge of the graces of *Bellanna* queene of the ocean, and knowinge that she alone possesst all these virtues which were in them deuided and that yet the best and most soueraigne place of that pallace was uoyde they were desirous to gratifie her with that honour in her life time which noe othere might hope to enioie after death.

As it is here conceived, the masque arranges the queens' display in the palace of Fame as the explicit reward of virtuous action:

which she vouchsafeinge at whic⟨h⟩e time he shewes the queene and the ladies sittinge in a *Portico,* they were not only kepte from obliuion but once againe made visible to the light. And to such a light as from whome euer she her selfe out of her trewest virtue acknowledged to receiue all her lustre. At this the musickes sounds while they are descendinge, and the gates openinge belowe the first 4 are discouered in a chariotte which comes forth drawne with Panthers, the 2 follo⟨wo⟩ers [second following?] drawne by Eagles and so the 3 whi⟨c⟩h is the last and most eminent with the statue of fame on the top of yt for her *Maiestie* drawne by Lions

In the description that follows of the triumphal procession, the hags are mentioned; and again the function of their presence is immediately emphasized as signifying their subjection to virtue's power:

> in which [chariots] they ride about the stage as in a solemne triumph ouer those vices which were flede before them, and so turninge all thre in face to the kinge, her maiesties chariot beinge in the midle they come forth and daunce in thire different habits accordinge to the different nations where they are.

The document concludes with a list of the queens:

> These be the names of the
> twelue Queenes.

> *Bellanna* quene of of [*sic*] the ocean
> *Penthesilea* queene of the Amazons
> *Thomiris* queene of the Scythians
> *Camilla* queene of the Voscians
> *Tenobia* queene of the Palmarians
> *Artemisia* queene of the Carians
> *Berenice* queene of the Ægiptians
> *Bundrica* queene of the Icenians
> *Valasca* queene of the Bohemians
> *Cnidace* queene of y^e Æthiopians
> *Atalanta* queene of the Ætoleans
> *Amalasanta* queene of the Gothes

If, as Jonson's editors believe, this is the masque's argument prepared (though badly copied) for approval of the project, the interpretive emphasis in the document is understandable. The account of the elements of the spectacle takes care to specify what the beholders will understand from it: after denying the power of any contrary influence over the Queen, the masque authorizes Heroic Virtue to introduce Bel-Anna as the recipient of all the glory that Fame ever has conferred on womankind.

Against the abstract coherence of this argument, Jonson's text is remarkable for its tendency to preserve the essentially dramatic effect of the masque's production. The effect of reading the two together is to see the argument as clarifying elements that Jonson's text acknowledges unfolded more gradually, even at times preserving in their full manifestation some of the ambiguities that attended their development to that point. In other words, the entire fabric of the poem that Jonson printed as *The Masque of Queens* has within it elements that qualify or even contradict the main thrust of the argument, colors and accents that could be said to defy the sense of the masque as instructive praise.

For example, what the reader of the argument knows at once about the hags and their relationship to the queens ("the opposites of glory") is something that Jonson's text is careful to insist that the spectators were called upon to conclude only after their eyes had been engaged with fantastic sights and their ears subjected to the charms that produce Mischief:

> Quickly, *Dame*, then; bring yoʳ part in,
> Spur, spur vpon little Martin,
> Merely, merely, make him sayle,
> A worme in his mouth, and a thorne in's tayle,
> Fire aboue, and fire below,
> With a Whip, i'your hand, to make him goe.
> O, now, shee's come!
> Let all be dumbe.

> At this, the *Dame* entered to them, naked arm'd, bare-footed, her frock tuck'd, her hayre knotted, and folded wᵗh vipers; In her hand, a Torch made of a dead-Mans arme, lighted; girded wᵗh a snake. To whome they all did reuerence, and she spake, vttring, by way of question, the end wherefore they came: wᶜh, if it had bene done eyther before, or other-wise, had not bene so naturall. For, to haue made themselues theyʳ owne decipherers, and each one to haue told, vpon theyʳ entrance, *what they were, and whether they would*, had bene a most piteous hearing, and vtterly vnworthy any quality of a *Poeme:* wherein a *Writer* should alwayes trust somewhat to the capacity of the *Spectator*, especially at these *Spectacles;* Where Men, beside inquiring eyes, are vnderstood to bring quick eares, and not those sluggish ones of Porters, and Mechanicks, that must be bor'd through, at euery act, wᵗh Narrations (*Qveenes*, ll. 87–110; vol. 7: 286–87).

The consequence of deferring the identification of the hags and their relationship to the masque's project is that by the time Mischief, as Jonson says in the marginal note to her first speech, "pursue[s] the purpose of theyʳ comming, and discouer[s] theyʳ natures more largely" (*Qveenes*, note p. to line 132; vol. 7: 288), the audience is deeply involved, as the audience of *Macbeth* always is, with creatures whose manifest perversion does not disqualify them from knowing things, however illicit, that we would know. As Mischief calls the roll of her attendants, all manner of suspicion, impudence, and malice might be aroused in the audience with satiric reflections on the masquers' entrance.

These are powerful if perverse fantasies, and a poet might take some pride in imitating them, so long as he is careful to disclaim their ultimate validity. In the body of his printed text, before Mischief's final invocation, Jonson's commentary notes how "the *Dame* . . . tooke occasion to boast all the power attributed to witches by the *Antients:* of w^{c}h euery *Poet* (or the most) doth giue some" (*Qveenes*, ll. 205–8; vol. 7: 294). Jonson's text, in fact, takes a reader to the very brink of the interpretive possibility that the hags' incantatory energy generates Fame; and this effect might have been even more pronounced in the production the text records. Dramatically, the second series of charms, followed by infernal music and a wild dance, precedes the entrance of the masquers seated on Fame's temple with the same momentum that produced Mischief.

In this, the crucial moment of the transformation of the masque's stage, the contrast between the account in the argument and the account in the text is particularly striking. The reader of the masque's argument sees at once that "the place is changed into a bewetifull and magnificent buildinge to shewe that the sounde of a virtuous fame is able to scatter and affright all that threaten yt." This clear statement of the meaning of the transformation of the stage is, in fact, what Jonson versifies in the speech of Heroic Virtue explaining his own appearance:

> When *Vertue* cut of *Terror,* he gat *Fame.*
> And, if when *Fame* was gotten, *Terror* dyde
> What black *Erynnis,* or more Hellish pride
> Durst arme these *Hagges,* now she'is growne, and great,
> To think they could her *Glories* once defeate?
>
> (*Qveenes*, ll. 375–79; vol. 7: 302)

But in the narrative account of the scene change in his text, Jonson's language seems to qualify this interpretation by conceding that something, once imagined, cannot be entirely obliterated:

> In the heate of they^r *Daunce,* on the sodayne, was heard a sound of loud Musique, as if many Instruments had giuen one blast. W^{t}h w^{c}h, not only the *Hagges* themselues, but they^r *Hell,* into w^{c}h they ranne, quite vanishd; and the whole face of the *Scene* alterd; scarse suffring the memory of any such thing (*Qveenes*, ll. 354–59; vol. 7: 301).

"Scarse" describes the faint perception of symmetry whereby the spectator appreciates the masque's design. Twelve epicene hags, "who, at they[r] meetings, do all thinges contrary to the custome of men" (*Qveenes*, ll. 346–48; vol. 7: 301) bequeath the stage to the twelve queens, who live and breathe now in a similarly epicene condition, as the imaginary projections of "Men-making Poets" (*Qveenes*, l. 386; vol. 7: 302).

The issue here is one with which the masque, as projected in its argument, does not engage but which is implicit in any reference to the goddess Fama: Fame traditionally presides over good and bad reputations; she not only immortalizes virtue but also perpetuates less edifying memories, sheerly false ones, or no record at all. The activities promoted by Mischief and her coven may seem to absorb all of Fame's fickleness and viciousness; but their exorcism from the world of the masque is not complete. When Heroic Virtue describes his daughter,

> She, that enquireth into all the world,
> And hath, about her vaulted *Palace,* hoorl'd
> All rumors, and reports, or true or vayne,
> What vtmost Landes, or deepest Seas contayne:

he cannot omit the necessary qualification of her effect that she, in the world of the masque, is supportive only of virtue:

> (But, only, hangs great *actions,* on her file.)
> (*Qveenes,* ll. 390–94; vol. 7: 303)

Moreover, when Heroic Virtue announces Fame's project, "To night, soundes Honor" (*Qveenes*, l. 396; vol. 7: 303), it is a prescription as much as a description of his daughter's duties, who, in other contexts, is so notorious for behaving otherwise.[9]

Heroic Virtue insists that Fame will no more immortalize rumor in *Queens* than he himself will permit any memory of the hags to linger on the stage. It is interesting that when the hags are described as reappearing for the triumphal procession, the argument's account of "a solemne triumph ouer those vices which were flede before them," while it is communicated in Fame's speech:

> And, let those *Hagges* be led, as Captiues, bound
> Before they[r] wheeles, whilst I my trumpet sound.
> (*Qveenes,* ll. 472–73; vol. 7: 305)

is not a part of Jonson's authorized description, which seems more engaged with the effect of *discordia concors* communicated by hags and queens sharing the stage:

> By this time, imagine the *Masquers* descended; and agayne mounted, into three triumphant *Chariots,* ready to come forth. The first foure were drawne w^{t}h *Eagles,* (wherof I gaue the reason, as of the rest, in *Fames* speech), they^r 4 Torchbearers attending on the *chariot* sides, and foure of the *Hagges,* bound before them. Then follow'd the second, drawne by *Griffons,* w^{t}h they^r Torch-bearers, and four other *Haggs.* Then the last, w^{c}h was drawne by *Lions,* and more eminent (Wherein her Matie was) and had sixe Torch-bearers more, (peculiar to her) w^{t}h the like number of Hagges (*Qveenes,* ll. 710–19; vol. 7: 314).

The impulse that the hags represent in the operations of Fame likewise remains a suppressed preoccupation of the songs:

> And, as [Fame's] browes the cloudes invade,
> > Her feete do strike the ground.
> Sing then *good Fame,* that's out of *Vertue* borne,
> For, Who doth fame neglect, doth vertue scorne.
> > > (*Qveenes,* ll. 727–30; vol. 7: 315)

Fame, infamy, and oblivion are not, in fact, as separable in Jonson's *Masque of Queens* as the interpretation in the argument would suggest. This is an ambiguity as much or more available to the spectator of *Queens* as to its reader. For the reader, its particular force does not become apparent until the very end of the text, in what Jonson calls his epilogue, "the celebration of Who were the *Celebraters*" (*Qveenes,* l. 775; vol. 7: 316).

For a modern reader especially, the list of the participating ladies is attended by the very irony implicit in Heroic Virtue's anxiety to confine his daughter's activities to noble objects: most of the ladies named in the epilogue have been ill-served by Fame. Moreover, the form in which they are granted what little fame Jonson can confer for their involvement in the masque gently deepens the irony: he lists them by title and family name ("Co. of *Huntingdon.* / Co. of *Bedford.*"), in contrast to the way he has listed the queens they have impersonated by the long and sonorous given names immortalized in other poets' verses. To be sure, not all of the ladies have received equal treatment at Fame's hands. For at least one, for example, the Countess of Essex, there has been infamy, although it came four years later and under another name, the Countess of Somerset. In 1609 her tendencies toward promiscuity and murderous intrigue were still matters of murmur, malice, and slander.[10] For some of the ladies there is a modest fame that, to a significant extent, Jonson, poetizing in other contexts, has been responsible for conferring. In his book of Epigrams, printed before *Queens* in the 1616 Folio, Susan, Countess of Montgomery, is celebrated for the propriety of her given name; and Lucy, Countess of Bedford, is praised as Lucy and as Bedford. In the latter case, Jonson even remarks that there is a propriety to the way she has appropriated Bedford for herself.[11] Finally, Queen Anne and her name have had a symbolic significance for Jonson since the accession of James, a significance he is proud of having devised in the coinage Bel-Anna, "to honor hers *proper,* by; as adding, to it, the attribute of *Fayre*" (*Qveenes*, ll. 663–64; vol. 7: 312). This name, Bel-Anna, is not, however, purely complimentary to her but rather a device to heighten her symbolic utility to the poet who would praise her husband. As early as the *Kings entertainment, in passing to his Coronation,* Jonson had thought in these terms. Noting that the date of the triumph (the Ides of March) suggests a union of Mars and Anna-Perenna, Jonson takes his cue from that happy accident to find in King James' wife a figure of the aspect of the King he wants to celebrate, wise diplomacy in place of war:

> these dead rites [of Mars and "Anna stil'd Perenna"]
> Are long since buryed, and new power excites
> More high and heartie flames. Loe, there is hee,
> Who brings with him a greater ANNE then shee:
> Whose strong and potent vertues haue defac'd
> Sterne MARS his statues, and vpon them plac'd
> His, and the worlds b[l]est blessings.
>   (*Kings entertainment*, ll. 587–93; vol. 7: 102)

Jonson's interest in her, which is the same as Fame's interest, consists of associating her name with that of King James by rechristening her Bel-Anna.

The scant individual reputations of these ladies is only one aspect, however, of the irony of Jonson's use of them in a masque on the subject of Fame. As nearly interchangeable entities within a type, they generate irony on another level. Collectively, they are the ladies of the court of

King James I, notorious for their indulgence in the courtly pastimes of masquing and banqueting associated with the household of the Queen, kept separate from and operated with an extravagance nearly equal to the household of the King.[12] In other words, as a group these ladies are known for their trivialized version of manly pursuits. Jonson's decision to associate them with women whose heroic exploits have given them each a place alongside of men invites reflection on the actual courtly habits of Queen Anne and her ladies.

It is likely, as I have already suggested, that Jonson viewed with some dismay the carelessness that the lady masquers exhibited toward the associations created by their masqued identities; he must be content with his part "to iustifie them all vertuous" (*Qveenes*, l. 479; vol. 7: 306). Fond as they doubtless were of their opportunity to individualize themselves in separately elaborate costumes ("These habites had in them the excellency of all deuice, and riches; and were worthely varied, by [Jones'] Invention, to the *Nations,* whereof they were *Queenes*" [*Qveenes*, ll. 699–701; vol. 7: 314]), there seems to have been no way for the fiction of the masque to capitalize on that variety and make it significant. Jonson's anticipation of criticism on that point is interesting:

> But, here, I discerne a possible Obiection, arising agaynst mee, to w^{c}h I must turne: As, *How I can bring* Persons, *of so different* Ages, *to appeare, properly, together? Or, Why (w^{c}h is more vnnaturall) w^{t}h* Virgil's Mezentius, *I ioyne the liuing, w^{t}h the dead?* I answere to both these, at once, Nothing is more proper; Nothing more naturall: For these all liue; and together, in they^r *Fame;* And so I present them. Besides, if I would fly to the all-daring Power of *Poetry,* Where could I not take Sanctuary? or in whose *Poëme*?

In the folio text, Jonson seems to have been provoked to go further still in the direction of a defense:

> For other obiections, let the lookes and noses of Iudges houer thick; so they bring the braines: or if they do not, I care not. When I suffer'd it to goe abroad, I departed with my right: And now, so secure an Interpreter I am of my chance, that neither praise, nor dispraise shal affect me (*Qveenes*, ll. 670–79 and note; vol. 7: 313).

Jonson's defensiveness moves the reader to imagine the scene that the court beheld without benefit of any gloss for certifying the queens' virtue with respect to the enterprises of men: twelve female warriors, a small battalion, in various attire. Before it can be authorized as poetical, conceived in terms of the idea of virtue which it is to represent, it is a vision at once threatening and ludicrous.

Hic mulier, or the man-woman as a type of vicious female, is a species notorious for its tendency to congregate, at least in the eyes of those who study it. A popular pamphlet a decade later than *Queens,* quips that one may see this type as "Masculine in Number, from one to multitudes":

> So I present these Masculine women in the deformities as they are, that I may call them backe to the modest comeliness in which they were.
>
> The modest comelinesse in which they were? Why, did euer these *Meare-maids,* or rather *Meare-Monsters,* that weare the Car-mans blocke, the Dutch-mans feather Vpse-van-muffe, the poore mans pate poul'd by a Treene dish, the French doublet truss'd with points, to *Mary Aubroes* light nether skirts, the Fooles Baudrike, and the Diuels Ponyard. Did they euer know comeli-nesse, or modestie? Fie, no, they neuer walkt in those pathes; for these at the best are sure but ragges of Gentry, torne from better pieces for their foule staines, or else the adulterate branches of rich Stocks, that taking too much sap from the roote, are cut away, and imploy'd in base vses. . . . It is an infection that emulates the plague, and throwes it selfe amongst women of all degrees.[13]

In Jonson's *Epicoene*, a play of the same year as *Queens*, the gentlemen Dauphine, Truewit, and Clerimont are equally horrified and amused by the prospect of the collegiates' corporate behavior:

> CLE. How now, DAVPHINE? how do'st thou quit thy selfe of these females?
> DAVP. 'Slight, they haunt me like *fayries,* and giue me iewells here, I cannot be rid of 'hem.
> CLE.O, you must not tell, though.
> DAVP.Masse, I forgot that: I was neuer so assaulted. One loues for vertue, and bribes me with this. Another loues me with caution, and so would possesse me. A third brings me a riddle here, and all are iealous: and raile each at other.
> CLE.A riddle? Pray'le'me see't? *Sir* DAVPHINE, *I chose this way of intimation for priuacie. The ladies here, I know, haue both hope, and purpose, to make a collegiate and seruant of you.*
>
> *(The silent Woman,* V.ii. 47–60; vol. 5: 255)

The emasculating woman, whether celibate, lesbian, or whore, adver-tises her independence by her affiliation with other women. In the eyes of those who despise her, she is both ludicrously typical of her kind and foolishly anxious to distinguish herself within that kind.

Jonson's imagination of a troupe of heroically attired females is thus

1. Inigo Jones' sketch for Penthesilea in *Masque of Queens*

accomplished in an atmosphere in which the images will be affected by contradictory associations, particularly when they are enacted by actual women already attended by some of those associations. In *Queens*, Jonson glosses Penthesilea in uncompromised heroic terms:

> Shee was Queene of the *Amazons*, . . . Shee is no where mentiond, but w'h the præface of Honor, and virtue; and is allwayes aduaunced in the head, of the worthiest Women. *Diodorus Siculus* makes her the Daughter of *Mars*. She was honord, in her death, to haue it the act of *Achilles* (*Qveenes*, ll. 483–91; vol. 7: 306).

But in *Epicoene*, he uses the name more commonly, in the mouth of Morose, to express horror at Morose's discovery of just what kind of monster he has wed: "I haue married a *Penthesilea*, a *Semiramis*, sold my liberty to a distaffe!" (*The silent Woman*, III.iv.56–58; vol. 5: 209). If, moreover, as a notation on Inigo Jones' sketch for the costume of Penthesilea suggests, the role of this queen in *Queens* was assumed by Lucy, Countess of Bedford, she precisely fits the poles of this ambivalence. Poets, Jonson among them, are on record as praising her ability to maneuver effectively at court; but a popular ballad-satire suggests that, as early as the days of her first prominence in the court of Queen Elizabeth, she was the object of some scorn for her assumption of initiative that her husband might more properly have taken.[14] These two meanings of the image of Penthesilea, as virtuous woman-warrior and as harridan leading a cohort of women against the enterprises of men, react in opposite ways with the hags of the antimasque, who either give way to the queens or linger to increase their impact with analogical force.

As a look at the Inigo Jones sketch for the costume of Penthesilea (Figure 1) objectifies the opposite ways that this character might be read in the masque, it also suggests a range of motives for which the role might be sought by one of the ladies, motives that include the exhibitionist tendencies appealed to by the details of the costume. Surviving sketches of costumes designed for queens not mentioned in the final text of the masque even prompt the speculation that a lady's preference for certain stylistic features might have exerted influence over elements of the fiction.[15] As the set and costumes were "intierly Mr *Iones* his Invention, and Designe" (*Qveenes*, l. 683, and see the whole passage, ll. 680–709; vol. 7: 313–14), negotiating those points, especially if they involved preferences of ladies that appealed to the designer's visual sense more than to the poet's conceptual one, must have been particularly liable to irritate Jonson. The details of costume are, in fact, a convenient way to objectify Jonson's basic problem in the masque of representing the doings of women in ways that do not interfere with the larger purposes of men.

The history of Jonson's involvement with the Queen's masques up to the point of *Queens* is nowhere told in detail, but what there is of it suggests that it was beset by just this tension between the Queen's fondness for spectacular display of herself in her court and Jonson's determination that the display would mean something. The first masque with which Queen Anne and her ladies entertained the new court in 1603, Samuel Daniel's *The Vision of the Twelve Goddesses*, seems to have impressed Jonson as a makeshift affair, arranged with no conceit beyond one that would allow the masquers to dress elaborately and exhibit themselves as a bevy of deities. Jonson apparently witnessed the production, because Drummond records his remark

> y^t Sr John Roe loved him & when they two were ushered by my Lord Suffolk from a Mask, Roe wrott a moral epistle to him, which began that next to plays the Court and the State were the best. God threateneth Kings, Kings Lords & Lords do us (*Conversations*, xi, ll. 155–59; vol. 1: 136).

Jonson's scorn of Daniel is especially interesting because the design of *The Vision* seems to be a form he revised in *Queens* by adding the antimasque. In his *Vision*, Daniel relies on emblematic properties in the costumes of each goddess as described and interpreted by a Sybilla to identify each character in the masque for the spectator; but Daniel makes no attempt to specify what lady masquer is to assume a given role, and his symbols seem to have been open to some dispute. If Jonson was among the "captious Censurers" of Daniel's *Vision*, as seems likely from the tone of the criticism as Daniel summarizes it in his defense of the masque in its printed text, then the charges Jonson himself feels liable to six years later in *Queens* and tries to prevent by admitting that "*chance*" controlled the casting must have seemed to Jonson a bitter return of his own contempt. Of his *Vision*, Daniel insists that, because all the symbols admitted considerable latitude of interpretation,

> vve vvere left at libertie to take no other knowledge of them, then fitted our present purpose, nor were tied by any lawes of Heraldry to range them

otherwise in their precidencies, then they fell out to stand vvith the nature of the matter in hand. . . . And therefore we tooke their aptest representations that lay best and easiest for us.[16]

Jonson would find this the *ars poetica* of a womens-poet; and yet he was to founder on the same rock, though, as we have seen, he finds another way to confess it, in *Queens*.

When the Queen's commission was awarded to him in the year following Daniel's *Vision*, he undertook to gratify the Queen's extravagant whimsy to "haue [herself and her ladies] *Black-mores* at first" (*The Masque of Blacknesse*, ll. 21–22; vol. 7: 169). In the text of *Blackness* (printed in a quarto of 1608 with *The Masque of Beauty*), Jonson claims nonetheless to have supplied the invention of the masque because he has made of the Queen's simple impulse a whole poetical conceit. The full predication of that conceit does not emerge until, in the subsequent *Masque of Beauty*, the twelve daughters of Niger from *Blackness*, increased to sixteen by another request of the Queen at some inconvenience to the fiction, are transformed by the blanching rays of Albion's sun. As Jonson would interpret the collaboration with his royal commissioner, he is man enough to imbue her eccentricities with a delightfully instructive meaning that can embrace the ladies as a lot. *Blackness* and *Beauty* were published in a joint quarto by Jonson with prefatory notes that describe their relationship to one another; and it is also as a single running text that they appear in the 1616 folio, with "*So ended the first* Masque . . ." occurring in the middle of page 901, after which only a bar intervenes before the title "The Second Masqve. Which was of Beavtie."[17] They thus appear, in the text, despite the two years separating their production, as a single poem. As such, they are the paradigm of *Queens*: if not precisely an antimasque/masque structure, nonetheless a continuous fiction that is arranged to display Jonson's ability to transform the Queen's fantasies into meaningful poetical expression.

Jonson's prefatory remarks to *Queens* make it plain that he is undertaking a continuation of the *Blackness-Beauty* project that is at the same time wholly new. He wishes to claim a prerogative in his role as poet, not simply the opportunity to react with ingenuity to the whim of the Queen:

> It encreasing, now, to the third time of my being vs'd in these seruices to her Ma.[ties] personall presentatio's, wth the Ladyes whome she pleaseth

> to honor; it was my first, and speciall reguard, to see that the Nobilyty of the Invention should be answerable to the dignity of they^r persons. For w^{c}h reason, I chose the Argument, to be, *A Celebration of honorable, & true Fame, bred out of Vertue*: obseruing that rule of the best *Artist,* to suffer no obiect of delight to passe w^{t}hout his mixture of profit, & example (*Qveenes,* ll. 1–9: vol. 7: 282).

The emphatic insistence on his own determination of the argument ("I chose the Argument, to be . . ."), the Sidnean echo in that argument ("*honorable, & true Fame, bred out of Vertue*"), the allusion to "the best *Artist,*" Horace ("*Hor. in Art. Poetic.*" being the marginal note to this phrase) all advertise that *Queens* is occasional art in a different and more important sense from *Blackness* and *Beauty.* Whereas in the former pair Jonson had made poetry out of the occasion defined by the Queen, in this masque he will use the occasion she provides as an opportunity to do something more freestanding and complete, to declare himself and his poetical project and, in so doing, to say what a poet is and what poetry ought to be. For this manifesto, the circumstance of the lady masquers is particularly apt: he will prescribe separate roles for them, sublimating their particular identities to his idea, representing women in just the way that the courtier learns to love them. Moreover, for the act of representation to be conspicuously heroic, he must triumph over actual women and, in their persons, the effeminate impulses in men and men's society that they represent. He will set his own antimasque against which he will work the transformation of his vision. The antimasque is the element of *Queens* that transforms it from a vision to a deliberately meaningful statement.

A remark by Jonson in the prefatory epistle attributes the impulse of the antimasque somewhat disingenuously to Queen Anne:

> And because her Matie (best knowing, that a principall part of life in these *Spectacles* lay in they^r variety) had commaunded mee to think on some *Daunce,* or shew, that might præcede hers, and haue the place of a foyle, or false-*Masque;* I was carefull to decline not only from others, but mine owne stepps in that kind, since the last yeare I had an *Anti-Masque* of Boyes.

Even if we take this at face value, it probably does not mean that the Queen requested an antimasque of hags. Rather, Jonson seems to be saying that, having been asked by the Queen for an antimasque, he invented its subject:

and therefore, now, deuis'd that twelue Women, in the habite of *Haggs*, or Witches, sustayning the persons of *Ignorance, Suspicion, Credulity*, &c. the opposites to good *Fame*, should fill that part; not as a *Masque*, but a spectacle of strangenesse, producing multiplicity of Gesture, and not vnaptly sorting w^{t}h the current, and whole fall of the Deuise (*Qveenes*, ll. 10–22; vol. 7: 282).

It is, of course, not the Queen but the King who has an interest in demonology; and it is against the order of Heroic Virtue, the concern of men, that Mischief and her company are posed. When we consider further the complicated way that the figures of the antimasque are related, by analogy as well as by antithesis, to the figures of the masque proper, Jonson's use of the hags achieves much more than variety. It converts the masque from a simple image of instructive praise to a complex analysis of the source of any reservations to that praise as it is being conferred. "Not vnaptly sorting w^{t}h the current, and whole fall of the Deuise" is a remarkable understatement, all in all, of what the antimasque in fact accomplishes.

The pattern of marginal annotations in the full text of *Queens* suggests that Jonson reviewed his production with a particularly attentive eye to the antimasque. The holograph copy of Jonson's text, which is the original of the 1609 quarto as well as of the more carelessly printed folio, opens with a dedicatory epistle to Prince Henry (reproduced in the quarto and omitted from the folio because the Prince was dead by 1616). In that epistle, Jonson says he compiled a text of the masque at the request of the Prince, who, having honored poetry with his ear, is now

curious to examine her w^{t}h yor eye, and inquire into her beauties, and strengths. Where, though it hath prou'd a worke of some difficulty to mee to retriue the particular *authorities* (according to yor gracious command, and a desire borne out of iudgment) to those things, w^{c}h I writt ovt of fullnesse, and memory of my former readings; Yet, now I haue ouercome it, the reward that meetes mee is double to one act: w^{c}h is, that therby, yor excellent vnderstanding will not only iustefie mee to yor owne knowledge, but decline the stiffnesse of others originall Ignorance, allready armd to censure ("To the glorje of our owne, and greefe of other Nations: My Lord Henry Prince of great Britayne. &c.," ll. 31–41; vol. 7: 281).

The gracious compliment to a patron's protective power as an excuse to write is an ordinary strategy, so we need not take this literally; but the crowded appearance of the pages in the first half of *Queens* suggests that something—the expressed interest of the Prince or his more troubled dismay at the disquieting effect of the antimasque on the masque, general criticism or bafflement, Jonson's own preoccupation with the hags as qualifying agents of his argument—something seems to have made him return to justify in particularly elaborate ways all of what the hags say in those curiously incantatory verses: verses that otherwise would stand by color and accent almost without sense.

Jonson's hags are at once a gratification of the professed interests of the King in demonology and witchcraft and Jonson's own more daring reflections on the deeper implications of such interests. The annotations acknowledge early on that the poet has read the King's book and then proceed to overwhelm that reference to his book with Jonson's own independently derived justifications for the wild images of his poetry. To the introduction of the eleven witches beginning to dance, Jonson's marginal note reads:

> d. See the *Kings* Maties booke (o^r *Soueraigne*) of *Dæmonologie. Bodin. Remig. Delrio. Mall: Malesi.* and a world of others, in the generall; but, let vs follow particulars (*Qveenes*, note to l. 44; vol. 7: 283).

As the King reads on, flattery must give way to instruction in the reasons for the power witches exert over men.[18] Jonson, moreover, goes beyond analyzing the phenomenon, or really, beneath such analysis, reproducing images of it; and the effect of the fantasy, wildly associative in the verse itself, is only barely controlled by the annotations. It is as if the charms originate deeper in the imagination than Jonson can rationalize easily:

> The Weather is fayre, the wind is good,
> Vp, *Dame*, o' yo^{r g.} Horse of wood:
> Or else, tuck vp yor gray frock,
> And sadle yo^{r h.} Goate, or yor greene ^{i.} Cock,
> And make his bridle a bottome of thrid,
> To roule vp how many miles you haue rid.

Notes justify this without explaining it:

> g. *Delrio. Disq. Magic. lib. Quæst vj.* has a story out of *Triezius*, of this Horse of wood: But, y^t wch o^r Witches call so, is sometime a broome staffe, sometime a reede, sometime, a distaffe. See *Remig. Dæmonol. lib. j. cap. xiiii. Bodin. lib. ij. cap. iiij. &c.* h. The Goate is y^e *Deuil* himselfe, vpon

whome they ride, often, to they[r] solemnities, as appeares by they[r] confessions in *Rem.* and *Bodin. ibid.* His *Mat.*[ie] also remembers the story of the Diuells appearāce to those of *Calicut,* in that forme. *Dæmonol. lib. ij. Cap. iij.* [i] Of the greene Cock we haue no other ground (to confesse ingenuously) than a vulgar fable of a Witch, that w[t]h a Cock of that colour, and a bottome of blewe thred, would transport her selfe through the ayre; and soe escap'd (at the time of her being brought to execution) from the hand of Iustice. It was a tale, when I went to Schoole. And somewhat there is like it in *Mar. Delrio. Disqui. Mag. lib. ij. Quæst vj.* of one *Zijto,* a *Bohemian* (*Qveenes,* ll. 64–69; vol. 7: 284–85).

Laughter at this business is certainly possible; but as it reverberates with the remembered fears of childhood, it is laughter in the dark.

An ambivalent appeal, to fascination and revulsion, must have operated on the King to an even more complex degree in the production of the masque. Danced by the male dancers of the King's Men, this spectacle of strangeness would have engaged him as much for what it was as for what it represented. When the vision of twelve warrior women swept it away, he would have been preoccupied by its lingering energy. The Queen and her ladies, statically turned out on Mr. Jones' *Machina versatilis,* are set off or set up by what has come before; no matter how we read or interpret the device whereby they have been foiled, they have been upstaged.[19]

As a pageant of monstrosity shadowing the queens, the hags do not surrender their power by vanishing; rather, they begin to exert it in less explicit ways that advertise the poet's essential difficulty with the project of representing women meaningfully. As vicious types of feminine conduct, the hags are degraded images of women. They are also, however, by their names, the impulses which any spectator must suppress in himself when he is asked to contemplate heroical femininity embodied in lady courtiers. In effect, the poet gives the reader, through the hags, temporary license to misread the more high-minded version of the masque's project that will be set forth in Heroic Virtue's speech; and then with that speech cancels that license by indicting it as typical of the brazen female behavior through which women have always perverted the works of men. Consequently, though the perspective of the masque shifts, there is no ambiguity to the representation of woman: as hag or queen, loved or hated, she is a caricature of male virtue. Mischief is conjured up for the spectator to indulge in and then to suppress in himself as an effeminate impulse. The epicene image of Mischief and her hags might cause the spectator to reflect that, in the perversions they represent, men and women are alike implicated; but, as all epicene images inevitably suggest, the feminine is the source of the monstrosity.

Queen Anne and her ladies, tricked out in their fantastic costumes and seated in the chariots of the progress from which they supervise the now restrained energy of the hags, seem in imagination oblivious to what has happened to their actual selves as they are used to represent something significant. In their chariots, on the page, they are silent women. The meaning of the spectacle belongs to the poet. However little sympathy we may have for them and the extravagant court of which they were a part, it is discouraging to think of them like that.

To be sure, as the text of *Queens* draws to a close, we are reassured that at court, on that Candlemas night in 1609, no thoughts so melancholy troubled the head of Queen Anne nor distracted her from the utterly ephemeral time, scarcely a page in the telling, that was her favorite part:

> Here, they alighted from they^r *Chariots,* and daunc'd forth they^r first *Daunce;* then a second, immediately following it: both right curious, and full of subtile, and excellent Changes, and seem'd performd w^{t}h no lesse spirits, then those they personated. . . . After w^{c}h, they daunc'd they^r third *Daunce;* then w^{c}h a more *numerous* composition could not be seene: *graphically* dispos'd into *letters,* and honoring the Name of the most sweete, and ingenious *Prince, Charles, Duke* of *Yorke* Wherin, beside that principall grace of perspicuity, the motions were so euen, & apt, and they^r expression so iust; as if *Mathematicians* had lost *proportion,* they might there haue found it. The *Author* was M^r. *Tho. Giles.* After this, they daunc'd *Galliards,* and *Corranto's.* And then they^r last *Daunce,* no lesse elegant (in the place) then the rest. w^{t}h w^{c}h they tooke they^r *chariots* agayne, and triumphing about the stage, had they^r returne to the *House of Fame* celebrated w^{t}h this last *song* . . . (*Qveenes,* ll. 731–60; vol. 7: 315–16).

This is action, but it is hard to imagine less consequential action than a dance graphically disposing letters spelling out the name of Prince Charles. Analogies to the intervals of sporting events in our day doubtless miss the exquisite quality of the dancing, though they are probably not inaccurate to the sense of power frivolously exerted in contrast to more effective maneuvers. The poet may be communicating through them, but these ladies have nothing to say to us. Finally, reading *Queens* becomes an exercise in imagining all the reasons why, to place these ladies in some relationship to Fame, Jonson's imagination had to tax itself so mightily.

WHEN WE WOMEN READ, particularly when we read for meaning rather than for (as we sometimes say) pleasure, the text becomes a kind of mirror of the psychological revision that education to our proper roles effects in us. We look, in our reading, for the larger elements of a poem's expression that give it significance, discounting its incidental particularities when they interfere with what we must understand as the informing idea. As we do this, we discount our own eccentricity to the project of education itself, which is still not, after all, our project. We produce works to be praised for their approximation of men's readings; we even, in some sense, adjust our looks to make them appropriate to the attitudes prescribed for us: the mischievous hag or the amazonian scholar, virtue's tutor. It is when we encounter actual, silly women in what we read that questions of meaning become occasions to calculate the price we pay to participate in significant discourse. *The Masque of Queens* is fascinating precisely because it takes its toll so directly. To make it mean something, we must despise or ignore the ladies in it. We must become, one way or another, the monsters men would make of us rather than admit our relationship to those women.

In the Oxford edition's discussion of the stage history of *Queens*, there is a notice (vol. 10: 496) of a production of the masque in the May Day festivities celebrated at Bryn Mawr College in 1906. No graduate of a women's college has any difficulty imagining the situation of this production; and, thanks to Bryn Mawr's traditional impulses, it is also easy to confirm one's imaginations. The Bryn Mawr College archives have preserved the script of the production, a program providing an account of its place in the festivities, and several photographs. The women who participated in this event, judging from the text and photographic record, made neither meaningful statement nor mischief with this masque. They simply played with it and, in interesting ways, criticized it. Some of what they did underscores issues I have tried to raise in my reading of *Queens*, so it is appropriate that an account of their play be my conclusion.

The title page of the program makes it immediately clear that the 1906 Bryn Mawr production of *Queens* was enacted in the spirit of a very fundamental mistake. "Belanna, Queen of the Ocean" in the cast list is preceded by an asterisk to this note:

*This part was played by Queen Elizabeth herself in the first presentation of the Masque; and Belanna, who is meant to typify Queen Elizabeth, embodies all the virtues of the other seven Queens.

This error, simply a mistake in the dating of the masque, makes a fair point against which to read interpretive commentary on the sense in which Queen Anne as Bel-Anna is virtuous: if this masque legitimately uses a queen as a type of the virtue to be immortalized by Fame, that queen must be, in some sense, famous. Assuming (by incorrectly thinking her to be Queen Elizabeth) that she was, these players also reduced the masque (the text is radically cut) to something more like *A Vision of Some Eight Great Ladies* preceded by a dance of witches.

A second major criticism is embodied in the cast list of the witches, named Hecate, Ignorance, Suspicion, Credulity, Falsehood, Execration, and Bitterness. (The numerical symmetry is not preserved; Murmur, Malice, Impudence, Slander and Rage are omitted.) Women play these roles as well as the roles of the queens. Consequently, a clearer sense of contrast between the witches and the queens is drawn: they are similar figures playing dissimilar roles. This observation is another way to appreciate how the amazonian monstrosity of Jonson's queens is emphasized by the preceding spectacle of the King's Men: they are dissimilar figures playing similar roles. A further consequence of the casting is suggested by the photograph of the witches (Figure 2) and illuminated by annotations on the working text. "Prostrate, on elbows, sit up, crouch, take hands . . . Draw off to our side . . . around Hecate . . . Faster, Faster, Faster": the viciousness of what these figures represent is dissipated by the energy of the dancing. I think this is, to some extent, an effect operating for the King's Men as well; but it is significant that a spectator of the Bryn Mawr production would be appreciating the grace of women at this point in the masque.

Finally, as another order of accommodation to the exigencies of casting, the queens are not only reduced in number to eight, but the remaining speaking parts of Jonson's masque, Heroic Virtue and Fame,

2. "Dance of Witches" from the production of *Masque of Queens* at Bryn Mawr College, May 1, 1906

3. Seven queens from the production of *Masque of Queens* at Bryn Mawr College, May 1, 1906

are omitted, with the elements of their speeches necessary to convey the action (there is considerable compression here) given to "Pentheselea." The simplicity of this revision was the first occasion I took to become conscious of the special distinction enjoyed by Heroic Virtue in Jonson's masque: he is the only character played unambiguously by an actor of his proper sex, and he is the figure that Jonson makes authoritative in the text. His is, I have argued, the authority of a high-minded poet, often mistaken for the author himself; but as I have also tried to show, Jonson the dramatic manipulator enjoys a more complex vision than Heroic Virtue expresses, in something like the same way that Dauphine "lurches" Truewit in *Epicoene*. The students of Bryn Mawr College, however, do not reproduce this sense of authorial sleight-of-hand in their version of the masque. They deposit authority straightforwardly in "the brave Amazon," the head of the worthiest women. I cannot identify the queens certainly in the photograph (Figure 3), but I imagine the mannish-looking one to the extreme right of the picture to be the sort of woman writer who might write what *The Masque of Queens* becomes in this production.

I enjoy looking at the photograph of these women. They are comfortable in the attitude they have assumed toward *Queens*. There is conspicuous ingenuity here, but it is not monstrous. Admitted to the sight, although their friends, we could laugh. It would be a pleasant interlude.

NOTES

1. I am quoting from Jonson's revised translation of the *Ars Poetica*, though phrasing in the first version of this passage, done in 1605, seems closer to the spirit of *Queens*. In particular, the mermaid image of line 5, "a blacke foule fish" in 1605, is less repulsive reconsidered as "some swarthie fish." In this essay, all quotations from the works of Ben Jonson will follow the texts of *Ben Jonson*, ed. C. H. Herford and Percy and Evelyn Simpson, 11 vols. (Oxford: Clarendon Press, 1925–52; corr. reprint, 1952–54). I locate works by title and line numbers followed by the volume and page numbers to this edition. My quotations do not record all the variations in type nor reproduce Jonson's notation symbols except when I will also quote the notes themselves; but all of these shifts and stops, to which the Oxford edition labors to be faithful, contribute to the effect with which I am here concerned, an effect that is obscured by more

recent, streamlined editions. In other words, a more immediate text provoked my "resistance." The term is from Judith Fetterly, *The Resisting Reader, A Feminist Approach to American Fiction* (Bloomington: Indiana Univ. Press, 1978).

2. This concession appears late in the *Defence*. In J. A. Van Dorsten's edition of *A Defence of Poetry* (Oxford: Oxford Univ. Press, 1984), it is on p. 72, l. 20, in the last part of the digression before the peroration. Sidney's own weakness for rhetorical flourishes is evident throughout the *Defence*, and Astrophil, of course, who is as unable to constrain his literary flourishes as he is powerless to sublimate his passion for Stella, is the best illustration of the analogy between *ars poetica* and *ars amatoria*.

3. In the fourth book of *The Courtier*, Bembo says that the soul begins its quest for beauty and goodness at the level of sense; but that reason and, failing that, the inhibitions of age will bring a lover to a higher understanding of the idealized object of his desire. Ultimately, the lover needs to control the woman that he loves to preserve the relationship between outward beauty and the abstract perfection of which it is a reflection. See Sir Thomas Hoby's translation of Baldasarre Castiglione, *The Book of the Courtier*, printed with an introduction by J. H. Whitfield (New York: Dutton, 1974), 313–14.

4. In his *History of King Richard III*, Thomas More apologizes for his digression on Mistress Shore: "I doubt not some shal think this woman to sleight a thing, to be written of & set amonge the remembraunces of great matters." See the English version of *The History of King Richard III* in the Yale edition of the *Complete Works of St. Thomas More*, vol. 2, ed. Richard S. Sylvester (New Haven: Yale Univ. Press, 1974), 56.

5. A facsimile of Jonson's 1616 folio has been printed for the Scolar Press with an introduction by D. Heyward Brock, 1976; and a page of Jonson's holograph manuscript of *Queens* (British Museum Royal MS. 18A, xlv) is reproduced in a plate opposite p. 290 of vol. 7 of the Oxford edition. Note the intrusion of Jonson's annotations in and around the text. Stephen Orgel's Yale edition, *Ben Jonson: The Complete Masques* (New Haven: Yale Univ. Press, 1975), 122–41, prints Jonson's notes separately and even relegates to an appendix the long description of the fictional queens (ll. 477–681). With his cleaner modern text, compare Orgel's reading of the masque in *The Jonsonian Masque* (Cambridge: Harvard Univ. Press, 1965), 130–46, which explores the significance of the clear contrast between the world of the antimasque and the world of the masque proper.

6. See the entry for Anne of Denmark in the *Dictionary of National Biography*. As befits her status, the entry runs to twenty-one columns; but it is laced with apologies for the lack of important matters in its content. Queen Anne has her recent biographer in Ethel Carleton Williams, *Anne of Denmark* (London: Longman, 1970).

7. "A Vergil" and "a Horace" with these attitudes toward poetry are characters in Jonson's *Poetaster*.

8. The document is printed by Herford and Simpson in an appendix to *The Masque of Queens* (vol. 7: 318–19). I have added some bracketed conjectures to their transcription. I mention below one guess I have about a motive for the change in the identity of one of the queens: Atalanta in the argument becomes Hypsicratea in Jonson's text. The other major change, in the animals drawing the chariots—from panthers, eagles, and lions to eagles, griffons, and lions—impresses me a decision motivated by the visual effect.

9. Joseph Loewenstein's *Responsive Readings: Versions of Echo in Pastoral, Epic, and the Jonsonian Masque*, Yale Studies in English, 192 (New Haven: Yale Univ. Press, 1984) contains a very stimulating discussion of Jonson's alterations to the figure of Fame from Vergil, Ovid, and Chaucer; see 111–18.

10. Most modern editions of *Queens* do not identify the ladies at all; but there is a handy list of all the celebrators in Jonson's masques in vol. 10, 428–45, of the Oxford edition. Trying to find these ladies in the *DNB* is a good way to consider women's relationship to fame or, in the case of Frances Howard, infamy. For a provocative summary of the principles informing Leslie Stephen's and, especially, Sidney Lee's stewardship of the *DNB*, see David Novarr, *The Lines of Life: Theories of Biography, 1880–1970* (West Lafayette, Ind.: Purdue Univ. Press, 1986), 1–2, 8–15. See also his entry for Virginia Woolf, 45–56. Novarr's study made clear to me what the method of this essay owes to Virginia Woolf and Victoria Sackville-West, to *Orlando* and *The Diary of the Lady Anne Clifford* they, respectively, wrote and edited.

11. See epigrams 104 (for Susan, Countess of Montgomery) and 76, 84, and 94 (for Lucy, Countess of Bedford).

12. For an example of the standard reading of Jonson's masques as coherent strategies of praise that is nonetheless accompanied by some acknowledgment of what the Jacobean court seems more realistically to have been like, see Graham Parry, *The Golden Age restor'd: The culture of the Stuart Court, 1603–42* (New York: St. Martin's, 1981), ch. 2, esp. 58–62.

13. The pamphlet *Hic Mvlier, Or, the Man-Woman* is printed in facsimile in *Three Pamphlets on the Jacobean Antifeminist Controversy* (Delmar, N. Y.: Scholars Facsimiles and Reprints, 1978). The introduction to this volume by Barbara J. Baines traces the impulse of the middle-class anxiety about mannish women to the pronouncements of the King through the sermons of his preachers. See Linda Woodbridge's very useful comments on the pamphlets in her *Women and the English Renaissance: Literature and the Nature of Womankind, 1540–1620* (Chicago: Univ. of Illinois Press, 1984), esp. ch. 6, 139–51. The quotations in my text appear in the unpaginated pamphlet on signatures A3 and A4v° to Biv°.

14. See my essay, "The Real Presence of Lucy Russell, Countess of Bedford, and the Terms of John Donne's 'Honour Is So Sublime Perfection,'" *ELH* 47 (1980): 205–34. To my citations there, I should add Margaret M. Byard, "The Trade of Courtiership: The Countess of Bedford and the Bedford Memorials; a Family History from 1585 to 1607," *History Today* 29 (Jan. 1979): 20–28.

As I was completing this essay, the Countess, it seems, was once again attracting attention. Compare Arthur F. Marotti, "Donne, Lady Bedford, and the Poetry of Compliment," a section of the third chapter of his *John Donne, Coterie Poet*(Madison: Univ. of Wisconsin Press, 1986), 202–32, with Barbara K. Lewalski, "Lucy, Countess of Bedford: Images of a Jacobean Courtier and Patroness," in *Politics of Discourse: The Literature and History of Seventeenth-Century England*, ed. Kevin Sharpe and Steven N. Zwicker (Berkeley: Univ. of California Press, 1987), 25–77. How differently the likes of her are still imagined: the politics of discourse indeed.

15. The sketches done by Inigo Jones for the costumes of the queens are reproduced in the two-volume work of Stephen Orgel and Roy Strong, *Inigo Jones: The Theatre of the Stuart Court* (Berkeley: Univ. of California Press, 1973), vol. 1: 139–53, juxtaposed there with other sketches and illustrations to suggest the fashions that Jones was following in these designs. Strong's catalogue entries for these sketches note, "The set of designs for *Queens* is unique in that all the masquers wore different dresses; it is notable for the splendour of the headdresses" (vol. 1: 139). The sense of male courtiers gossiping about the rivalries among the ladies for distinction and variety in their masquing dresses can be gotten from a comment of Dudley Carleton to John Chamberlain on *The Vision of the Twelve Goddesses*, in a letter (S. P. 14/6, #21 for January 15, 1604) printed in *Dudley Carleton to John Chamberlain, 1603–1624: Jacobean Letters*, ed. Maurice Lee, Jr. (New Brunswick, N.J.: Rutgers Univ. Press, 1972), 53–60.

16. *The Complete Works in Prose and Verse of Samuel Daniel*, ed. A. B. Grosart (Printed for Private Circulation Only, 1885), vol. 3: 189. See my essay, "Samuel Daniel's Poetical Epistles, Especially Those to Sir Thomas Egerton and Lucy, Countess of Bedford," *Studies in Philology* 74 (1977): 431–34, for a more fully worked out discussion of my sense of Daniel's compromises in *The Vision*.

17. The 1608 quarto actually includes three masques, the Haddington masque being printed in it with continuous signatures through the volume. There is, however, no mention of this third masque on the title page. See the Oxford edition, vol. 7: 163 and 167.

18. Orgel notes (see his edition, p. 526) that Jonson's reference to the King's *Demonology* at the mention of the witches' first beginning to dance is mistaken: "James does not discuss witches' dancing."

19. In an autograph dedication of the quarto edition of *Queens* to Queen Anne, Jonson feels compelled to explain why he dedicated the printing of the masque to the Prince rather than to the Queen herself. The letter is printed in the Oxford edition, vol. 7: 279. Its defensive tone may be conventional; but that tone has contributed to my suspicion that in the presentation of the masque at court, the hags compromised the queens, at least to the spectators.

Contributors

Patricia Francis Cholakian is visiting assistant professor of French at Hamilton College. Her publications include the introduction to a facsimile edition of Gournay's *Le Proumenoir*, co-authorship of *The Early French Novella*, and articles in *The French Review*, *Romance Notes*, *Theatre Journal*, and *Prose Studies*. She is now working on Marguerite de Navarre's *Heptaméron*.

Anne J. Cruz is associate professor of Spanish and Portuguese at the University of California at Irvine. She is the author of *Imitación y transformación: El petrarquismo en la poesía de Boscán y Garcilaso de la Vega* and co-editor of *Renaissance Rereadings: Intertext and Context*. Her articles on Spanish Golden Age poetry and prose have appeared in *Romanic Review*, *Romance Notes*, *Revista Canadiense de Estudios Hispánicos*, and *Ideologies and Literature*. She is currently finishing a book on the picaresque novels of the Spanish Golden Age.

Sheila Fisher is assistant professor of English at Trinity College. She is the author of *Chaucer's Poetic Alchemy: A Study of Value and Its Transformation in The Canterbury Tales*, published in Garland Press's Distinguished Dissertations Series. Her essay on women and the revision of Arthurian history in *Sir Gawain and the Green Knight* appears in Christopher Baswell and William Sharpe's collection, *The Passing of Arthur*. Her current project is a study of women and systems of exchange in *The Canterbury Tales*.

Janet E. Halley has published articles on Sir Thomas Browne and Henry Vaughan, and on the language strategies of Familist heretics, in *English Literary Renaissance*, *The George Herbert Journal*, and *Representations*. Her essay on Eve's subjectivity appears in Julia Walker's volume, *Milton and the Idea of Woman*. She has recently graduated J.D. from Yale Law School and is currently clerking in the U.S. Court of Appeals, Sixth Circuit. She is an executive editor of the *Yale Journal of Law and the Humanities*.

Elaine Tuttle Hansen is associate professor of English at Haverford College. She is the author of *The Solomon Complex: Reading Wisdom in Old English Poetry*. Her articles on Old English poetry and on Chaucer have appeared in such journals as *Speculum*, *Journal of English and Germanic Philology*, and *Women's Studies*, and she has also published essays on Margaret Atwood, Margaret Drabble, and Marge Piercy. She is currently at work on a study of feminization in Chaucer's fiction.

Roberta L. Krueger is associate professor of French at Hamilton College. She has published a number of articles on medieval French romance and edited, with E. Jane Burns, the issue of *Romance Notes* devoted to "Courtly Ideology and Women's Place in Medieval French Literature." An editor of *The Medieval Feminist Newsletter*, she is currently writing a book on the female audience of Old French romance.

Margaret Maurer is professor of English at Colgate University. She has published essays on the writing of Samuel Daniel and John Donne in *Modern Language Quarterly*, *Studies in Philology*, *Studies in English Literature*, *ELH*, and *Genre*. She is now writing about Sidney and Shakespeare.

Elizabeth Robertson is assistant professor of English at the University of Colorado at Boulder. She specializes in Anglo-Saxon, Middle English, and women's literature from the Middle Ages to the present. She has written a book, tentatively entitled *An Anchorhold of Her Own: The Role of the Female Audience in the Development of Middle English Literature*, which will be published by the University of Tennessee Press.

Marguerite Waller is associate professor of English at Amherst College. She has published a book, *Petrarch's Poetics and Literary History*, and articles on Dante, Wyatt, Shakespeare, Hollywood film, and feminist theory. Her current research uses poststructuralist and feminist theory to perform ideological analyses of early modern texts and their late modern readings.

Index

Seeking the Woman in Late Medieval and Renaissance Writings was designed by Dariel Mayer, composed by Tseng Information Systems, Inc., printed by Cushing-Malloy, Inc., and bound by John H. Dekker & Sons, Inc. The book is set in Times Roman. Text stock is 60-lb. Glatfelter Natural Antique.